THE GRAIL

The Lies. The Truth.
The Answer.

By
Tanishka

DEDICATION

To my ancestors, who helped me remember

TABLE OF CONTENTS

INTRODUCTION

Most of what has been written about *the Grail* to date has been the result of research conducted by male historians from a rational perspective. In this book I decode *the Grail* from a feminine perspective. I walk in the footsteps of groundbreaking women like Marija Gimbutas, a world-renowned archeologist and anthropologist, who reinterpreted evidence of Paleolithic and Neolithic civilizations from her understanding of feminine symbology and sacred traditions and author, Barbara Walker.

Initially I received the information intuitively through visions and automatic writing. I then researched the subject matter and interpreted my findings through the lens of the sacred feminine mystic tradition, drawing upon my work as a teacher in this area for the past twenty-five years.

Whilst there is evidence of *the Grail* in many cultures, dating back to Mesopotamia, it is in the land of the Celts, specifically Wales where Uther Pendragon and his son, *King Arthur* hailed that *the Grail* is most strongly associated. This is the land of my ancestors, both matrilineal and patrilineal, who have assisted me in joining the dots to glean the big picture; that being an ancient religion of love that I see as the key to restoring the sacred balance on Earth, so life may prevail.

The Holy Grail is often referred to as 'the greatest secret of all time'. I have since learned this secret is manufactured. Created through the deliberate suppression and distortion of a truth considered so powerful it posed a direct threat to those who assumed power during the Age of Empires. This is the underlying reason for the persecution of those who sought to disseminate *the Grail*, the sacred feminine wisdom teachings and practices that were outlawed by the Roman empire.

While there is much conjecture over the exact identity of *the Grail,* it is widely accepted as part of the ancient Celtic mystic tradition. Knowing this, it makes sense that a mystery such as *the Grail* can't be deciphered without an understanding of the mysteries of life, which was once the area of expertise afforded priestesses trained in the mysticism, the path of the sacred feminine. That said, I have not done this alone. Specifically, I would like to acknowledge the Druid priest, *Wolfstar* who alerted me to the fact *the Grail* was conducted over the 9 days of mid-Winter, the audience member in Glastonbury who drew the origins of *the Grail* cross on a napkin for me, the *Stag King* who paid me a house call and my Welsh ancestors who have guided me for years to recreate the various practices that, at the time, I didn't realize were part of the ancient *Grail* tradition.

My Journey to Decode The Holy Grail

My search for truth and meaning began at age 21 when I received 2 copies of *The Prophet* by Kahil Gibran. However, it wasn't until age 26 that my search for meaning became my central focus. This was catalyzed by my belated initiation into my womanhood by the late, Amrita Hobbs; one of the pioneers of this work in Australia. I then searched for a local women's circle to join and when I couldn't find one, created my own. Then one fateful night, in a moment of desperation I called out to the Universe for female role models and shortly thereafter met Jennifer Powell, a wise woman who looked like she'd walked out of Middle-Earth who introduced me to the mythos of the sacred feminine. This inspired me to leave my dysfunctional life in the city and head to the hills! I spent a year in a cabin in the woods on a self-imposed sabbatical. Like the ancient Greek philosopher, Pythagoras, I studied and cross-referenced mystical traditions. These included astrology, numerology, Tarot, Kabbalah, symbolism, archetypes, fairytales, mythology, yoga and eastern philosophy. I meditated, did self-guided rituals and automatic writing. This was punctuated by 3 months of grieving my old life, until I experienced a day when reality, as I knew it, challenged the perceptions of my rational mind. I experienced a 24-hour period where both the day and night were only 2 hours in duration, during which time I observed the ground ripple like water. When I awoke the next day, I felt a lightness of being I hadn't felt since I was a child. I had experienced a kundalini awakening. Known as 'The Force' to Jedis and chi, prana or Shakti to yogis, I had experienced an activation of life force through the energy centers within my central nervous system, creating an epiphany of self-realization and insights. I knew myself beyond this incarnation as an eternal being. I recalled past lives and felt completely at one with all of existence. In the ancient mystery schools of the East this awakening of the central energy channel of *Sushumna* was the path to awakening gnosis - the ability to channel truth. This experience prepared me to serve as an oracle, a messenger of truth.

To serve as an oracle one must clear their energy field of dense energies, such as unexpressed emotions. For the more crystal clear we become, the clearer one can serve as a channel, transmitting truth like a beacon from the quantum field of infinite intelligence.

This awakening was followed by an experience of being 'ridden' and called to serve by the dark Goddess, *Kali Ma* on Beltane, the ancient rite of Spring. This involved dancing into a trance state (without substances) experiencing a rising of inner heat that mirrored the huge pyre of fire erected for the rite. I gave myself over to the inner fire which moved me, as if possessed by the spirit of Great Grandmother Spider dancing the *Tarantella*. This was followed by violent purging for hours!

After these ancient teachings started flowing through me. Teachings I remembered I had taught as a *High Priestess* at *Avalon* and in Babylon. One night I stood beneath the Cosmos renewing my vow to serve the greater good as a priestess of the mysteries. It was then I took on the name, *Tanishka;* a name I'd been given as a nickname by Polish immigrants I'd worked with prior to my sabbatical. I then recalled this had been my name in previous incarnations when I was a Tantrika in southern India and later, as a Romany gypsy, giving oracle readings. I understood the frequency of this name would assist me in recalling the gifts I'd honed in those lifetimes. By the year's end I was teaching. My workshops and ceremonies grew into the *Star of Ishtar* mystery school offering a range of services, including a 9 month initiate priestess course, rites of passage initiations for women's life stages and teacher training. (Ishtar was the Goddess of Love in ancient Babylon.) Throughout this time, I continued to serve as an oracle offering private readings which honed my intuition.

Through the privilege of being a keeper of secrets, midwifing people of all ages through their moments of crisis, my insight into the human condition was accelerated.

Then in October 2008 I heard an inner voice telling me it was, "Time to activate *the Grail* codes." Shortly afterwards I began channeling teachings during the dark months of Autumn and Winter; the most feminine times on the seasonal wheel that were once revered in *the Grail* tradition. I distilled the ancient teachings I received into a series of *Sacred Union* books.

Three years later, during my menses, when my psychic senses were heightened, I received a vision of an ancient ceremony being performed by women who were initiating men in the forest on a mid-Winter night. In the vision I was conducting these ceremonies. I had a flash of remembrance, "This was *The Holy Grail*." Over the next three years I channeled more insights about *the Grail* during the dark months. My body assisted by aligning my menses with the Winter Solstice, the time *The Holy Grail* was observed. I was then invited to go to the central desert of Australia for the end of the Mayan calendar in December, 2012. The land initiated me intuitively to perform a number of water ceremonies. I prepared by opening my seven energy centers using Sanskrit mantras and kundalini kriyas to receive the ecstatic healing energies of the Goddess. Then I entered into a multi-orgasmic trance state and experienced energy flowing out of my fingertips, which I used to charge the water molecules with rainbow holographic light. I was informed through evaporation and precipitation the codes would be disseminated across the land. Despite this powerful initiation I was disheartened to find the group ceremonies were undertaken by people under the influence of various substances. When the shadow dynamics in our group started erupting as daily dramas, I suggested we have a morning check-in circle to process what was present for us each day. I soon discovered my traveling companions had not developed the ability to speak their truth from the heart in circle as an opportunity to publicly reflect on their choices and behaviors. As we went around the circle everyone just responded, 'I'm fine' and passed the talking stick. Meanwhile, the drama continued to escalate.

At the main ceremony with around a hundred people who'd been called to the 'Red Center', the final straw came when, afterwards everyone retreated to their individual camps to get high and I saw a bumper sticker on a hippie van that said, 'One World, One Tribe'. It occurred to me if we can't even sit together around a fire and connect without substances, how can we unify our world?

I was then given a vision of the Earth covered in spirals. The spirals were men and women gathered in circle during the solar and lunar vortices, creating ascending spirals to elevate the frequency of the collective. When I returned home, I was told about an online platform where I could create a course so I created the first online training course for women to facilitate *Red Tent* women's circles as a monthly practice, honor their *Graal* (menses) and align with the lunar cycle.

The following year I created an equivalent template for men to gather in alignment with the solar cycle in brotherhood like 'knights of the round table' to support their annual archetypal hero's journey. I didn't realize at the time these practices were to prepare men and women for *the Grail* rites. It was over these three years I gained access to a global audience of half a million people on Facebook with my daily lunar guidance after Natasha Odnoral gifted me her page, *The Moon Woman* which at the time had 7000 followers.

Then in 2013 I received guidance to do my first national speaking tour. At the time I was a sole parent supplementing my mystic work with welfare payments so this request seemed like an impossible feat. Fortunately, someone suggested I create a crowdfunding campaign and I raised the funds with pre-sale tickets. One month before the tour, I received my second vision of *the Grail* ceremony and when I came back into the present moment, I saw a stag deer standing at my front door! Initially I did a double-take as I thought what I'd seen out of the corner of my eye was my landlord walking past my kitchen window with a wheelbarrow full of sticks, not the antlers of the King Stag! When I realized the Lord of the Forest was paying me a personal visit, I got down on my knees and crawled to the door, bowing in humility and trying not to scare him away so I could thank him for entrusting me with the teachings of *the Grail.*

I then understood the real reason for the tour. I was being asked to share my revelations about the *Grail*! I spent the next few years spending all I had to take my *Grail* presentation wherever I was guided to go. This included Ubud in Bali, then the USA: Colorado, Sedona, Arizona, Albuquerque and LA, then to the UK; London and Glastonbury.

The call to the UK began when I was awoken by a voice pre-dawn on 3 consecutive mornings repeatedly saying the word, 'conjunction' with an image of the elemental spirits (faery folk) who lived within the Glastonbury Tor, asking me to come and do ceremony. I did an online search for 'conjunction 2016' and saw there would be a Venus superior conjunction the following year. During which, the planet of love would pass behind the sun, coinciding with an astrological aspect known as a Grand Cross. I sensed a crop circle would happen on this date…which it did and we did ceremony within it. The link to view that crop circle is in the resources section.

I was then shown an image of the mandorla, the intersecting circles that represent *Sacred Union*. I had an image of a ceremony with 12 men and 12 women in this configuration, so I set about trying to inspire 12 men and 12 women to join me for a pilgrimage of ceremonies along the ley lines in England to anchor the harmonic balance of opposites into the energy grid of the Earth during this astrological event. Only 4 women responded to the call to gather. I was gutted. The least of which, was that I lost travel, accommodation and meals expenses for 24 people that could've bought my first home. However, my greatest sadness was that the sacred masculine was not represented. Thanks to local help some beautiful brothers joined us for ceremonies at Stonehenge, Avebury, Cornwall, Glastonbury Tor, the White Spring and the Chalice Well. I was then invited to Ireland and visited New Grange, an ancient *Grail* site and the Hill of Tara where many *Grail* kings had been sworn in.

With the help of my dear friend, Annabel, I created a homeopathic essence from my *Graal* and another for the sacred masculine using shavings from the antler of a stag that had been used in Druidic ceremonies for generations and gifted to her at her dad's funeral. These were used in conjunction with a *Sacred Union* crystal, shell and flower essence I'd been guided to make at several portal dates.

As part of my preparation, I also created a series of

mandalas under the tutelage of Karen Scott to activate *Sacred Union* within my blood codes and energy field. The first was a painting of my inner twin flame serpents as the *caduceus*. The second painting was a *Sri Yantra* within the eighth chakra; the godhead and the final painting was a Mandorla featuring me, a *Magdalene* holding the chalice of my *Graal* within the Vesica Pisces.

I was then sent to New Zealand, to present *the Grail* teachings at a yoga festival and one of my students connected me with a Maori elder who had received a similar vision for the ceremony that I'd been guided to do in Glastonbury. When we met at dusk, we meditated to ask why we'd been brought together and I was told to anoint him with my *Graal*. (I'd started bleeding an hour before our meeting). While I felt nervous asking a complete stranger if I could anoint him with my menses, he responded with complete ease saying all bodily fluids were revered for their alchemical properties by his people and we agreed to do ceremony at midnight on the beach where I'd felt most connected with the *Earth Mother* as a child. After a 40 year absence it was an emotional homecoming.

He explained his niece had been practicing traditional Maori menstrual rites on that beach and had just received a grant to write her thesis on that topic. When the moment arrived and I anointed him on the third eye with my *Graal* he dropped to his knees, prostrate on the sand for some time, and later explained he'd seen me as a multi-dimensional being of rainbow light. I explained I was a vessel for *Ishtar*, the rainbow

Goddess who bridges Heaven and Earth. He was told to gift me his whalebone fish hook amulet that had been passed down through his lineage. Humbled, I gave him the small jade fish hook I'd just bought and cleansed in a thermal waterfall. I received the understanding these amulets would act as portal keys during our simultaneous ceremonies for the Grand Cross.

In 2018, after my daughter relocated to her dad's, I did a 2-month trial move to Ubud, Bali where the kundalini is amplified due to the interception of the two main dragon lines (energy meridians) within the Earth. Understanding this, the Balinese people do ceremony at dawn and dusk every day to balance the energies of light and dark. Here my soul felt supported energetically to expand, after living in the restrictive energy of the group mind in the West that's programmed into a perpetual state of fear about time and money. I enrolled in a kundalini Tantra yoga retreat for the first new moon of 2018 but the Dark Goddess, *Kali Ma* had other ideas! The retreat began with a pre-dawn walk to a water temple that banned menstruating women. My *Graal* started to flow with such strong contractions, that both a hike and immersion in cold water were out of the question. As my *Graal* spiraled down, so did my consciousness into the center of the Earth where the *Black Madonna* initiated me with teachings about the three taboos that were once part of *the Grail* mysteries and gifted me thirteen menstrual chants. I delivered those teachings as a 3-part series called, *Initiation: The Sacred Power of Blood, Sex and Death* which are listed in the resources section. I returned to Australia to facilitate and film a training course teaching rites of passage ceremonies for women - sacred blood rites initiated by the cycles of our wombs in conjunction with astrological transits. Ceremonies that were once part of *the Grail* mysteries and this formed my final initiation before I started the next phase of my work, initiating men into *the Grail* tradition.

With the support of my *Red Tent* sisters, I packed up my home in the forest outside of Melbourne, Australia and burnt a body cast to acknowledge the end of my mother phase. Then I moved to Bali for 2 years, punctuated by tours of Europe and Australia where I facilitated *Sacred Union* workshops and Forgiveness ceremonies for men and women to heal the gender war.

It is only in 2021, after years of gestation and rough drafts I am ready to write the final draft of this book on *the Grail* in the hope it will serve as a catalyst to awaken those still in a sleep state, as *the Grail* heraldry is shown to do in the *Judgment* card of the Tarot. This is the last major lesson we undergo as a soul before experiencing a return to a whole and healed state of awareness depicted in the final card, *The World*.

JUDGEMENT.

CHAPTER 1

The Ordinary World:
Houston, We Have a Problem

Feel overwhelmed by the stats about our global decline every time you open your newsfeed? From the extinction of species, to the pollution of the elements or the violence perpetrated on the innocent...you're not alone! Cortisol, our stress hormone, is constantly being dispensed into our bloodstream as we receive digital notifications and headlines that flood our sympathetic nervous system, hindering clear cognitive function and in many cases, right action.

The truth is, nothing in our lives has prepared us for what we are now facing on a grand scale...chaos, destruction and death. Most of us in the modern world weren't initiated when we came of age to confront these fears, unlike those reared in indigenous cultures so we are ill prepared to confront the darker side of life and assume our adult responsibilities. Without rite of passage initiations, we have not sufficiently matured so when faced with an epic challenge, such as our current world events, it's understandable many respond by cowering in fear, seeking someone to blame or disassociating, rather than face it directly.

The lack of initiation into adulthood is due to widespread colonization by dynastic empires that severed our longstanding cultural traditions. Without access to the sacred rites that once assisted our collective psyche to mature, we are stunted psychologically and emotionally. Why? An immature collective is easier to enslave and control. Just as children defer to the authority of their parents, feeling unable to navigate life alone, we are kept disempowered, ignorant and over-regulated so we look to governments to govern us. After generations of systemic disempowerment, the majority doesn't need overt force to comply with unreasonable demands as their immaturity makes them prisoners; complicit in their own enslavement.

We have overlooked immaturity as the root cause of our global problems because we tend to perceive ourselves as clever, based on the evidence of our 'man-made' achievements. However, the state of our relationships and our environment tell a different story. The decline of both human relationships and our habitat illustrate we destroy more than we create. This is not because human beings are bad and deserve to become extinct. This is the abusive narrative we've been conditioned to believe. To stop the pattern of destruction we simply need to recognize how undeveloped the feminine side of our collective psyche is and take steps to remedy our immaturity. To validate this claim, one needs only look at how our modern culture worships the external signs of youth and devalues the inner qualities we gain with age. Why?

The masculine governs the external world and the feminine governs the inner world. We have neglected the growth of our inner world, so our outer world is sounding the alarm. Without wisdom to guide us, we are paving a road to Hell with good intentions…all in the name of progress.

It Wasn't Me!

Up until recently, like teenagers, we have been primarily concerned with our personal needs and wants, and then as 'shit got real', many reacted like siblings in the backseat of a family road trip, squabbling over who is to blame. Others figure, "Why blame us?!" when our so-called leaders, abdicate responsibility like a hot potato…probably because their hands are full juggling perks, prostitutes and pay-offs. While the minority have attempted to respond in practical ways, the vast majority have waited for an external authority to fix things. This passive sentiment is echoed by John Mayer's song, *Waitin' on the World to Change.* Yes, when religion looked unlikely to provide the promised savior, many looked to the government, only to become completely disillusioned as it became apparent those in public office were doing the bidding of privately-owned corporations who funded their ascent to power.

My intention here is not to invalidate the efforts of all the well-meaning individuals who, like me, have been signing petitions to ban plastics, reading labels to boycott palm oil, donating money to save rhinos and planting trees on weekends. I am simply suggesting an allopathic approach to our global crises is as futile as sticking your finger in the cracks of a dam wall that's destined to break. We must acknowledge the underlying cause for all these seemingly unrelated issues as a matter of priority. For as long as we expend all our energy reacting to the symptoms and neglecting the cause, the unraveling of the fabric of life will continue faster than a run in the pantyhose of a Radio City Rockette.

So...Will Religion or the Government Save Us?

No, let's face it, the whole system is corrupt to the core, like Wall Street in the Big Apple so while the circus of debate continues like background music on the deck of the Titanic, it's inevitable our modern civilization must fall. Why? Our modern society is based on the values of ancient Rome...even the architecture of state buildings replicates those of ancient Rome. Similarly, just as the Roman Empire fell due to its arrogance, acted out as an insatiable ego-driven appetite for status, glory, power and wealth to prove its power and dominion, so too, our modern world is destined to meet the same fate. It is crumbling due to its corrupt foundations, destabilizing every aspect of life as we know it. This is why everyone who's trying to hold it together is literally cracking up under the strain. The question is, will our group mind transform by embracing our collective breakdown as an opportunity for a breakthrough or will we, as an unconscious collective, take everyone and everything down with us? This depends on one thing, whether we humble our egos and mature.

Social Sustainability: Growing a Grass Roots Foundation

If focusing on our maturity levels seems like a sideward step, ponder this; if someone is not functioning in age-appropriate ways, they cannot keep a pot plant alive, let alone muck in and help save a planet. So too, if we are not personally sustainable, we cannot create sustainable relationships, environments, or care for other life forms. I speak from experience. In my family of origin, we flushed a lot of goldfish, signaling my parent's coping mechanisms were frayed, like so many behind brick veneers in the suburbs. Such unstable interpersonal foundations have been the norm, or *The Simpsons* wouldn't have struck such a universal chord. Only by acknowledging our immaturity and reinstating healthy social structures as scaffolding to support us can we grow and fulfill our true potential. Only then will we be able to effectively deal with the crises now at hand.

Crisis = Danger / Opportunity

There's nothing like a crisis to reveal someone's maturity levels. When immature, we respond to crises with fear, anticipating only danger. When mature, we see crises as an opportunity for growth. This is why we're now seeing such a divide between those clinging to the old paradigm, who are looking to governments to save them, and those trying to actively seed a new paradigm through innovating change at a grassroots level.

Those who feel internally like frightened children want to be taken care of by an external authority to feel safe, so they comply without question. While those who feel internally like teenagers will look to see what their friends are doing and follow suit to gain approval and acceptance. Meanwhile, those who feel internally like adults will assert their internal authority by questioning, researching and informing those unaware of what's really going on what's at stake. However, just as you wouldn't impose X-rated adult content onto a child because their psyche couldn't handle it, those who are essentially children in adult bodies feel traumatized when well-meaning folk try to wake them up by exposing them to the global shadow in the light of day. Much easier to shoot the messenger by dismissing them as mad (a conspiracy theorist) than entertain the repercussions of their message. This is a response people are entrained to do with their daily dose of mind programming by the corporate-owned media. Similarly, this is why those operating at the level of teenagers are more likely to join with their oppressors, like victims of *Stockholm syndrome*, criticizing, judging and bullying those who aren't conforming. Like teens, they rebel against those who are asking them to grow up by confronting hard truths that challenge their accepted reality. This leaves those investigating the extent of the global shadow trying to discern who has 'eyes to see and ears to hear.'

Watching Superhero Films Will Not Save the Earth

Our impaired maturity is why, as this cataclysm of epic proportions is unfolding all around us, just when we need a hero most, the majority are suspended in a state of childlike passivity, gaming in virtual worlds and watching films about superheroes instead of actually responding as real-life heroes. Whether it's *Star Wars*, *Avatar*, *Braveheart*, *The Lion King*, or Marvel and DC's cinematic franchises, simply consuming formulaic re-enactments of *The Hero's Journey* will not save the world in this, our time of need.

This is most noticeable in the collective masculine. That isn't to suggest all women are mature but women are initiated by their bodies, so once you start cycling as a woman you are confronted with your power to create life and bear the responsibility of raising it. That recognition matures the psyche. Men in a patriarchal society do not receive an equivalent blood rite to initiate their psyche and mature. This is why indigenous cultures insisted all men were initiated through rites of passage to mature psychologically and emotionally.

The problem is not that men identify with superheroes. In fact, it's wonderful that most young boys dream of being a superhero...of making the world a better place, serving the greater good and upholding justice. I know my heart swells with appreciation whenever I see a preschooler proudly wearing their superhero suit and I thank them for showing up to save the world. The question is, why do the vast majority of young men end up betraying their primary urge and core values when they come of age, by settling for a job that contributes to the corrupt Military Industrial Complex - the dark side of The Force, instead of serving the greater good?

Most haven't explored their feminine side; their unconscious feelings and motivations, let alone identified the ways they've been emasculated by patriarchy. Yes, men have suffered equally, but in less overt ways than women...a subject we'll explore later. Suffice to say, men's internalized shame about being male manifests as personal disempowerment. This is why the majority of the men indulge in fantasy scenarios where they save the world single-handed, instead of working together to adequately respond to the challenges immediately facing us. So yes, Houston, we have a problem, and it can't be fixed with technology or science. Let me assure you guys, if you're feeling uncomfortable, this book is dedicated to your empowerment rather than scapegoating you through blaming and shaming but to do that we have to acknowledge there's a problem. In fact, this book is a step-by-step roadmap to awaken the hero and save the world!

Awakening The Hero and the Mystic

Without rites of passage, most men have not directly faced their fear of failure and as a result, struggle to awaken the hero within. Equally, most women have not faced their fear of persecution and madness and as a result, struggle to awaken the inner mystic. These are just two of many archetypes that inhabit our psyche but they're the two most needed in this time of chaos and crisis. Without initiation, most people have no idea of the many facets of masculine and feminine expression that together comprise empowered, authentic manhood and womanhood. I single out these two aspects as they pose the greatest threat to the dominion of the empires, those that oppress us for without the hero and the mystic we lack the wisdom to see clearly and the courage to act when needed.

These are two of the archetypes *the Grail* tradition empowers within the individual and the collective and the two most disempowered by patriarchy. Before the rise of the Roman empire, men and women throughout the Western world were initiated into *the Grail* wisdom tradition. Without initiation into *the Grail*, many men struggle to overcome their inner demons. This prevents them embodying the archetypal hero to realize their goals and dreams and results in them being haunted by the fear their existence is meaningless.

Similarly, many little girls are fascinated with the magic of nature and love to dress as fairies. However, for the last two millennia females have received the message, in both subtle and overt ways, that it's unsafe to explore and embody the archetype of the mystic.

Why? Those who have dared throughout patriarchy were viewed as evil or crazy. They were burnt, drowned, locked away or ostracized. Why? Without *the Grail,* the archetypal mystic is feared and oppressed and without initiation, modern women struggle to positively embody their inner mystic, who is key to accessing their inner guidance. This usually results in women shutting down their subtle perceptions and feeling shame about their sensitivity. The exciting news is that it is all about to change!

The Return of the Cupbearer

We are now entering the Aquarian Age, a 2000-year astrological age, symbolized in myth by the cupbearer. This is a sign it's time for the *Grail*; the sacred vessel to re-emerge. It's time for us to transcend the quest for power, and seek to fill our cup with love by becoming receptive to Spirit that speaks to us through the heart. Those who seek *the Grail* are motivated by their hearts to seek truth, knowing intuitively the truth will set them free from enslavement; by freeing their minds so the heart can be heard. This is why those who sought *the Grail* sought truth as a path to true love. The seeker of *the Grail* is portrayed in the Tarot as *The Knight of Cups*. This card shows a *Grail* knight, a man on white horse who seeks truth, love and wisdom. He holds a goblet which is empty, indicating his mind is receptive to new ideas, for one must be earnest and humble in their search for truth.

Likewise, I trust you wouldn't have opened this book if it didn't call to your soul so I invite you to trust your inner calling, if some of the material presented challenges your conditioned beliefs. For just as love challenges the rational mind, so does truth. I do not ask you to blindly accept what I say as true, but rather sit with it and see what resonates. I encourage you to be skeptical, filtering all information through your own intuition, rather than cynical, rejecting new ideas without due process. In other words, filter and retain what serves you and leave the rest. What I know to be true is we cannot transcend the existing paradigm of war that operates through the Military Industrial Complex without the wisdom of *the Grail* that provides a path back to love, borne of wisdom.

So, without further ado, it is time to look behind the veil into the greatest mystery of all time, *the Grail.* I will do my best to serve you as an oracle, a vessel for truth, to unveil the illusions that distorted *the Grail* and enabled tyranny to reign. For we are now in the 11th hour, and there is no greater issue of importance. This is why so many are seeing the synchronistic sign 11:11. For those of you familiar with the archetypal *Hero's Journey* popularized by Joseph Campbell, you will recognize I have applied this framework for this book, as it was once an intrinsic part of *the Grail* tradition. (More about that later.)

As with all heroic adventures, we start by acknowledging the problem and what we've outgrown. Next, we'll journey the 12 heroic stages to map the quest for *the Grail,* explaining all facets of *the Grail* tradition enroute. For you can only find something if you know what you're looking for. (This is why so much misinformation was perpetuated about *the Grail,* to stop us finding it.)

While the primary focus is on awakening and empowering the sacred masculine, *the Grail* does this by reclaiming the true feminine. Since both reside within us, I anticipate both men and women will find this book healing through its validation and empowering with insight. For both the feminine and the masculine must be healed within our psyche if we are to move forward as sacred and sovereign beings. So, let's start with the most well-known *Grail* parable…

The Fisher King: A Parable for our Times

There was once a land that was sick…the cattle did not reproduce, the crops wouldn't grow, men were dying, children were orphaned and women wept, all because the king was wounded. The prophecy said when the king was healed, the land would be healed…

This is the ominous opening to *The Fisher King*, the story of an old man who is materially rich but spiritually poor, unable to find pleasure in his privilege. He has a physical wound in his groin, preventing him from participating in the nightly festivities of his court. A sad figure, he is unable to stand or drink from the chalice offered to him. He is perpetually restless, distracted by his pain. His only focus is on how to relieve his discomfort.

One day he consults the guidance of an oracle, who decrees only a young fool has the power to heal him…one who is pure of heart and asks the right question. Annoyed by this cryptic riddle, he resigns himself to fishing by day and social distraction by night.

One day while he is fishing on the lake, a sincere and honest youth approaches him to ask where he can find lodging for the night. *The Fisher King* secretly hopes this is the young man who will fulfill the prophecy and heal him by asking the right question.

He welcomes the young man to stay, and after dinner, the youth is shown to his room. Then, in the middle of the night, the youth is awoken by a strange procession passing by his door. First, he sees a maiden carrying a lance with a single drop of blood. She is followed by another maiden carrying a golden platter and then a third maiden bearing a golden chalice. Though intensely curious, he doesn't dare ask what is going on, for he recalls his mother's parting words, "Don't ask too many questions, lest people think you rude."

In the morning, when he awakens, the castle has disappeared, and he realizes that what he glimpsed was, in fact, *The Holy Grail*, the very thing he had dedicated his life to find. Then it dawns on him. He missed the opportunity to discover the mystery of *the Grail* because he didn't ask the women in the procession what they were doing. When he realizes the cost of his choice, he is haunted by the enormity of his failure…having found *the Grail*, he did not seize the opportunity to comprehend it when it was before him.

A Deconstruction of the Parable

The elderly character of *The Fisher King* is a symbol of the wounded masculine. His life is without meaning or purpose. His estate, once bountiful, has fallen into decline, reflecting the barren state of his soul. The tale warns if he cannot find a cure for his wound, his land will become a wasteland.

This fateful tale was once a teaching parable in *the Grail* tradition. A warning of the fate that befalls a man who doesn't seek the *Grail*; initiation into the wisdom tradition of the sacred feminine. *The Fisher King* depicts the endgame of a man who dismisses the importance of the inner soul quest in favor of an external pursuit of personal power through the acquisition of status, knowledge, influence and wealth. It is a tale whose consequence echoes through our modern world, holding a mirror up to the dominant cultural values of our time.

The Lesson For Men and Masculine-Dominant Women

While I address men directly, for whom these lessons are primary, I would encourage women, especially those who are masculine-dominant, to equally heed these lessons, given how prevalent it is for women to sacrifice their feminine side to be taken seriously in a man's world in an effort to ensure their safety.

The story of *The Fisher King* highlights the power of our choices. This is illustrated by a crushing blow to both men in this tale, catalyzed by their choices that serve as a warning. Without direct participation in *the Grail* rite, neither can solve the riddle needed to relieve their burden. As a result, the youth must endure 20 years of chaos and confusion, haunted by his failure before another opportunity to access *the Grail* presents. Whereas the elder leaves no trace, indicating no legacy, revealing his life amounted to nothing, as it was void of true meaning.

The core teaching of *the Grail* parable, *The Fisher King*, is that man and the land are one. The wasteland reflects the wasted potential of a man who thinks only of himself and not how to serve the land and her people. Ultimately, what man does to the land, he does to himself, and vice versa. When we comprehend this, we understand there is no long-term gain in exploiting the land for personal gain. In the end, one who does, pays the ultimate price. This is something understood by indigenous cultures who lived sustainably before colonialism.

The Fatal Flaw of the Hero

As with all mythic heroes, the protagonist's downfall is his ability to take right action. This refusal to seek guidance results in a state of ignorance and eventual destruction - his own and everything around him. *The Fisher King* is not humble enough to ask questions or seek answers to the meaning of life. He is a man considered wealthy by those whose focus is rational and material, valuing only what they perceive through their physical senses. From this perspective, *The Fisher King* appears to have it all; a stately manor, social status, worldly power and material wealth. However, if we view him from a psycho-emotional perspective, we see a man who has dismissed the richness found in the inner realms, leading to an unenviable state of inner torment. This means he is unable to enjoy his daily life, making him a figure of pathos.

The Fisher King is a herald of entropy, for he is not in right relationship with his inner self. This prevents him from being in right relationship with all other life forms. His wound, manifested physically, indicates an internal mindset of dis-ease, for he is soul-sick, enslaved by toxic thinking and disconnected from his heart. So long as his mind overrides his feeling function, he remains unavailable to enjoy the natural richness life has to offer so he is unable to experience pure joy, the essence of true abundance.

Only by living with an open heart can we perceive life's simple pleasures. When the heart is closed, we remain trapped in a soul cage, tormented by our jailer, the inner critic who finds fault with everyone and everything, including ourselves. This state of unrest undermines our energetic frequency. This disturbance is felt first within the subtle bodies of the mind and emotions and then the physical body. Having sustained this state of being for some time, *The Fisher King* is rendered ineffectual, unable to instigate the change he so desperately needs.

The mind, in and of itself is not bad. Analytical by nature, the function of our mind is to anticipate danger in order to avoid it. However, without balancing this function with the intuitive wisdom of the soul, our mind inevitably becomes unbalanced. This manifests as hyper-vigilance and controlling behavior in a futile attempt to create safety and security in a world where the only constant is change. This leads to neurosis and obsessive compulsions, driven by fears that undermine wellbeing. This is why today we see anxiety disorders now twice as prevalent as all other mental illnesses[1] indicating our mind-dominant culture is operating under the strain of mental imbalance.

With his rational-material focus, *The Fisher King* has spent his life in an unfulfilling pursuit of short-term gain. This is the unconscious behavior of someone who unconsciously seeks external challenges as a distraction from their core wounds. Such as *The Fisher King's* compulsion to accumulate material wealth to prove his worth, indicating his lack of intrinsic self-worth.

It is only through taking the journey within to discover the totality of our multifaceted soul that we can glean an appreciation of our true worth, which is beyond measure. Without taking this quest to truly know ourselves, we can never identify our soul calling and live a life of real meaning. *The Fisher King* dies, oblivious of his character flaw, due to his refusal to become self-aware.

Impotence: The Disempowered Masculine

As *the Grail* parable of *The Fisher King* warns, when the masculine is weak, the land and her people will perish. Today, many of our men are in such a state of personal crises they are impotent to act on that which threatens their existence and this manifests physically as erectile dysfunction. The high volume of Viagra sales and pornography evidences men's desperate attempt to feel potent and powerful through artificial, external means.

The physical condition of erectile dysfunction compounds a man's pre-existing low self-worth and disempowerment. In our patriarchal culture men are pressured to perform sexually. This stems from an unconscious compulsion to prove one's power as a man, often through acts of domination of the feminine; be it nature, women or feminine-dominant men. The bitter irony is such internal pressure makes one a lousy lover as they're unavailable to themselves, their partner and the present moment due to their personal neurosis. Men are also conditioned to attain external power by pursuing wealth, status and influence to prove their power as men. I see this as an unconscious compensation for low self-worth. The only way to grow self-worth and empowerment is through gaining self-awareness. This is the significance of the wound in the groin of *The Fisher King*, suggesting impotence. It is not simply a lack of physical virility, but his impotence to act. He lacks the ability to take the right action by addressing his personal dysfunction so he can be a force for good in the world. Since the masculine energy polarity is active, the opposite of the feminine polarity, which is receptive, his inability to take appropriate action, as needed, signals a lack of male power.

His passivity indicates he is operating unconsciously from the shadow feminine part of his psyche; the unacknowledged and undeveloped feminine. This occurs when a man does not receive mystic initiation and instruction from the empowered feminine. Over time he becomes eclipsed by his wound, habitually passive he experiences a decline in his physical mobility, until he is completely incapacitated.

Like Father, Like Son

While *The Fisher King* and the youth, *Parsival*, are not blood kin, we see the inter-generational wound illustrated. The youth, *Parsival*, is also impotent to act, suggesting his lack of positive male role models. *Parsival*'s wound is not yet physical, but surfaces as an internal neurosis. This results in paralysis from over-analysis. Put simply, he fears taking action, lest he makes the wrong choice so he embodies failure with his refusal to make an effort. Had he dared risk looking like a fool, he would've learned through trial and error, but by not making any effort, he embodies the adage, 'Nothing ventured, nothing gained.'

Parsival lacks confidence in his inner authority to make his own choices, indicating, like *The Fisher King*, he is essentially 'half a man', as he has not become whole by integrating the feminine side of his psyche. He lacks clarity of mind as he has not yet awakened his intuition, a function of his inner feminine. Without the ability to attune to his inner knowing for guidance, he defers to the opinions of others, such as the internalized voice of his mother. Dominated by the incessant chatter of his rational mind, he experiences confusion, leading to procrastination which limits his opportunities. It's worth noting in this parable it is the disempowered feminine who is Parcival's inner authority as his mother cautions him not to seek the truth for fear of what others will think. Here we see history repeating as the next generation misses the moment of opportunity to become whole by seizing the gift of feminine wisdom when it is before them.

The Fisher King is a tragedy of epic proportions. For not only does the protagonist lack the ability to take the action needed to heal himself and the land, he is so disempowered he can't even stand. This signifies he can't take a stand for the convictions of his heart's deepest truth; what he believes in and is most important to him. As a result, he lives a meaningless existence. Without anything to live for, he is a man at risk of death, whether that's via a reckless act or a slow decline borne of self-negating choices. This is why male suicide rates continue to climb, sounding the alarm that is being muffled by a media black ban on the taboo topic of suicide. Meanwhile, countless men are enacting their death wish slowly via addictions to numb their psycho-emotional pain.

"I'd rather die standing than live on my knees"

Stéphane Charbonnier

The Fisher King is a man whose psycho-emotional maturity is stunted due to his inability to know his own heart. This results in his physical body bearing the burden of his unexpressed feelings and desires. A solitary figure with no apparent emotional attachments, he is a man who has avoided intimacy with himself and others. Without exploring the crucible of human relationships, his priorities and values have remained unchanged since his youth. Here we see the emptiness that awaits those whose main priority in life is acquiring status symbols that represent 'the good life' - those who fall victim to the law of diminishing return. That being, the more you have of something, the less you enjoy it. Without awareness of the universal laws governing us, *The Fisher King* does the same thing day in and day out. By day, he fishes, and by night, he lives through others as a voyeur. Neither pursuit is soul-fulfilling. Both activities are nonsensical as they serve no purpose, so what ensues is a dystopian circus, an endless cycle of dysfunction, repeatedly doing that which brings no relief while hoping for a different outcome; a miracle of salvation.

This is not uncommon behavior in our modern world. Many enact this 'Groundhog Day' saga. They wake up, do the habitual activities that offer no real fulfillment, hoping to win the lottery to change their fate, while passively watching other people on their devices, with mass voyeurism normalized since the advent of television. This never-ending circle is the rat wheel of our modern world due to the lack of initiation into the life/death/life cycle of feminine mysteries. Without this initiation, it's understandable people fear change and resist the endings required for growth. We can only embrace change when we make time to question our choices.

Without developing the feminine side of our nature, we don't prioritize the space and time needed for reflection, so our past patterns aren't identified and transcended. It is only through introspection we stop going round in circles and ascend into the sacred spiral of our own evolution. If we don't know how to do this, we remain frozen in time, unable to progress to our next psychological and emotional stage. *The Fisher King* is the epitome of someone who has not examined the cause and effect of their past actions to assume accountability for their choices. Despite his chronological years, *The Fisher King* has failed to mature, so he becomes a frail old man instead of a wise elder.

This is inevitable if we don't seek the wisdom of the cycles, the teachings inherent in *the Grail* tradition that assist us to grow, mature and age with grace. As a result, the ageing process of *The Fisher King* is tortured, a fulfilment of his fear of change, ageing and death. As he deteriorates, so does his land, as nothing can thrive without understanding the natural cycles; be it the human psyche, one's physical health, interpersonal relationships, or the fertility of the land. Without the wisdom of *the Grail,* the masculine aspect in both men and women remains immature, sabotaging love, health and purpose. The legacy of such an individual is one of unconscious destruction, to themselves and all life, as they unwittingly create a life that isn't worth living.

This ominous tale warns those who dismiss or dominate the feminine, do so at their own peril. Without *the Grail,* we see the vast majority of men and masculine-dominant women seeking to emulate the external success of *The Fisher King* without realizing the cost to themselves and the land. All because they're so desperate to prove themselves a success in order to gain approval. Until we address this wounded thinking that subconsciously drives progress at any cost, we won't stop the downward spiral of destruction and entropy that threatens the sacredness of life prevailing.

"One day...there would come a time, when the earth being ravaged and polluted, the forests being destroyed, the birds would fall from the air, the waters would be blackened, the fish being poisoned in the streams, and the trees would no longer be, mankind as we would know it would all but cease to exist."

An excerpt from the Rainbow prophecy as retold by a Cree woman over a century ago.[2]

CHAPTER 2

The Call to Adventure:
Will You Seek the Grail?

Now we've acknowledged how immaturity and disempowerment stems from a lack of initiation, it's time to offer the cup of feminine wisdom to restore our birthright of sacred knowledge. Like a herbal healing elixir, the truth may be bitter and hard to swallow, but is necessary to expose the toxic thinking that causes our wounds to fester.

Just as potent herbal medicines were imitated and replaced by petrochemical-based pharmaceuticals, *the Grail* has suffered a similar fate. It has been replaced with a poor imitation that has done more harm than good. I am referring to the hierarchical religions created by the empires. I will explain the connection between *The Grail* and Christianity in greater detail later on. For now, I'll start by revealing what I know to be the truth about *the Grail,* an ancient mystic tradition that empowered individuals through the integration of the empowered feminine. For the restoration of the true feminine is necessary if we are to dispel the societal enchantment that cast the mystic feminine as evil. A spell that still causes women to suffer from self-loathing and men to suppress their feminine traits for fear of being dominated. Both of which sabotage true love and enable tyrants to rule. In this chapter, we'll unveil the enchantment that has kept the archetypal hero disempowered in a sleep state. For only through facing the truth, can the hero in all of us rise and end the paradigm of war.

What is the Grail? Discerning Fact from Fiction

Considered the greatest mystery of all time, *The Holy Grail* has been surrounded with ongoing speculation down through the ages regarding its true origins and identity. Claims have been made *the Grail* is:

❖ A vial of precious blood

- ❖ A blinding white light
- ❖ The Celtic cauldron of plenty
- ❖ A secret book or gospel
- ❖ The philosopher's stone
- ❖ The chalice Yeshua used in the Last Supper
- ❖ The blood of Yeshua collected while he was on the cross
- ❖ The bloodline of Yeshua and Mari signified by her womb

Why? *The Grail* has remained shrouded in mystery because, like all mystic traditions, it was not written down. Its gifts were reserved for those willing and brave enough to face their fear of the unknown through the act of initiation. I'll now explain the origins of these theories and share my understanding of the original sacred wisdom tradition known as *the Grail*. I'll also reveal why *the Grail* was considered such a threat to Rome and was subsequently shrouded with falsehoods.

Celtic Versus Christian Grail Tales

What has been written about *the Grail* can be divided into two camps; that of early Celtic legend, detailing a mystic quest undertaken by noble knights and the later claims it was the blood of Christ.[3] When one considers both versions from the standpoint of sacred feminine mystery teachings, it's obvious which points us in the direction of truth, and which attempts to steer us away from it. Even more compelling are the lengths to which the deception has been perpetuated for thousands of years, indicating just how feared and ultimately powerful, this ancient mystic wisdom tradition truly is.

The Original Grail Legends from Traditional Folklore

While *the Grail* was practiced long before antiquity, it enjoyed a resurgence during the 12th century when the first documentation alluding to *the Grail* was recorded in two very similar tales. The most renown was a romantic tale written by Chretien de Troyes, titled *Perceval Le Gallois*. An Arthurian love poem, it outlines a humble young man's pursuit of truth and love and conveys the tale of *The Fisher King*. This poem was never completed due to the untimely death of either the author or his source. Such a fate suggests foul play as four subsequent writers attempted to finish and embellish his poem during the 12th and 13th centuries.

Then there is the Welsh romance, *Peredur, Son of Efrawg*, part of the *Mabinogi* collection of Welsh prose handed down through the oral storytelling tradition of the Druidic bards who traveled from town to town, sharing the mystic lessons of the Celtic myths. The *Mabinogi* collection is regarded as the earliest literature of Great Britain. This traditional Welsh folktale bears many striking resemblances to *the Grail* story written by Chretien de Troyes. Both were published during the 12th century, and in each story, the young hero is raised solely by his mother in the forest due to his father's premature death. This indicates both youths were raised with feminine values and seek answers to what it is to be a man. As a result, both protagonists desire to find meaning through a noble cause and seek their missing father figure by serving a *Sacred King*. Like *Parsival, Peredur* aspires to serve in *King Arthur's* court after he meets a group of knights. This indicates their yearning for true brotherhood to ease their sense of isolation.

Both young men meet a woman along the way whom they fall in love with and wish to marry. This illustrates *the Grail* is intrinsically linked to the quest for true love. The similarities continue…both meet an older man who challenges their world view, and both tales feature some kind of ceremony involving mystic women where the masculine is injured or killed. In the former tale, this is indicated by 3 drops of blood on the lance, representing the triple-fold Goddess, the cyclic feminine. In the latter tale, it is symbolized by[4] the severed head of *Peredur's* uncle, presented on a silver platter. When reinterpreted from a patriarchal view, such occurrences may understandably incite fear of the feminine. However, with initiation one understands the mystic feminine is an ally who assists the hero to undergo an ego death that's necessary for his true self to emerge so he may fulfill his potential. For a man who is mind dominant will never know his true heart and will forever be destined to suffer.

The Original Philosopher's Stone

Long before *Harry Potter* reawakened interest in the philosopher's stone, the rendition of *the Grail* quest by medieval German knight and poet, Wolfram von Eschenbach, claimed *the Grail* was a 'philosopher's stone' that fell from the sky and possessed powers to bring longevity and happiness. This claim stemmed from ancient Syriac texts that refer to the foundation stone that lays hidden within the primordial depths of the Earth. *The Grail* romances speak of noblemen's journeys to the center of the Earth to find their sovereign power. This is why British kings were crowned on a *Stone of Destiny*. This symbolized that the *Earth Mother* as their cornerstone; on the understanding their foundation of power lay in their connection with her. Eschenbach's version focused on the qualities a man must possess to procure true love and how love inspires a man to be chivalrous and do great deeds.[5] Again we see *the Grail* themes of nobility, love and mysticism recurring.

I suspect his version was inspired by the ancient Irish folktale, *The Dagda's Cauldron* which features the sacred stone that once determined a High King's right to rule. The possession of this sacred stone represented a man's spiritual connection and commitment to serve the land and her people. The investiture ceremony for ancient kings saw them lay their heads on the sacred stone of coronation of those who had gone before. Such a privilege was only afforded to a man who was grounded in wisdom after being reborn from the Earth via the mid-Winter *Grail* rites. This is why *Sacred Kings* were said to rule from 'the center of the Earth'.[6] The following quote from the Bible illustrates how the Romans opposed this sacred tradition.

"Do not make idols or set up an image or a sacred stone for yourselves, and do not place a carved stone in your land to bow down before it."

Leviticus 26:1[7]

The Appropriation of the Grail

In the 12th century, the French poet, Robert de Boron, wrote a poem titled Merlin, whom he claimed was the antichrist; a son of the devil and a virgin.[8] It should be noted that a *virgin* was once a term used to describe a priestess of *the Grail* tradition. His slur clearly indicates his attitude towards mysticism and those who practiced it. De Boron created the concept of the 'sword in the stone' claiming *Arthur* obtained the British throne by pulling a sword from an anvil that sat on a stone in a churchyard on *Christmas* Eve.

Robert de Boron was also the first to associate *the Grail* legend with Christ. His other published work, Joseph *d'Arimathie* asserts Joseph of Arimathea, the uncle of Christ, received a vision of *Yeshua* handing him *the Grail*. He claimed it was used in the Last Supper and later by Joseph of Arimathea to collect Christ's last remaining drops of blood as he hung on the cross. While I concur, he may have received a vision indicating *Yeshua's* connection with *the Grail* mysteries, I suspect associating the holy blood of *the Grail* with the blood sacrifice of Christ by the Romans was an overlay influenced by his Christian convictions. If we consider *Yeshua's* mother was referred to as a *virgin*, we can see how fitting such an association was, despite the misinterpretation.

Boron's poem asserted Joseph's family brought *the Grail* to the *vaus d'Avaron*, in the west of France, which later poets changed to the mystic isle of *Avalon* in the British Isles. It is interesting to note after the crucifixion, there's evidence showing Joseph and *Mari* traveled through France enroute to England, where they established the *Avalon* Mystery school that seeded *the Grail* wisdom teachings and practices in *Brigid's Isles*, later renamed the British Isles, just as the Goddess, *Europa* was conquered and divided.

Bloody Hell!

Once this assertion was made linking Christ's blood to *the Grail,* numerous claims followed from competing parties declaring they had the cup that had collected Christ's blood. One of the most well-known came from the Vatican, who asserted *the Grail* was the *Holy Chalice of Valencia,* an ornate ceremonial goblet stored behind glass in the Montserrat cathedral in Spain. This artifact is now a tourist attraction, despite[9] the style of the cup not being congruent with first-century goblets, along with a convoluted backstory about how the cup ended up in Spain. Personally, I find it significant that Spain was home to the Catholic inquisitors who persecuted those who sought to uphold *the Grail*, and it was the apostle, Peter, who was said to have retrieved the goblet. The disciple who openly opposed *Mari*, the *Magdalene*.[10]

Another well-known claim came in 1910 from a team of archeologists in Syria who discovered a silver chalice depicting Christ and his disciples. They claimed Christ used their cup in the Last Supper.[11] Still today, there are rewards offered to anyone who can locate the 'missing' cup from the Last Supper used by Christ, believed to be *the Grail*. All of these distractions simply create more confusion to conceal the truth about *the Grail*.

Personally, I don't resonate with the notion that *the Grail* was a cup used to collect the blood of Christ while he was bleeding from wounds suffered during his crucifixion. The concept of gathering blood from a tortured man is as repugnant to me as treasuring blood borne of pain. I see this as a direct inversion of the original *Grail* that honored the sacred blood of the womb as the life-giving blood that had the power to heal. This was the sacred blood that didn't carry the lower vibrational signature of blood that's caused by wounds.

The Symbolic Cup of Death

I do believe *the Grail* was part of the Last Supper, the sacred act of communion *Yeshua* shared with his Beloved, *Mari* and his disciples before his crucifixion, just not in the way we've been led to believe. Why? His partner, *Mari* was a *Magdalene*. This was the title given to the priestess women who initiated both men and women into *the Grail* tradition. In this ancient tradition, the drinking from the sacred cup signified one's willingness to humble their ego. The cup of the feminine mysteries was symbolic of the death and rebirth that takes place each month within the womb and psyche of a menstruating woman, when a woman was said to be most internal and closest to God. To drink from this cup signified one's willingness to surrender the ego to Divine will. This is a theme common to all shamanic traditions where ceremonial drinks alter the initiate's consciousness, catalyzing an ego death. This is why *Yeshua* was reported to have said, the night before his crucifixion while praying in the Garden of Gethsemane, "Take this cup away from me. I don't want to drink its poison." This is an acknowledgment that *the Grail* is a cup of death. Not a physical death as was later interpreted, but a psycho-emotional one necessary for the maturing of the psyche.

This earlier symbolism of *the Grail* cup, was distorted in the Christian rite of the Eucharist, so that the cup signified the ingesting of sacrificial blood from a persecuted messiah. Today this pseudo blood rite is one children are still indoctrinated into as young as 7, an age when they lack the maturity and capacity to grant informed consent. Given the power of any ritual act, I see this as a form of ritual abuse, albeit unconscious and well-meaning.

My intention is not to condemn those indoctrinated into Catholicism, for when the concept of ego death is foreign, we view death as physical and final. In fact, it is the fear of death that keeps us in an immature state. Once we undergo an ego-death we become more afraid of not living fully by embodying our potential.

The fear of death is, therefore, a powerful means of manipulation on a populace who is immature.

This literal interpretation of the mythic quest for an ego death is why we see violence constantly suggested as the answer to external opposition, rather than personal transformation. Patriarchal portrayals of heroes constantly anchor the expectation one must risk physical death via acts of violence to succeed. As a result, immature men resort to brute force and aggressive behavior while immature women and emasculated men enact their rage via passive aggressive, covert means such as poisoning their spouse with a literal cup of death rather than drinking a metaphorical one to liberate themselves from their own patterns of dysfunction. Even more common are those who slowly drink themselves to death rather than transmute their pain into wisdom. Whether the violence is enacted on ourselves or others, or is overt or covert, it stems from a lack of empowerment and self-love...both of which the true *Grail* addresses.

The Grail Prepares Us For True Love

The Grail often appears as a call to adventure via the unexpected arrival of a new love interest. In fact, the meeting with the Goddess is one of the universal stages on the archetypal hero's journey. In all *Grail* myths, the questing hero meet a fateful woman who challenges him to grow beyond their existing self-perception and worldview. The cup of love the magical woman offers the hero is *the Grail.* By accepting the offer to journey with her; one who consciously cycles, he will be initiated directly into the circle of life through her highs and lows. Her womb and its cycles will initiate them both in a constant yin/yang cycle of life and death, via light and dark experiences, evoking strengths and shadows as sure as night follows day. That neither men or women are taught how to navigate this ongoing challenge in intimate relationships is why we see relationship breakdown so prevalent today.

The Grail is the cup of initiation into the world of the feminine. Love always requires a sacrifice; this is why the word sacrifice once meant to 'make sacred'. This originally referred to the sacrifice of the ego through one's ability to let go of their childish ways and dedicate themself to something more noble...not a blood sacrifice of physical life. This is the distortion that occurred without the wisdom of *the Grail* to guide us.

Without *the Grail* we perceive those who are different as a potential threat. We perceive opposition as the enemy to be defeated, conquered or seduced to do the bidding of our ego. Should the other exert their free will, we scapegoat them to avoid self-examination, thereby refusing our hero's call to adventure. Similarly, those who run from an opportunity to explore true love with their opposite may experience a sense of temporary safety, as their ego hides from the inevitable ego-death that awaits them, but eventually they'll be consumed by their own unresolved psycho-emotional issues. Why? Without psycho-emotional maturity, we lack self-love. This is evidenced by *The Fisher King's* wound indicating a lack of self-care and responsibility. Without an internal foundation of self-love, *The Fisher King* cannot form a lasting bond with another. When an invitation of love is offered, symbolized by *the Grail* chalice, he is unable to participate in the act of communion. We see this in those who avoid emotional entanglement due to the fear-based doubts of their mind. Irrational fears, such as a fear of change, the unknown and intimacy.

The Deception of Dynastic Bloodlines

More recently, there have been claims that *the Grail* refers to the genetic bloodline of *Yeshua* and *Mari*. Claims made popular by the best-selling book, *The Da Vinci Code* by Dan Brown, a novel that sourced inspiration from the book, *Holy Blood, Holy Grail*, written 20 years earlier by Michael Baigent and Richard Leigh. While I don't disagree, it's entirely plausible secret societies sought to track their bloodline, given the emphasis dynastic families place upon their genetics. I assert this has nothing to do with the true origins of *the Grail*. It is yet another distortion that succeeded in creating greater confusion by associating *the Grail* with a quest for power and status, based on genetic rights of claim.

So, What are the True Origins of the Grail?

Before the advent of patriarchy, traditional cultures honored women as sacred vessels whose wombs shed life-giving blood. *Gra-al* is an ancient Mesopotamian word meaning 'nectar of supreme excellence' (blood), which was consumed by antediluvian Gods and kings.[12] Either as a ritual drink or in *Graal* infused desserts, such as mooncakes and moon-shaped croissants to enhance wisdom and longevity! The *Graal* was revered as the elixir of the *Sangraal*, meaning 'holy chalice' or 'sacred vessel'. So, *the Grail* didn't simply refer to the womb of *Mari*, the *Magdalene* as claimed in the book, *The Da Vinci Code*, but to every woman initiated into *the Grail*, as the ancients understood the power of a woman's womb as a receptacle for creation. Not just physical children but intentions seeded in alignment with the Cosmic womb at the Galactic Center.

This is why *the Grail* was represented in sacred ceremony as a cup, bowl or receptacle. Patriarchy reduced to the role of the mythic cupbearer, to Ganymede, a servant boy who poured wine for the Olympiad Gods, who used him to satisfy their sexual urges. Before this distortion, the cup bearer was an earnest young man like *Parcival,* who sought to serve *the Grail* by seeking truth, embodying love and serving the *Earth Mother*, while upholding an honor code. While *the Grail* is most closely associated with the Celtic tradition, the motif of *the Grail* cup featured in ancient Sumer as the *Gra-al*, the 'cup of the waters' and the Rosi-Crucis, meaning 'dew-cup' in both the Egyptian and Hebraic tradition.

Distilling Cyclic Wisdom

The Grail didn't just refer to the physical womb, but the accumulated wisdom contained within the womb of an initiated Grail maiden. When someone sought *the Grail,* they were seeking feminine wisdom so each questing hero received the help of a female guide. These were women who had accrued and distilled wisdom within their wombs by consciously journeying the cycles of nature and the Cosmos within their bodies. These wise women assisted men to make sense of their inner terrain. This role as a spiritual guide was later stripped from women and appropriated by male clergy; priests, rabbis and gurus until recently when women were permitted to hold these positions, but confined within the patriarchal constructs of religion.

In the ancient world everyone was initiated into *the Grail* tradition. For women, this occurred when they began cycling with the moon. *Grail* maidens were taught how to revere the wisdom of their cycle and the cycles of nature as a path to wisdom. For men, this began when they reached the age of 21 and were invited to join the annual rite of passage known as *The Holy Grail*. This was a rite held over the Winter Solstice to assist men through their annual psychological death and rebirth during the darkest day, the most feminine time of year…their equivalent of menses (the death phase). This is why men received a key on their 21st birthday, signifying their access to the mysteries of life. This custom was appropriated and distorted to represent a key to the city; the world of men.

Seekers of the Grail

Down through the ages, we have heard how elusive the search for *the Grail* has been, especially by men who took up the search in earnest. This is because *the Grail* represents that which is received intuitively; *gnosis*. For fertile women, intuition is most easily accessed during their menses, when they are psychically expanded and open. Post-menopausal women have even greater access to their intuition, due to increased sensitivity with age. Since the masculine psyche is rationally dominant, the search for *the Grail* was considered more arduous for men and therefore required a significant commitment and dedication.

For a man to receive divine insight, he first needed to become receptive; an empty vessel. In other words, he needed to develop his feminine side. Contrary to popular belief, this is not simply achieved through mastering domestic chores! This is a sad indictment of what patriarchy associates with femininity. Rather it is through awakening the inner mystic, as seen in *Star Wars*, *Avatar* and *The Karate Kid*, where the hero learns to perceive and receive information through their subtle senses. To prepare men for the mystic experience of *gnosis*; receiving intuitive truth, men in the ancient world were initiated into *Grail* practices. This included teachings, initiation rites and ceremonial sharing circles that aligned with the greater cycles to tame their dominant rational minds.

Since men weren't initiated directly through the life/death/rebirth cycle via their bodies, as women are each month, women-initiated men into *the Grail* mysteries. Men would gather each month in sacred circle to prepare for the annual rite of *The Holy Grail*, led by a priestess. This preparation assisted men to face their fears so when they were evoked by the darker months of Autumn and Winter, the most inward, feminine seasons, they didn't self-destruct. This training ensured men developed the strengths of their inner feminine so they could consciously traverse their annual 'dark night of the soul' evoked by the Winter Solstice.

The Winter Solstice, known in the Celtic tradition as *Yule*, is the longest night of the solar year. It was understood to be the most perilous time for the male psyche, when not balanced by an empowered and integrated feminine side. Since the sun is the natural power source for the male psyche, as the solar light wanes, masculine strengths like confidence and optimism wane like Superman's strength when exposed to kryptonite. It is the weakening solar light that catalyzes their psychological 'dark night'. This is why men who are not initiated into the wisdom teachings of the feminine are more at risk of depression, illness, injury and suicide during mid-Winter. Especially those residing closer to the poles who often experience more extreme polarized psycho-emotional states. This is also why so many immature men chase the sun, residing in tropical climates to avoid the darkness of Winter.

The Meeting With the Dragon

The Yuletide initiation of *The Holy Grail* was also referred to as 'the meeting with the dragon'. The dragon symbolized a man's dark side. This annual initiation for men of all ages was considered the holiest of holies, as it demanded a complete humbling of the male ego through a confrontation with one's greatest fears. The local *Magdalene* presided over this sacred rite. She was the *High Priestess* who taught *the Grail* mysteries to both men and women to ensure they lived in right relationship with themselves, others and the Earth.

The Grail tradition and the rite of passage known as *The Holy Grail* were central to the ancient Earth-based religion of our Anglo-European ancestors as their survival depended on their symbiotic relationship with the Earth. So much so, men would take vows to serve the *Earth Mother* when they were initiated during their initial *Holy Grail* rite to ensure their actions honored the circle of life. Only after a man wedded himself to the Earth, the original rite of Matrimony, was he considered mature enough to enter into *Sacred Union* with a woman. For women were revered as a microcosm of the *Earth Mother*. Hence all the tales that featured kings who sent potential suitors away to 'slay the dragon' to prove themselves worthy for marriage. It's little wonder that without *the Grail* tradition, we see many men ill-equipped for the rigors of partnership and family life. This results in many men lashing out, running away or shutting down, creating endemic trauma.

The Taming of the Shrew

Patriarchy distorted this earlier tradition that sought to tame the male ego by insisting the wild, soulful nature of the feminine should instead be tamed by the ego-dominant masculine. This was done to create order, since the immature masculine fears chaos; the feminine principle. Hence the patriarchal marriage vow that saw women pledge to 'obey' that was never asked of men. We see this same pattern in the macrocosm with Earth-worshiping peoples expected to bow down to the might of rationally-dominant cultures who exploit their resources and labor. While in the microcosm of human relationships, wild-spirited women had their spirit broken with persistent programming modeling domestic compliance. This was illustrated as the societal ideal with plays like, The *Taming of the Shrew* by William Shakespeare, *Pygmalion* by George Bernard Shaw and films *like My Fair Lady* and *Pretty Woman*...and ad nauseum on television, billboards, radio and magazines.

This deep-seated conditioning is why we will not create true equality through external measures, such as gender equality legislation or initiatives, if we fail to comprehend and address the root cause. That being, the fear of the feminine by those who are immature and ego-dominant. Put simply, the true feminine is a force of nature that instigates change. The Goddess is the embodiment of chaos and transformation. That is the role of the feminine. To the immature ego, change and the unknown is terrifying, so every effort is made to control and dominate the feminine, the force of nature that induces change. This 'fear of the feminine' - the textbook definition of *misogyny*, requires the submission of the feminine to the will of the immature ego for the fear to be temporarily appeased. It's worth noting men and women who subjugates the feminine part of themselves will seek to oppress this aspect in others. We're all guilty of misogyny, internally and externally as we've all been conditioned to think and act in misogynistic ways. Acknowledging this is essential to our healing process.

The Grail doesn't just liberate the feminine in men and women. It celebrates and honors the role of the feminine. This is why *the Grail* tradition was perceived as a direct threat to the empires, illustrated by the vigorous oppression of the feminine. I refer to the mass persecutions that resulted in the genocide of countless women from 1300 – 1600CE. These campaigns served the political purposes of both the church and the medical establishment who forbade women from practicing herbalism or studying medicine, despite medical science being founded on women's herb lore. Today we see big pharma continue their witch hunt, oppressing natural medicine and the healing arts through political lobbying that dictates funding and legislation, all at a cost to public health.

As with all oppressive regimes, the stripping of intrinsic rights only has to be done to one generation until it becomes accepted as the norm. Without *the Grail* to heal our *psyche* with wisdom and soul-based practices, we see many modern medical practitioners doing more harm than good, despite taking the Hippocratic oath, to 'harm none'. This is because the inner realms of the psyche, meaning 'soul', require a mystic approach rather than a clinical, biological one. Despite good intentions, a rational approach, with its myopic focus on alleviating symptoms will often exacerbate mental illness and emotional dysregulation.

The Essence of the Grail

The ancients understood love was the most powerful force in existence, essential for health and healing. Today the medical system dehumanizes and traumatizes both staff and patients alike with its budget-driven decisions and rigid protocols that reflect fear, not love. Primarily a fear of being sued and losing money, status and power. Previously, before the mechanization of humanity it was understood love had the power to heal and ignorance had the power to wound. The film, *Patch Adams* calls out this shadow side of the medical industry, as does the book, *The Road Less Traveled* by Dr. M Scott Peck.

There is no capacity for love without maturity and wisdom, as those who are immature are focused purely on their own gain so humbling the ego, through observing the wisdom teachings of the natural cycles that govern us, is essential if we are to avoid *dis-aster*, which means 'to go against the stars'...the Cosmic cycles that initiate our psyche.

I know *the Grail* as the ancient religion of love. A mystic tradition that taught people how to develop their capacity for love; not just romantic, courtly love, which *the Grail* has become synonymous with, but all forms of love. Self-love, brotherly love, sisterly love, romantic love, erotic love and devotional love, expressed as acts of service. Each is an initiation path to embody love, once undertaken by *Grail* initiates in alignment with their corresponding solar, lunar and seasonal cycles.

The Grail taught men and women how to increase their capacity for love. This was done incrementally, as it was understood one could not master romantic love before embodying self-love and brotherly / sisterly love. Each initiatory path involved an inner descent to meet disowned aspects within the psyche and integrate them. With each subsequent descent, the initiate would become more self-aware, resulting in more wise, empowered and loving choices.

Today we see unrecognizable remnants of *the Grail* tradition in our modern lives, their meaning diluted and distorted. This is because *the Grail* was so central to life in the ancient world, it had to be incorporated by the empires. It is my understanding that the mystic tradition of *the Grail* formed the basis for the Christian festivals including *Easter* and *Christmas*, just as the mystic traditions of Sufism and the Kabbalah were the foundations for the patriarchal religions of Islam and Judaism. The earlier mystic traditions contained the essence and true power of the Divine. Potency that was lost when they were appropriated into political vehicles for amassing power and control.

All of the earlier mystic traditions were feminine in their approach. They instructed initiates to experience union with the Divine directly through personal experience. The emphasis was on awakening the soul to temper the traits of the ego. This was achieved through self-awareness rather than imposing rules to be obeyed under threat of punishment. The power of the rites lay in the act of participation. So rather than watching rituals performed by clergy (men in feminine attire) as was the custom in the religions that followed, *the Grail* required active involvement, even from prisoners who were released to attend specific rites to ensure their maturity!

This was so the collective consciousness continued to evolve with the divine design of the greater cycles; the Fibonacci spiral sequence. *The Grail* was essentially a complex web of social structures that together, created a framework to promote social sustainability. This, in turn, ensured the sustainability of the land. Quite a commonsense approach, unlike the propaganda I received in religious education as a young child in a secular school that dismissed the Earth-worshiping people as superstitious pagans who performed rituals to please and appease the Gods.

Social sustainability is often overlooked in the global conversation about ecological sustainability. Hence, we still see a divide between eco-villages that strive to sustain the Earth and ashrams that strive to sustain connection to Spirit. I hope we shall soon start to see intentional communities that seek to combine the two realms of Spirit and matter, Heaven and Earth through incorporating the ancient *Grail* practices. For *the Grail* is a framework for social permaculture, a gardening philosophy that seeks to create a culture of permanence based on the patterns of nature, to combat the impact of consumerism.

The Loss of Culture, Identity and Sovereignty

In 392 CE, the Roman Empire passed legislation to outlaw all forms of Earth-based worship. Those who dared keep the old religion alive were tortured and killed. So, the persecution of mystic women started long before the 500-year European witch hunt that spread to the colonies.

This legislation is why those of us of Anglo/European descent lost access to our ancient birthright of sacred knowledge and customs. This is a loss the vast majority are completely oblivious to since this is not the history we have been taught in school. The colonization of our ancestors disconnected us from our indigenous lands and traditions. As a result, many today don't perceive themselves as indigenous to any part of the Earth. This sense of separation has contributed to the demise of both the health of individuals and the *Earth Mother*. Ultimately it is this loss of connection and culture that broke the wild spirit of the Celts and Europeans.

The loss of native culture is a travesty many of us acknowledge concerning indigenous cultures in our land of residence, but don't apply to ourselves and our own ancestry. This lack of appreciation for our own cultural loss makes us susceptible to ongoing manipulation due to our sense of 'white guilt' and endemic shame that compounds our collective disempowerment. Without strong cultural roots, we lack a greater sense of identity, dignity and self-respect. Without a clear cultural identity, we are more likely to adopt a way of life that offers us a new identity, through accumulating status symbols that reward our compliance with an ideology that offers no real fulfillment.

It is worth noting that the significant contribution of culture to our psyche is why the mantle of keeping culture alive was once bestowed upon the priests and priestesses as a sacred charge of utmost importance. This is why I believe wholeheartedly we will not restore our human rights without reinstating our original sacred rites, as they form the basis of our birthright as sovereign beings.

The Roman Empire's oppression of *the Grail* tradition resulted in severing ancestral cultural practices on a scale never seen before. It was these lineages that had previously ensured each subsequent generation received their sacred birthright. That being, the rites of passage deemed necessary to fulfill one's potential as a man or woman. Without these sacred ceremonies and teachings to initiate young men and women into adulthood and through their life transitions, each subsequent generation became more disconnected from their roots and unstable. This made them more reliant on the dominant cultural ideology being perpetuated by the empires run by dynastic families that today control both industry and the media machine that drives their profit. This mind programming has also created social pressure to conform with patriarchal gender roles, resulting in a shadow expression of gender that causes polarization and conflict, both internally and externally.

Without sufficient understanding of the multi-faceted aspects of feminine and masculine expression within the soul of both men and women, we have experienced an escalation of gender politics. That is, viewing gender from the perspective of the mind, rather than the soul. Today we are witnessing the endgame of this trajectory with many of our youth generation aspiring to be 'gender neutral', rejecting the concept of gender altogether. Understandably, they are refusing to comply with the disempowered gender representations perpetuated by our distorted mythos. However, they are rebelling without any clear idea of what it truly means to be authentic, empowered and multi-faceted men and women. Only by taking up the inner quest to truly know ourselves can we heal the gender war internally and externally. (More about that later).

When we don't know who we are, it's understandable we struggle to create soul-fulfilling lives of purpose and meaning. For without direct initiation into the mysteries of life, we remain disconnected from the essence of life and what gives our lives meaning. Without meaning, we are lost and lacking direction, so our lives feel empty and insignificant. It is this inner dilemma that results in reckless and destructive choices.

The Grail once provided clear guidelines for youths to embark on a life of chivalry, truth, purpose and meaning, along with ongoing practical support to fulfill one's soul potential in a spirit of service. Without *the Grail,* it's understandable that many people live lives of quiet desperation and perpetual distraction while wondering, "What's it all for?" When our lives lack true meaning, we are less inclined to value ourselves, others and our environment. This inner desolation puts many at risk of depression, suicide, interpersonal dysfunction and violence, all of which are then enacted on the Earth.

Ending the Paradigm of War

In 2020 the US spent or committed to spend $6.4 trillion on war.[13] Look at your annual income tax return, and you'll see how much your government takes out of your earnings to fund the military without your explicit consent. War is the biggest business there is, which is why those with the most wealth and power invest in both sides of a conflict. To see who profits from the Military Industrial Complex, check out the link provided in the resources section.

Without mystic wisdom traditions like *the Grail* to guide us into maturity and sovereignty, we have accepted war as an inevitable part of life. This is because we are groomed for war from the moment we enter the educational institutions that uphold Patriarchy. Like soldiers we assemble on parade, line up for class, wear uniforms, and ranks are assigned to those who excel. We may even have to swear a pledge of allegiance. We are assigned a house team and encouraged to compete to defeat the enemy and win. To show our school spirit we have one of three options; play on the field using brute force to dominate our opponent, cheer on the home team from the sidelines or sound the battle alarm by marching in military style formations playing war anthems. This conditioning repeatedly provokes a 'winner takes all' mentality that plays out as compulsive competition rather than creation via cooperation. By way of contrast, *the Grail* tradition anchors feminine values, through regular community-based practices that strengthen a spirit of brotherhood and sisterhood, just what we need to rebuild a cohesive society once the despots are removed from their ivory towers and held accountable.

So foreign is the concept of brotherly love. If you search online for images of brotherhood, the results are currently limited to pictures of men in combat or ritual combat, aka team sports. We even see *the Grail* appropriated as the prize in the *World Cup* with soccer players drinking from a shared chalice. This is because we have been conditioned to associate brotherhood with war, conflict and competition rather than a concept synonymous with cooperation, harmony and peace.

Why? *The Grail* once met a primal need, initiating young men with a sacred blood rite when they came of age. Without this, men unconsciously seek out a destructive blood rite to prove their manhood in the form of bloodshed so they can bond as *blood brothers* through inflicting wounds. This is the subconscious conditioning that perpetuates war and ritualized war...blood sports like football, that satisfy the bloodlust of bloodthirsty voyeurs in gladiatorial arenas during the darker months of the year. Our patriarchal culture that seeks violence as a bonding ritual hurts our young men by placing on them an expectation that they sacrifice their wellbeing for glory. 28% of NFL footballers experience brain injury since the human skull has no shock absorbers, unlike animals, like the woodpecker, who have adapted to direct head impact. The doctor who exposed this was silenced until the number of suicides of ex-footballers struggling with the long-term effects of head trauma demanded it be acknowledged. Meanwhile the game continues in all educational institutions, grooming young men to sacrifice themselves for short-term reward, while glorifying violence as entertainment.

What's the connection? History reveals the cultures that denied the sacred power of the holy blood became the most bloodthirsty.[14] Only when the sacred blood is understood and honored for its sacred power, will our world become less violent and bloodthirsty. When men can publicly show affection and enjoy the support of brotherhood without first engaging in acts of violence to prove their masculinity, will we see our society transform from a war-based culture to one of peace that values a brotherhood of man. Similarly, when women are taught to revere and honor their wombs as sacred, gathering in *Red Tents* and *Moon Lodges* to support each other through their monthly descent, will we restore a culture of sisterhood amongst women.

"When the women give their blood back to the earth, men will come home from war and earth shall find peace."

Hopi Indian prophecy

CHAPTER 3

Refusal of the Call:
Being Sensible

The previous chapter was a call to adventure, an invitation to seek *the Grail*. So now you may be tempted to put the book down and walk away. Why? Any soul calling evokes our ego's fears. "Change the status quo…who, me? I think you've got the wrong person." Yes, it's human behavior to do avoidance in response to a big challenge. This is why so many potential heroes don't take the first step to become a greater version of themselves as their fears eclipse their courage, indicating a lack of belief in themselves to overcome adversity.

It's worth remembering, we only find courage by directly confronting our fears. Without the willingness to 'feel the fear and do it anyway', we offer a list of excuses, such as our existing responsibilities as the reason for our refusal. These are plausible, sensible reasons, as to why we cannot get involved in a cause greater than us. Such reasons make sense, so we're not likely to be called out on our cowardice, unless we cross paths with a mystic. In fact, quite the opposite, we may be praised for 'coming to our senses' by refusing the call by those closest to us, who fear change.

What's In It For Me?

We tend to avoid taking the road less traveled and entering the mystery of life because it offers no guarantees. In fact, quite the opposite, such a quest demands complete trust and surrender. This is counter-intuitive for an ego-dominant individual who won't commit, unless there's a proven formula, a specific outcome or a prized goal ensuring a good return on their investment of time and money. For time and money are the two masters the ego serves. Not because the ego is bad, but because it is scared of losing what's most valued in society, fearing it will never have enough of either. This is why time and money are the two reasons we most commonly cite to refuse an opportunity that calls to our soul. Time and money are the knee-jerk excuses that sabotage our inner growth. Why? The mind sees time as linear, rather than cyclic and eternal, so it fears not having enough time to prove its worth by achieving its ambitions.

Equally, the mind cannot perceive one's true value so every day is a race against time to prove one's worth. Hence there's a predominant belief that there's no time to delve into the meaning of life...unless it will directly assist the achievement of one's goals for those looking to 'fast track' their success. This is why the vast majority won't seek answers to the meaning of life until their ego has been humbled through some kind of major loss, usually the loss of what they valued most. Until such an ego-death occurs, taking time out to listen to the advice of a mystic seems utterly foolish, even crazy.

I Am Not Mad

Ironically, those who most harshly judge others for expressing less conventional viewpoints are often the ones who most fear being seen as mad. Such as the trolls on social media who abuse those expressing counter-culture viewpoints or the talk-show hosts who mock mystics because they threaten their rigid worldview and self-identity. These are the folk who subscribe to the idiom, 'I think, therefore I am.' This kind of pubescent bullying is akin to those in the closet of self-denial about their own homoerotic urges who enact hate crimes of violence on those who have liberated themselves out of the closet. Why? It is human nature to externally attack our disowned aspects.

Those afraid of losing their mind will similarly make excuses to avoid intimacy. Why? The act of falling in love is considered a temporary madness. To be available to the experience of falling in love or experiencing the mystical rapture of devotional love with the divine, one must abandon their rational constructs and directly face their fears. Namely, the fear of looking like a fool. Challenging for those who are rationally dominant and therefore, hyper-critical. Those who cannot conceive of life beyond the rational mind's constraints will dismiss those they can't comprehend as inferior, on the presumption their mind is weak and therefore susceptible to delusion. This arrogance of the ego is what keeps many in a perpetual state of ignorance, judging what they cannot understand.

One must abandon the fear of not having enough time and money to serve something greater. This means risking harsh judgment from others to be true to one's own heart. When our heart is more dominant than our mind, we will follow a higher calling to pursue love, truth and wisdom at any cost. Only through pursuing these ideals can we lift the cloak of gloom and cynicism that torments the ego and manifests as a morbid fascination with the dark. This is why prime time viewing features a glut of forensic crime shows and murder mysteries. To transcend this voyeuristic exploration of the darker side of life we need to confront our fears directly. Only then can we restore our lost state of innocence. Innocence is not to be confused with ignorance. The return to innocence is when one comes full circle and experiences liberation from their own negative thinking. It's a lightness of being that comes with renewed trust in a higher power as an all-encompassing intelligence. This is why the oracle states the only cure to heal the wounded masculine, is a meeting with a young fool.

Parsival, the name of the youth in *The Fisher King*, means 'Pure Fool', a derivative of the Arabic, *fal parsi*. That he is considered the one most likely to succeed in curing the ailment of the king signals we must risk looking like a fool to discover the true bounty of life. What appears as foolish, is in fact, receptivity to true learning and growth. This is perhaps the greatest challenge for the learned mind which is full of preconceived ideas, facts and opinions. Such a mind often seeks to bolster one's identity and status, by debunking the mysteries of life. I refer to those who delight in proving others wrong in order to assert how clever they are, such as science fundamentalists. Those who worship the mind and seek to accumulate facts, often to avoid the feeling function of the heart. Without realizing it, they deflect the opportunity to learn by asserting how much they already know. By way of contrast, one whose mind is open will ask questions like a curious child to discover what is not readily seen or has been deliberately concealed.

The closed mind of *The Fisher King* is what results in him being his own worst enemy. Like the saying, 'You can't teach an old dog new tricks' he is old and cynical, unwilling to risk his status and reputation to bow to the wisdom of the mystic feminine. He has lost connection with his inner youth; his joy of learning and delight in discovery. This is why, in mystic traditions, truly wise sages often appear light-hearted and foolish, like the very young. They have transcended their critical mind, liberating them from the fear of what others think, so their manner is uninhibited and spontaneous. Like the archetypal fool, *The Fisher King* must learn to drop his prejudices, his intellectual knowledge, his pride, and his arrogance. Only then will he be truly able to listen to the guidance of the feminine to discover the riches of *the Grail* firsthand and heal his unbalanced psyche. It is interesting to note, the word, *mentor* was the name of the guide to the questing hero in the epic, *The Odyssey*. While the character known as Mentor was male, his mentor was the Goddess, *Athena*, indicating the wisdom of the feminine is the ultimate guide of the soul.[15]

Why Don't We Stay in Kansas, Toto?

The rational mind, our appointed protector, likes the comfort of what's familiar, where the risks are known to us. This is why we may tell ourselves we're being responsible by staying in a job or a marriage that's unfulfilling. However, our inability to move forwards indicates irresponsibility to ourselves, as we demonstrate an inability to respond effectively to our authentic feelings and needs.

We may avoid this acknowledgment by casting ourselves as the martyr, seeing ourselves as noble, protecting others, and not burdening them with what we know or feel is true. However, even if our concealment of truth is well-meaning, such deceit robs others of the choice to make truly informed decisions. Alternatively, we may avoid growth by casting ourselves as the victim, blaming others for our circumstance and misery, rather than acknowledge our power to choose.

We may swing between the polarities of victim/martyr rather than avoid the fear of stepping into the unknown. However, if we're really honest with ourselves, we'll dare to acknowledge that our comfort zone, in reality, is not very comfortable. Those who sabotage their growth disconnect from their true feelings with countless distractions. As we age, this becomes less possible, as our soul seeks to become more dominant, urging us to seek greater connection and meaning. Inevitably, we become aware of how empty our life feels if we've ignored the call of our soul. This is why many men and masculine-dominant women experience a mid-life crisis. Now, with the world in a state of crisis, we're all having to examine our choices, regardless of our age.

The Handless Maiden: The Betrayal of Love

This is another *Grail* wisdom parable that speaks to the power of choice. Both this story and *The Fisher King* are included in Robert Johnson's writings on *the Grail.* I recommend his writings which are very insightful, although his strong Christian bias influences his interpretation of *the Grail*. As a counterpart to *The Fisher King*, *The Handless Maiden* speaks to the wounded feminine and identifies the origins of her wound as *The Devil's Bargain*. The fateful choice that betrays our soul and our loved ones - a lesson for men and women alike.

The story opens with a meeting between a miller and a stranger, who is the Devil in disguise. The stranger offers the miller an opportunity to mill more grain, much faster and with less effort...for a fee. This captures the attention of the miller whose daily work is labor intensive. The proposition of more return for less output makes rational sense, so he asks the stranger, "What is the fee?" To which the Devil replies, "Just that which stands behind your mill."

The miller presumes the stranger is referring to the old tree behind his mill, so in his haste to seal the deal in his favor, he readily consents to pay the fee, unwittingly making a bargain with the Devil.

The Devil promptly holds up his end of the bargain by providing the miller with the mechanical knowledge needed to establish a waterwheel to power his mill, thereby increasing his productivity and profits. This agreement greatly enhances his standard of living, and he and his wife quickly become accustomed to their new lifestyle. So much so, he forgets there is an outstanding price to pay.

One day the stranger returns to make good on his claim. Dressed in his finery, he arrives on the doorstep of the miller's home and announces he will now take what is behind his mill. The miller takes him out behind the mill where they find his only daughter. The Devil declares she is his due payment. Only then does the miller realize the true cost of his bargain. It is a cost far greater than he could've imagined because his mind could not have conceived of such treachery. The Devil promptly takes the young woman as his property, cuts off her hands and carries her away. This signifies the stunting of the burgeoning feminine and the theft of her potential.

This symbolism is repeated in various tales, such as the play, *The Merchant of Venice* by William

Shakespeare where the merchant, *Shylock*, seeks a pound of flesh in exchange for his favor. Similarly, in the myth of the Inuit Goddess *Sedna*, her hands are cut off, and thrown into the ocean due to a betrayal by her father.

The Devil's Bargain: Our Power to Choose

These tales show us how easy it is to sell our soul for something much lesser in value when we are naive; unaware of the shadow side of human behavior, in ourselves and others. Like the saying, 'Better the Devil you know' unless we see our own dark side, we won't see it in others. Such naïveté is more likely when we've not received an initiation to confront our own shadow; our unconscious behaviors, when we come of age. This is what *the Grail* tradition once provided. Without such an initiation, we remain like a child, easily tricked by those whose motives aren't pure.

So long as we are unaware we will attract those who seek to take advantage of us. This may be someone who flatters our vanity, placates our insecurities or promises the fulfillment of our desires. As I write this the criminal global cabal is seeking to introduce its dystopian New World Order through excluding from society those who won't comply with their unreasonable demands. Meanwhile, those who blindly trust the government, like a child would a parent, cannot contemplate the abuses of power being committed behind the scenes so they are submitting like lambs to the slaughter in the most devastating Devil's bargain humanity has ever seen.

Those who haven't taken the road less traveled to explore their own psyche in depth are more susceptible to being taken in, as the rational mind looks to external authority rather than observe the intuition of the higher mind. Since the ego seeks power and comfort, if we're ego-dominant we're more likely to hastily agree to offers that promise us what we want in the short-term, without ensuring we have all the facts to discern the long-term impact and scrutinize the terms. When we are soul-dominant, rather than being enchanted, seduced or intimidated we will pay attention to the vibe we get from the other party or an uneasy feeling in our gut. Ultimately, if we hear an offer that promises us the world if we just submit our will to carry out another's bidding, we ought to then ask, 'What's the catch?'

In the story of *The Handless Maiden*, the daughter is betrayed by her father's greed. He places his desire above consideration of other possible factors. Perhaps it is significant he has no idea of the likelihood his daughter will be standing behind the mill. This could imply he was unaware she liked to spend time with the tree that stood behind the mill. This motif is significant when we consider *The Tree of Life* represents the awakened sacred feminine. Her father's lack of awareness of others suggests he's so focused on creating wealth, he has lost sight of what is of greater value; quality time and connection with his family. It also signals he has no idea of the impact of his choices on the feminine.

Such a betrayal of others only occurs when we have betrayed our own soul. In this case, by valuing material gain over time connecting with oneself and loved ones. In the industrial age, we have been conditioned to betray the true self. We are indoctrinated to overlook our inner needs for external gain. This is why it's considered normal to stay in a job we loathe, or appease societal expectations at a cost to ourselves. The more we betray our soul, the more soul-sick we become. Each subsequent betrayal clouds our ability to discern what is true and right for us at any moment, leaving us susceptible to manipulation and deception.

Like *The Fisher King*, the story of *The Handless Maiden* encourages us to awaken our power to affect our fate. We do this through increased awareness of the effect of our choices. This awareness empowers us to take the time needed to scrutinize offers and negotiate fair terms on our own behalf. This describes our ability to take responsibility for our harvest. If we neglect to do this, we will forever see ourselves as the victim of circumstance, casting all the blame on perceived perpetrators rather than seeing our own part in the dance. This refusal to acknowledge our own shadow is how we stunt the growth of our feminine and remain immature, symbolized by the loss of the maiden's hands. The hands symbolize the part of us that can seize opportunities and create our heart's vision.

Ultimately, whether we exist in a state of Heaven or Hell is determined by our ability to apply this lesson. This runs counter to the way we've been conditioned, to view fate as fickle and arbitrary, leading us to fear, blame or appease an external Divine force rather than examine the karmic fallout of our own thoughts, words and deeds and be accountable for our choices.

Just as the feminine element is water, one of the functions of *the Grail* tradition was to assist initiates to become reflective like water in order to take responsibility for one's choices. This ensured no experience was wasted, as the lessons learned could be applied to avoid future losses and deception. Without acknowledging the cost of our own ignorance, we have continued to blindly allow deception on a grand scale as a species. Fortunately, the more grand the deception has become, the more people have awakened to it. We take back our power when we realize it is our betrayal of ourselves that results in the betrayal by those benefiting from the corruption in our world. So rather than focus our energy vilifying those at the top of the pyramid of power, we need to consider how we are each holding such an unsustainable hierarchical order in place. For unless we are willing to identify our part in the dance and unplug from a system that serves a few, at a cost to the many, we will remain in Dante's Inferno without a hall pass.

Is It Just Me, Or Is It Getting Hot in Here?

It is our good, but naive intentions that lead us on a slippery slope to Hell. This occurs when we collectively make childish choices, often motivated subconsciously by FOMO; the fear of missing out. For instance, we may continue to work for a corrupt enterprise in exchange for the security of a regular wage and benefits. We may overlook unethical policies and a toxic work culture to ascend the corporate ladder of success to create the patriarchal notion of a 'better life' for ourselves and our families. However, the more self-aware and connected to our feelings we become, the stronger the call to honor our conscience. Increased awareness creates an inner conflict between our thoughts and our feelings; the ego and the soul, until we submit to the will of the heart, that knows the difference between right and wrong. Such inner tension is why most Fortune 500 CEOs suffer chronic insomnia, muscle pain and headaches, not a state of being to be admired or emulated.

This is how all the dystopian crap currently happening on the planet is actually serving our evolution. As more of the shadow truth is exposed, we are challenged to act accordingly. So those who are abusing their power are simply a catalyst, like the irritating grain of sand that results in an oyster creating a pearl. Without their corrupt covert agendas coming to an alarming climax, we would undoubtedly continue to trade our personal power for the illusion of safety and security.

The world as we know it will change when we reach a tipping point of awareness in the collective consciousness. Meanwhile, our current world crisis is a catalyst for that consciousness shift. As more people make the shift to bow to the authority of their own conscience, it's inevitable we'll create a society that's self-governing rather than continue to defer to external top-down governance. I'm not suggesting total anarchy is the way forward. Rather, a new approach. One where we de-centralize power and put it back into the hands of we, the people at local levels. Imagine as world where the airwaves disseminated consciousness-raising content to support everyone to attune to their conscience rather than messages that condition us to consume. After all, even a child knows right and wrong. The truth is simple, unlike a lie which is complex, incongruent and rife with inconsistencies, such as the mandates being imposed worldwide in UN member states. And for those who say a Utopian ideal isn't realistic, I offer the example of the Earth-based people who lived peaceably for thousands of years during the Neolithic period, before the rise of the empires.

The Truth Will Set Us Free

Without consulting the wisdom of the heart, it is inevitable internal pressure will build if our choices don't align with our core values. We may try to silence our conscience with mind-numbing distractions or substances, but ultimately, we cannot escape ourselves. While an internal showdown may be initially painful, when we bring the light of understanding to the fears that underpin our self-negating choices, we inevitably liberate ourselves with self-honoring choices. When we honor ourselves, we honor those around us, even if they initially protest. Like the great quote by Gloria Steinem, "The truth shall set us free…but first, it will piss everyone off."

Good to remember this when we are summoning the courage to be true to our own heart, in the face of potential opposition. For a lie to ourselves is a lie to those nearest to us. So too, not making a choice, is still a choice, albeit a passive one, and any denial of our deepest truth puts us at risk of our soul opting out via a sudden accident or illness. This tends to happen when we resist the call of our soul and our daily life becomes a living Hell due to our unwillingness to acknowledge a need for change.

The Wolf in Sheep's Clothing

It is a bitter irony that we may not seek *the Grail*, the wisdom of the soul because we fear looking like a fool, and yet, if we do not, we are more likely to be taken for a fool by those seeking to take advantage of others. Just as the Devil appears to the miller, as his saving grace; the answer to his prayers, we must learn to discern truth from illusion or we will invariably make a bargain with the Devil on the false assumption the one who seeks to harm us, is our Savior. For example, having blind faith in those afforded high status in society like doctors, clergy or politicians, whose motives may be clouded by their own bargain with the Devil, such as the status of their title, commissions from pharmaceutical companies, the promise of career promotion or financial payoffs from private investors.

Use Your Antennae

The fastest way to avoid being taken for a fool is by attuning to your intuition. This is what often manifests as our first impression. Considered a woman's 'sixth sense', it's a subtle sense that both men and women have access to when they develop the mystic feminine within. *The Grail* practices assist men and women to develop this gift. Intuition helps us pierce illusions and know in an instant what is true in any given situation.

While intuition has recently become a buzzword amongst ethical entrepreneurs, the vast majority of the group mind still defer to the external voice of authority, such as the media, academia or science, rather than attune to their internal guidance system as their primary authority. Honing this skill is essential if we are to break free of the constraints of third dimensional reality and become self-governing sovereign souls. This requires investing time in knowing ourselves. This is why the stone at the temple of Delphi, Greece read, 'Know Thyself'.

If we are not willing to have an authentic relationship with ourselves, we cannot hope to have any real form of authentic, soulful connection with another. Without a connection to our souls, we have no real capacity to love, so we may give up on love and settle for codependency. When we don't believe love is possible, we are more likely to seek power as a substitute. This is not usually a conscious choice but an attempt to stay safe or bolster our self-esteem when we experience disappointment, loss and grief.

Compassion For Those Eclipsed By the Dark

We need to remember that those who seek to dominate other life forms do so because internally they feel small and afraid. Like the wizard in the story of *The Wizard of Oz*; a small man hiding behind a large projection of power. After all, a tyrant's greatest fear is being exposed for their weaknesses. In a patriarchal culture what are perceived as weaknesses are usually the feminine character traits that humanize us. When we understand power and control are sought by those who are most fearful of being dominated, we can view tyrants with compassion, rather than feel intimidated by their displays of grandeur and assertions of power. Once we know their Achilles heel, all we see is their lack of true empowerment. Like *The Fisher King*, they may appear to have great power and privilege, but they are plagued by inner torment. So rather than fear or despise those at the top of the power pyramid, we can pity their own enslavement to compulsive desires, such as the need to constantly achieve to accumulate proof of their value. Such maniacal activity is not sustainable, as one can't ever outrun their own sense of inadequacy, without facing it directly. And those who disconnect from their feelings to avoid their insecurities are as self-destructive as they are abusive towards others.

Those who have a seat at the table in the patriarchal halls of power have, for the most part, fallen prey to the adage, 'Absolute power corrupts absolutely'. This speaks to their loss of personal integrity, the erosion of their soul. This occurs when one compulsively tries to placate their ego's fears. Like the *Star Wars* villain, *Darth Vader*, meaning 'dark father', who appears more machine than man, the more one climbs the power pyramid, the less human they become. The more bargains they make with the Devil, the more they become like him, an agent of the dark. Those responsible for heinous acts and corruption will inevitably pay the ultimate price, even if they appear to have gotten away with murder. No one can escape their own conscience or the repercussions of the universal law of reciprocity; cause and effect. When we understand this, we don't feel a compulsion to enact vigilante justice, which simply perpetuates a karmic cycle of war.

PANDORA

Love or Power: What Is Your Choice?

If the *Grail's* main intention is to promote a culture where love prevails, and we live in a society where *the Grail* has been oppressed, it stands to reason that love holds the key to healing the existing paradigm where power reigns, destroying all that we love.

Love is, therefore, the ultimate form of activism. If our actions are motivated by love for the greater good, not ourselves, we all win. Those who have amassed the most power during the longest-running game of Monopoly ever played have done so at the expense of others. Whether that's sacrificing the innocent, making profits via sweatshop labor or assassinating whistleblowers and those who stand in their way. Yes, the ruling elite are those who have dominated others to serve their own interests. Ironically, those who claim to be philanthropists and benevolent monarchs are often the worst offenders!

"We look forward to the time when the power of love will

replace the love of power. Then will our world know the

William E. Gladstone

If love, as the answer to the world's problems sounds like hippie, flower power nonsense, consider how Mahatma Gandhi successfully ended the rule of the British empire in India. He inspired people to rise up against their oppressors because his love for his people was so fierce. He risked his own life, repeatedly engaging in provocative acts of non-compliance with unjust laws. This is the behavior of a sovereign being. One who follows the conviction of their heart's conscience, rather than blindly complying with rules imposed by an external authority. Secondly, he emphasized non-violence when attacked by oppressors. Non-violence in the face of injustice further highlights inappropriate abuses of power and promotes fellowship by appealing to the perpetrator's conscience. When Ghandi's compatriots did retaliate with violence, he risked his own life by going on a hunger strike. He did this so his people would see the pain their violence caused to his heart. This action touched them and the violence ceased. Gandhi illustrated love in action and showed we can achieve miracles when we trust in the urges of our heart and follow it earnestly, even in the face of grave opposition.

Our challenge now as a species is to find our way back to love. We inspire those around us to rise to the occasion and be the best version of themselves when we are loving. Equally, when we lack self-love, we project our unresolved issues onto those around us. When our core wounds from childhood are unhealed, we inadvertently perceive, speak and act from a wounded place, and this wounds others, creating more pain and conflict. So, the healing of past trauma is the most crucial contribution we can make to the world around us. For it is a lack of healing, borne of self-neglect, that undermines our belief in love. It is our cynicism about love that leads us to co-create unconscious power dynamics. Whether that's in our families, schools, workplaces, sports or social clubs. When we lack healing and empowerment we are unwittingly complicit in contributing to group dynamics where a dominant ego rules, overtly or covertly. A hierarchy then forms according to the levels of allegiance to the 'top dog'. This subtle compliance is done to ensure one's own social survival, to avoid being the group scapegoat. The more power on offer at the top of the pyramid, the more ruthless the tactics employed.

Unconscious group dynamics create a culture of fear, corruption and endemic trauma, as disempowered individuals seek to dominate others to avoid being dominated. This is the lowest expression of humanity. However, even if we come from a conscious and loving home environment, at age seven, our locus of reality shifts from internal to external, and we become more aware of how others see us. This is when we are more likely to succumb to social pressure to enhance our status. This intensifies during our teens and twenties when the ego is often most dominant.

Hence toxic group dynamics are fed by destructive mind programming that's disseminated via entertainment targeting the youth generation. Through social media, virtual games, TV shows and movies the belief is anchored, 'everyone loves a winner'. Yes, we are repeatedly instilled with the concept that we must achieve to earn respect and acceptance (love.) We are told to make something of ourselves, fit the projected model of social acceptance and prove our worth to be worthy of love. This results in a preoccupation with achieving the perfect body or job to attract a partner or perfect grades to gain parental approval. This sends the message we are intrinsically worthless. Only when we accept the call to adventure to explore beyond the ladder of competition will we discover our worth is infinite as divine beings whose essence is eternal love. Only then, do we break this enchantment and stop trying to fit in by appearing acceptable or impressive.

CHAPTER 4

Meeting the Mentor:
The Magdalenes, Keepers of the
Grail

W e've now arrived at the fourth stage of *The Hero's Journey*, known as, *The Meeting with the Mentor*. This is when the hero meets the mystic who provides him with a map and guidance to navigate his quest. *The Hero's Journey* is an archetypal journey that was once a key part of *the Grail* tradition. It taught men how to fulfil their potential by observing cyclic wisdom. It also emphasized how essential it is for men to embrace an inner descent to integrate the feminine part of their psyche. Before detailing the connection between *the Grail* and *The Hero's Journey*, I will first introduce you to the women who mentored men in this quest and explain in more detail, why women performed this role.

This chapter also serves as a roadmap to understanding the true power of the feminine for men and masculine-dominant women who may be tempted to skip ahead on the presumption this info is unnecessary or irrelevant. To do so would be at one's own peril. For the mentor's function is to make sense of the terrain the hero will encounter, often through providing a map. Not a map outlining external goals, like a business plan or training schedule, but a map charting the inner realms of the psyche. This is because the hero's internal issues will inevitably be provoked by their outer challenges. The mentor assists the hero by identifying the inner lessons they must master to succeed in their outer challenges. Without a mentor, many heroes lack the self-confidence to start their quest, let alone navigate the inherent obstacles. Many others waste precious time and energy shadow-boxing their saboteur, unable to identify the true nature of their struggles. The mentor serves as an external conscience for the hero and gives them the necessary support to ensure they stay on course and don't succumb to self-doubt and give up when the going gets tough.

Follow The Star and Live The Impossible Dream

Just as a fisherman wouldn't go to sea without first checking the weather and the tides, in the ancient world, a questing hero wouldn't embark on a mission without first enlisting the help of a mystic, one proficient in navigating the stars. Yes, the ancients didn't just navigate their sea voyages by the stars. They consulted the stars to guide their inner journeys. By observing the lessons of the Cosmic cycles, they could anticipate the nature of each challenge to discern the best course of action. This was done by observing and applying the lessons of the mythic journey illuminated by the timing of planetary transits. The mythos of *The Hero's Journey* aligns with the sun's transit around the zodiac wheel.

When astrology and mythology are combined, they provide a clear map to chart a path to victory. Without comprehending the relationship between myth and astrology in our modern world, we tend to devalue the true power of both, viewing them as mere entertainment. So no, you won't activate your heroic strengths by reading your horoscope in the local paper or watching Hollywood reenactments of myths. However, you can activate your potency through combining these esoteric agents to make sense of your inner world, just as exoteric science helps us make sense of our outer world. So, it's inevitable that without this framework to understand, heal and empower the psyche, we perceive our struggles as perplexing and random, unable to join the dots to see the big picture of our 'uni -verse' - the one heroic story we all traverse.

Got Fears of Abandonment? You're Not Alone

The mentor didn't just provide a map like a DIY set of building instructions, leaving the hero to figure it out independently. Despite portrayals by Hollywood, showing fledgling superheroes like *Spiderman* or *The Greatest American Hero* receiving a suit with special powers and no manual. Unlike IKEA, a true mentor sticks around to help the hero decipher the map, offering practical guidance as needed. This is why ancient chieftains, kings and queens would consult a court astrologer or an oracular priestess to advise them when making significant decisions. Similarly, Egyptian pharaohs would enlist metaphysical counsel to assist with dream interpretation. This was done to ensure coherence between their inner and outer world, not merely as a fear-based superstition as we've been led to believe.

The legends of mythic heroes also provided a template for the symbolic lessons of the soul. Just as devout Christians today might ask, "What would Jesus do?" When unsure how best to progress, the ancients would consider the example of heroes like Hercules, Thor or Gilgamesh...all of whom sought the guidance of a mentor. Yes, all the great mythic heroes sought help, as they understood it was essential to fulfil their aspirations. Meanwhile, today, many men resist asking for street directions for fear of looking stupid. This is because Hollywood portrays heroes saving the world in 90 minutes, single-handedly while cracking smug one-liners. At most, they receive practical instructions detailing their assignment but no soul guidance, the essential ingredient needed to outwit the inner saboteur, who is a far greater threat than any external villain. Without wise counsel to face one's inner foe, the hero in all of us inevitably succumbs to their fears and repeatedly sabotages their efforts or their entire quest. The heroes who learn to outwit their inner foe, such as *Shrek*, by removing the chip on their shoulder, win our hearts in a battle far greater than the glory attained by defeating their external rival.

"Wars do not make one great."

Yoda

The original mentors were schooled in the mystic arts, so they were familiar with the inner realm of the feminine, the unseen world. This was the prerequisite needed to help the hero navigate the terrain of the psyche. In the ancient world, this role was usually fulfilled by a wise woman, a priestess initiated into *the Grail*. Some of the most popular films to date have featured mystic mentors, rather than mundane representations of the mentor such as a coach, boss, teacher or inventor. This indicates our thirst for greater meaning as we feel inspired by the example of characters like *Yoda* in *Star Wars*, *Mr Miyagi* in *The Karate Kid*, and *Morpheus* in *The Matrix* who each awoke their hero's latent mystical gifts. They did this by assisting them to discover a new perception of reality. This is because the ultimate function of the mentor is to awaken the feminine archetype of the mystic within the hero's psyche.

Like the examples mentioned above, most modern quest dramas on the silver screen feature a male mentor. In fantasy films, this is more likely to be a sage who has developed the mystic traits of the feminine within himself. Whereas in action films, the mentor is more likely to be an alpha male; a bad ass, like a gangster, someone who is considered the antithesis of femininity. We never see a butch action hero humble his ego to listen to the advice of a woman. Although more recently, we have seen the character *of Jake Sully* in the sci-fi film, *Avatar* be mentored by *Neytiri*, a fierce heroine with superior hunting and fighting skills which earns the respect of male movie-goers. While she signifies a step forward, we're yet to see a true feminine mystic be positively portrayed as a mentor.

Films have served as our modern myths, reflecting back our archetypal stories, enacted by screen Gods and Goddesses. However, these representations have been heavily influenced by the patriarchal mindset and agenda, so they've distorted our perception of the hero's quest. So, while it was once commonplace for men to seek insight and mentoring from mystic women, the lack of representation of wise women has devalued the wisdom of the feminine. If mystic women are portrayed, it's usually a negative representation, such as an evil, power-hungry sorceress or a hag who is feared or ridiculed or a sexy young babe who has psychic superpowers. Women's wisdom has been dismissed as 'old wives' tales'. As a result, esoteric science has been lampooned as kooky, flaky, woo woo and hocus-pocus while exoteric science, limited by what one can perceive via their lower senses, is elevated to a dais of truth beyond question. What is the cost, not just to women, but to the hero who lays dormant within the collective psyche when women's wisdom is suppressed?

The Silencing of Feminine Wisdom

The ruling elite employed this oppression of mystic guidance to undermine wisdom as the mark of true power and authority. This has reduced the status of the feminine in society. Before the rise of empires like Rome, mystic women were revered and respected. The Roman Empire outlawed the practice of Mysticism and persecuted priestesses of the old tradition so men would more readily swear their allegiance to the state of Rome, rather than see it for what it was, a Devil's Bargain. Today we see the echo of vows taken by men to honor duty to the state over love, with many men overworking to achieve status and wealth while becoming strangers to their families. Without initiation into the mysteries of life, the archetypal hero remains immature, seeking short-term gratification, often at a cost to themselves as well as the greater good. Over millennia this has created a culture where power and status are valued and sought over love and wisdom. This cultural conditioning also undermines male/female relations, both internally and externally. This robs many potential heroes of much-needed guidance and support.

Why? Men and masculine-dominant women who are immature tend to run from women who assert their inner authority; intuition. This is because interacting with an empowered woman evokes unresolved feelings of powerlessness. Feelings they may have experienced in relation to their mother growing up as an immature man or masculine-dominant woman is still trying to individuate from their mother by doing the opposite of her instruction or example. This often plays out as enacting impressive feats to prove one's autonomy, capability and success. When one is on a quest for glory instead of truth, they resist help from the feminine, viewing it as cheating or a weakness. Accepting such help may evoke fears of being exposed as a fraud or a failure, based on the belief that, unless they achieve their desired goal solely on their own merits, they cannot claim the victory as proof of their worth. This neurosis underpins destructive behaviors like ruthless competition, workaholism and the need to assert dominance at any cost. Until we address this underlying wound, we will see the escalation of unsustainable development. Such as phallic skyscrapers, utility vehicles the size of army tanks and McMansion housing developments. All of which are created by a competitive mindset as primitive as an alpha gorilla beating his chest. Kind of ironic when we consider this kind of progress is what we've considered proof of how advanced we are, compared with those who lived more simply, in harmony with nature; the feminine.

It stands to reason, those who try to dominate the feminine or reject assistance from the feminine tend to be those who have rejected the feminine traits in themselves. This is because they equate any embodiment of feminine traits with a loss of personal power. Ironically, without developing feminine traits, the hero can't escape his compulsion to seek external validation to compensate for his lack of authentic empowerment. And the more one seeks power externally, the more they neglect and sabotage their personal relationships. This includes their relationship with themselves.

This is the awareness that pierces the illusion that a rich and powerful man is a great catch as a relationship partner. This is a patriarchal fallacy that places pressure on men to overlook their inner riches to create outer wealth. Only when a man has seen through this charade, often after a costly divorce, is he truly ready to seek something of greater value. For only a heart that's been broken open is receptive to hearing the voice of wisdom.

Mentors of the Grail Maidens and Grail Knights

Mention the name, *Magdalene* and the assumption is usually made that you're referring to *Mary Magdalene*. A woman whose true identity has been disguised and corrupted, like *the Grail*. That's because a *Magdalene* was a woman who served *the Grail*. As stated earlier, the title of *Magdalene* referred to a priestess who initiated both men and women into *the Grail* mysteries. There were many *Magdalenes*, just as there were many *Merlins*, the male equivalent who served as a *High Priest*.

The *Magdalenes* were revered as spiritual leaders within their communities. They taught people how to honor the Great Wheel; the circle of life. They did this by teaching people how the greater cycles of nature and the cosmos initiate us to grow wise. This understanding enabled people to live in right relationship with the natural cycles that govern us. Matriarchy was not about women ruling men as the women in positions of sacred power acknowledged the only 'true ruler' were the cycles of nature, the universal laws of quantum physics that govern us all. When the circle of life is honored, all of life is kept in balance and revered as sacred. This is what we have lost and what is essential for our survival as a species. This is why the film, *The Lion King*, struck such a chord, for it acknowledged this sacred truth.

The *Magdalenes* taught women how to live in alignment with the lunar cycle to be in right relationship with their womb and their feminine energy. Similarly, the *Magdalenes* taught men how to live in alignment with the solar cycle that governs their heart and masculine energy. They also taught men how to truly love a woman by understanding how women's fertility cycle changed their demeanor like the ever-changing phases of the moon. The *Magdalenes* also taught couples how to live in alignment with the seasons by observing how the seasonal wheel influences patterns of relating. This awareness supported couples to grow with the seasons, so their love blossomed with wisdom over the years and endured the challenges of the dark months when the ego is dominant. Without this understanding, it's not surprising we see a 50% divorce rate.

Watching Over Their Flock

Long before *Yeshua* was described as a shepherd of his flock, the *Magdalenes* presided over the soul needs of the collective. The title of *Magdalene* meant 'watchtower'.

"Mary Magdalene's introduction in the Book of Luke 8:2 describes her as 'Mary, called Magdalene' - that is, 'Mary, called the Watchtower'. This distinction referred to her high status in the community as a spiritual guardian, a 'watchtower of the flock'. This is why Jacapo di Voragine, a 13th century archbishop of Genoa stated Mary' possessed the heritage of the castle of Bethany' the correct translation being the tower of Bethany as there was no castle. So, the rouse about her being a woman of low standing from a small fishing village

called Magdala is coincidentally a red herring."[16]

Laurence Gardner, The Magdalene Legacy

The elevated location of the *Magdalene's* offices symbolized the higher perspective they offered to raise others as to reside in the watchtower, one had to ascend, both literally and metaphorically. Patriarchy inverted this tradition, converting watchtowers into places that gathered military intelligence, used for amassing power and control, rather than places dedicated to gathering divine intelligence to liberate the group soul. Today's watch towers operate as a network of surveillance cameras and data collection systems. Prior to the digital age, they were castle turrets used as fortress lookouts and prison cells to incarcerate enemies of the state.

One of the most famous prisoners to be locked away in a tower was the priestess *Cassandra*, daughter of *King Priam*, King of the ancient Grecian city of Troy. Like many noblewomen, she had trained in the mystic arts as this increased a woman's value as a prospective wife as a spiritual advisor to men in positions of power. *Cassandra* is famous for having foreseen the fall of Troy with her gift of precognition. Her proclamations of truth were a source of embarrassment to her father, so he locked her away in a tower. Hence patriarchal writers describe *Cassandra* as 'cursed to speak the truth' portraying precognition as a curse which encouraged people to fear and disown this latent ability.

Similarly, the turrets within the Tower of London were used to punish the perceived enemies of the crown, the ruling sovereign. It is significant this is where the crown jewels of the British monarch are kept on display. Royal accouterments that are an appropriation of the earlier symbols of sacred sovereignty associated with *the Grail.* Such as the golden orb that mimics a pomegranate, a fruit revered by women's mysteries. Pomegranates feature a naturally occurring crown atop the fruit and contain ruby red seeds, signifying the regal status and cyclic wisdom mystic women acquire by digesting the bitter seeds of past experience catalyzed by the release of the seeds of their wombs each month during their menses.

The royal scepter is an appropriation of the measuring ruler that once indicated one's right to rule, based on one's ability to chart and interpret the natural cycles. Originally these ancient calendars were fashioned out of bone or cow horns that bore incisions for the 13 lunar months. Paleolithic tribes used them to chart their nomadic course in accordance with the phases of the moon, essential for their survival.

Meanwhile, today we see the symbol of the watchtower synonymous with rich, young and naive princesses in Disney castles. It is here the patriarchal princess resides, awaiting her rescue by a young man from a wealthy family of high rank. This distortion anchored the notion that the ideal woman was from elite stock increasing her value as a prize breeder, lauded for her physical beauty and youth and her ability to bring forth heirs. Previously the earlier role models of womanhood, *Magdalenes* were sovereign women who were revered for their humility, wisdom and empowerment.

In the advanced ancient cultures that honored the wisdom of the feminine, the *High Priestess*, the highest-ranking *Magdalene*, shared rulership with the king of the land. He oversaw the external needs of the people and she, the inner needs. Hence *Yeshua*, who embodied the archetype of the *Sacred King*, trained in mystery schools in the East to prepare for his destined role of *High Priest King* partnering *Mari*, a *Magdalene*, as *High Priestess Queen*. This was the custom in the culture of Mesopotamia, whose civilization was initially influenced by higher dimensional beings, known as the *Annunaki*.

The *Magdalenes* were the keepers of the *Grail*; custodians of cyclic wisdom teachings, initiation ceremonies and sacred practices that together comprised *the Grail* mysteries. They wore red robes indicating their commitment to walk the 'good red road', the path of Earthly wisdom, the way of the Goddess. Referred to as *The Ladies in Red*, they dedicated their lives in service to the *Earth Mother* and upholding the sanctity of the holy blood of the fertile feminine that enables life to prevail. Perhaps this is why the song, *Lady in Red* in the 1980s was a hit for previously unknown artist, Chris De Burgh. The Romans appropriated this tradition to create the order of Vestal Virgins whose sole charge was to keep the flame alive that signified the life force of the empire. They distorted the word, virgin to mean sexually chaste and buried alive priestesses who didn't remain so.

In the Tantric Hindu tradition of ancient India, *Magdalenes* were referred to as *Red Dakinis*, meaning *Sky Walkers*. This term was the inspiration for naming the protagonist, Luke Skywalker in the film, *Star Wars*. According to the late historian Laurence Gardner, a *Magdalene* was also referred to as *The Moon Woman* because of the lunar lore she taught. I discovered this after one of my students asked me to take on the Facebook page she had created, called The Moon Woman...a name that became synonymous with me when the page went viral in the days when Facebook operated on organic likes and followers. Another term the *Magdalenes* were known by was *Scarlet Women*, a term later used by the medieval Roman church to brand and punish women as adulterers. In Greek they were called *Hierodule*, meaning 'Sacred Women' a word later transformed (via medieval French into English) to *harlot*. In the early Germanic tongue, they were known as *Horés* - which was later Anglicized to *whores*. It's interesting to note, the term, *Horés* originally meant, *'Beloved Ones'*.[17]

The Red Path of the Dark Goddess

One of the sacred symbols associated with the *Magdalenes* was the red rose. While the white rose denoted purity; the color associated with the Heavenly Father, the red rose signified initiation into the sacred feminine mysteries of the *Earth Mother*, known in the West as *the Grail* and in the East, the Red Path of Tantra. Symbolically, a woman who wore white still belonged to her father like an innocent girl. Whereas a woman who wore red signified she had been initiated into the ways of the sacred feminine to 'know herself'. This threshold catalyzed an internal shift that enabled her to individuate from the influence of her father so she belonged to herself as a sovereign woman in her own right. This is why traditionally brides in the lands colonized by Rome wore white and those in the east wore Red. The red rose symbolized the blood-engorged vulva of the feminine, considered the sacred gate of death and birth in Mysticism. This portal is the mouth of the Dark Goddess, which is why the vulva, especially a hairy, menstruating vulva, incites fear in those who are uninitiated and often afraid of change, death and the unknown. That is why women down through the ages in various cultures engaged in *Anasyrma*, the most ancient and powerful gesture of the feminine, raising one's skirts collectively to reveal the power of their sacred opening to shock men out of desecrating the gift of life on the battlefield. A tactic that has worked due to men's fear of the yoni (vulva).[18]

The fear of the yoni, the face of the Dark Goddess is why we see so many uninitiated women today diminishing the power of their genitalia. They do this without comprehending the fear of rejection that motivates the removal of their pubic hair, the injecting of hormonal implants to cease menstruation and the mutilation of their labia to appear less fertile and powerful. This is all done to appear acceptable to those who fear the power of the feminine, such as immature lovers who reflect the internalized misogyny of uninitiated women. I also suspect this is why in my experience, men have been reluctant to passionately kiss the mouth of the Dark Goddess, yet show no resistance to receiving oral worship. I write this not to shame or judge men but to be transparent in educating how significant this is.

A man's ability to wholeheartedly embrace the Dark Goddess holds the key to unlocking the deepest part of an empowered woman's soul. A man who has transcended the cultural conditioning that shames the dark feminine is a rare find. A man or masculine-dominant woman who lavishes love on the primal feminine, be it her hairy vulva, her menses, or her ability to name the shadow, will receive erotic devotion like no other. This is what heterosexual porn attempts to mimic; the worship of the wild masculine by the wild feminine. Instead, it shows disempowered women who have disowned the wild feminine pretending to worship the disempowered masculine. Such pretense is painful to watch for anyone who knows the real passion of absolute erotic abandon inspired by total devotion. Equally, uninitiated women may deter a man from going 'down there', reflecting their own rejection of their unmentionable dark feminine. This prevents women from experiencing deeper orgasms due to their erotic inhibition and internalized cultural shame about their womanhood. Such a woman will keep her defenses up by playing the role of the perfect partner, performing sexually rather than entering the mystery through an act of unbridled surrender.

In the Arthurian language of flowers synonymous with courtly love that's long been associated with *the Grail,* red roses represent the passion of erotic love. For one who is willing to surrender their ego to experience union through erotic love will experience the liberation of the soul that sexual ecstasy offers, the promise of which is intoxicating. Thanks to the act of marriage becoming more about providing security for assets and children, a legacy of the business alliances brokered between dynastic families, rather than an act of true love we've been led to believe that chaste and often unrequited love is true love. This results in portrayals of true love as tragedies of epic proportions, like the romances of *Tristan and Yseult, Romeo and Juliet* or more recently, *Love Story* and *The Fault in Their Stars.* These tragedies convey yet another hallmark of the puritanical twist Christianity placed upon the *Grail;* the belief that true love equals suffering.

As stated previously, the path of *the Grail* is one of initiation. So too, one who enters the holy vessel of a woman through the sex act experiences a loss of innocence, catalyzing a psychological death. For men who have not been circumcised this initial experience of intercourse often provides a blood rite of initiation due to the foreskin tearing. This is equivalent to a woman's hymen breaking during penetration which also produces blood. The patriarchal practice of circumcising boys as babies robs them of this rite of passage when it is age appropriate. (I'll speak more about that later on.)

Through the sacrament of erotic love, an initiate will meet the most primal part of themselves. This is why the sacred opening of a woman has been demonized, for fear of her primal, sexual power. The greater the fear of a woman's sexuality, the greater the fear of losing one's identity, status and power – one's ego. The stronger the ego, the weaker the soul and the less true love is possible. Without a willingness to surrender one's carefully constructed facade, there can be no real soul connection or growth. The measure of our fear of the primal power of the feminine can be seen in our attempts to bypass her initiations by replacing them with medical interventions. Today manmade science claims her power as its own with conception replaced by artificial insemination, birth replaced by caesarian sections, the breaking of the foreskin during sexual initiation replaced by medical circumcision and the natural passage of death avoided at any cost with medical procedures that prolong life at any cost, even when the quality of life being preserved is poor. Without these primal initiations to meet the Dark Goddess directly, we remain disconnected from our primal power.

Without looking directly into the face of death via a life experience that serves as an initiation with the Dark Goddess, we seek to avoid change, due to a fear of the unknown. This results in evasive behaviors that stunt our maturity. Since change is unavoidable, eventually we will find ourselves trapped in the abyss of the unknowable, experiencing inner torment and depression, unable to process our fears. It is when we find ourselves lost, afraid we will never return to the sunny disposition of our youth, that we are finally ready to meet the Dark Goddess. For until such a conscious meeting occurs, we remain trapped in the *Underworld*; the darkness within. Our escape depends on our ability to accept the help of an agent of the Dark Goddess. Such as a mystic priestess like Ariadne or the crone Goddesses, *Hecate* or *Hel* who helped the heroes of olde navigate their way out of the dark labyrinth within. Just as *Gretel* did for her brother, *Hansel*, when they became lost in the woods.

Regardless of our gender, without instruction from the mystic feminine we fail to grasp the lessons of the dark and suffer an eternal 'Winter of discontent'. That is, until we experience soul realizations that pierce the illusions of our ego. Otherwise, we remain in stasis, like an extra on the set of the zombie apocalypse, barely able to function in our everyday world. It is at this point of total despair we reach out asking for Divine intervention. It is after this turning point in our heroic adventure that supernatural aid will appear in the form of a mentor to assist us to find our disowned aspects so we may re-emerge from our descent more aware, empowered and humble. So ask and it will be given!

We Need Each Other

Just as women need men to protect them from dark forces in the external, physical world, men need women to protect them from dark forces in the inner, non-physical world. Until we appreciate this equitable exchange, the feminine will be viewed as the weaker sex and not respected; seen as a burden to be carried or a commodity to be bought and sold. Such societal arrogance will only change with initiation. For example, men who attend the home birth of their children are humbled by their meeting with the primal feminine. So too, men who are made aware of the perilous inner descent women take to the *Underworld* each month when they menstruate will no doubt be more courteous and respectful towards women. Not because chivalry is expected or equal rights legislated, but because they understand and respect the shamanic power of the feminine. This is the real reason *Grail* knights and kings were chivalrous towards the feminine and took vows to honor and protect the sacredness of the feminine. Without *the Grail,* we see a society where the reversal is the norm, with violence towards the *Earth Mother* and women at an all-time high and many who profess to support women's rights and status, covertly indulging in fantasies that humiliate, degrade and dominate women in the sex act via porn.

Why the World Went to Hell in a Hand Basket

We often avoid what we fear and judge what we don't understand. This leads us to inadvertently dismiss what we most need and suffer the consequences. For example, if we associate the unseen realm as a dark place of punishment aka Hell, it makes sense we avoid descending to the depths to become more self-aware. Ironically, without consciously exploring the depths within, we unconsciously create Hell through unaware choices. That means parts of our psyche remain unexplored, locked away in our subconscious, like the folkloric character, *Bluebeard* who's most shamed aspects were hidden away, causing him to destroy those who discovered them. For what we hide, even from ourselves are the aspects we fear are unacceptable. Healing comes when we seek to understand, embrace, and integrate these wounded parts. Through this process we create a balanced and integrated psyche which leads to healthy choices in all areas of our lives.

In the ancient world, they had a different perception of the subconscious. They revered the *Underworld* as the womb of the *Great Mother*. The patriarchs renamed this realm, Hell, appropriated from the name of the Norse Goddess, *Hel*. *Hel* was a priestess who previously assisted heroes, like *Thor*, to emerge from the *Underworld* with a more mature outlook. Christianity instilled the belief that the lower world was a place of punishment inflicted by a vengeful *Sky Father* God. This insinuated the worst punishment one could inflict was a journey to the inner realm of the feminine. As a result, people feared going within. They feared initiation, they feared mystic women and they feared the dark, perceiving it as evil. This fear prevented subsequent generations from going within to face their fears, a process necessary for growth and maturation.

Today we label those trapped in the *Underworld* as mentally ill and prescribe chemical treatments in an effort to numb their psychological torment.

Fortunately, we are seeing a growing number of progressive therapists who are soul-based in their approach. This means they utilize the tools of the inner landscape, such as the power of myth, symbols, archetypes and ritual to explore the psyche. This is the ancient feminine approach to healing adopted by the famous healer, *Asklepius* which he applied in his 300 healing temples throughout ancient Greece. Such an approach works on the premise that illness is caused by unresolved trauma within the psyche. For more insight into that, I highly recommend watching the film, *The Wisdom of Trauma*, featuring the work of Gabor Maté.

The Relationship Between Trauma and Power

When one is overwhelmed by unresolved trauma, they are more likely to hand over their autonomy; their power of choice, to an external authority such as medical institutions, government agencies or the media to think for them. When the psyche is not whole and healed, we become more easily disoriented and overwhelmed as our unprocessed pain erodes our trust in ourselves as decision-makers. When the group mind is immature and bombarded with trauma-inducing information and systems that dehumanize and invalidate the soul, mass psychosis ensues.[19] This is understood and leveraged by those who seek absolute power and control. This is why mystics have been persecuted for so long. They pose a direct threat to totalitarian regimes, like the one now visible that has been systematically orchestrated over millennia. Essentially, the more traumatized someone is, the easier they are to rule. The more integrated someone's psyche, the more they can hold their own in the face of opposition and assert their intrinsic rights as a sacred and sovereign being. In a nutshell, healing equals empowerment. To date, women have been more proactive in attending to their need for healing and empowerment. Men's empowerment often focuses on how to achieve external success rather than how to heal the psyche. Traditionally women assisted men with this task...something which is taboo in a patriarchal culture.

The Return of the Magdalenes

Never before has there been a more urgent need for the return of the sacred feminine to play a long overdue role in the healing of the World Soul. It is the sacred charge of the *Magdalenes* to assist the collective in confronting and healing our relationship with the three taboos; blood, sex, and death. These are the three subjects that, if experienced directly, initiate our psyche into the *Underworld* via a loss of innocence. Without mentoring to reframe our experience from a mystic perspective our psyche remains trapped in the Underworld. This can manifest as depression caused by unprocessed fears, guilt and shame. This is why these sacred taboos carry a lot of power. Power that can harm or heal. This is why even the words; blood, sex and death carry a provocative, emotional charge, because of the power they contain.

The word *taboo* comes from the Polynesian word, *tapua* meaning 'sacred power'. The ancients understood taboos held the key to our deepest fears, so they created initiations to ensure people understood their sacred power and approached them with humility and reverence. Without mystic initiation to assist us to be in right relationship with our cultural taboos, their sacred power has been abused. Instead, blood, sex and death have been used to intimidate and enslave the innocent and naive by those who have sought power at any cost.

It is worth noting one can only be controlled by those seeking absolute power to the degree they fear the dark. That's why it's so powerful to initiate people to face their fears with support and insight, so they are empowered to transcend their fears and liberate their psyche. For when we are unconsciously initiated into experiences of blood, sex and death without adequate preparation, the shock of the novel experience remains unintegrated within our psyche. This stunts our maturity as part of our psyche remains frozen at the age of our unintegrated experiences. This is why the number one search term on pornography sites is 'teen', representing the psychological age of most users who lost their virginity as teenagers. When we address this issue with benevolence, we will reduce the risk of young people being groomed by predators. Ultimately, it is our unprocessed fears and trauma that makes us susceptible to being a victim or a perpetrator.

Due to the lack of acknowledgment, acceptance and accountability for our societal taboos, they tend to accumulate shame. This leads people to publicly distance themselves from associations with blood, sex and death while seeking them out privately. This creates a split in the psyche, like the infamous *Dr Jeckyl and Mr Hyde*, where one aims to show their lighter side in public and hide their darker side in private.

Without integrating the lower, primal parts of our psyche, many disassociate from vilified aspects to be more acceptable to themselves and others. Ironically, the more we strive to be good and pure, the more likely we swing to the other polarity and crave the forbidden fruit, expressing our desire in destructive ways. We see this behavior in priests who sought to be pillars of purity and then violated the temples of the innocent. This fall from grace occurs when we seek the white path of spiritual union with the Father God and don't balance it with the red path of Earthly wisdom of the Mother Goddess. Without being grounded in humble self-acceptance, we become unbalanced, falling victim to spiritual ambition. This may play out as striving to have the perfect mindset, body or moral fortitude.

It is simply a fact of life we must face and integrate our shadow to take responsibility for it, or like the vicar in the film, *Chocolat*, we will binge on what we've abstained from in a Dionynisian frenzy during our hour of weakness. Women as earthly embodiments of the Goddess naturally gravitate towards sensate pleasure. This is why women have been scapegoated by patriarchal religion as evil temptresses. However, it is not women, but abstinence that creates a compulsion to indulge the senses in destructive ways. What is denied holds a tempting fascination.

One need only look at popular culture to see our distorted relationship the collective psyche has with these three taboos. For instance, while we may not see ourselves as puritanical or sexually repressed, we may refer to ourselves as a 'naughty girl', 'bad boy' or suggest a 'dirty weekend'. All of these colloquial terms illustrate how immature our cultural attitude is towards sex. So too, menstrual blood is considered unmentionable in 'polite' company. In fact any sign of it is avoided at any cost. Most men would be unaware how careful women are to avoid wearing light clothes for fear of a leak being seen in public during 'that time of the month'…or the anxiety women feel if they bleed onto bed sheets that aren't theirs or God forbid, their stomach looks bloated, instead of flat despite the fact once a month the fertile female uterus doubles in size.

Sex, blood and death often go hand in hand so if our relationship with one is unresolved it will play out as a dysfunctional expression of another. For example, in 2020[20] when the media incited the group mind's ultimate fear; death via hysteria about COVID-19, the use of pornography dramatically increased. The degree to which people allowed themselves to be disempowered by their governments during 2020-21 evidences how essential it is we take back our power as a species by understanding the sacred power of our cultural taboos. To listen to a podcast series I did about this with my sexologist friend, Kristen Murray Alexi, visit the resource section.

Reframing and healing our relationship with our taboos is yet another reason we need to reinstate the tradition of *the Grail*. Why? Global human trafficking statistics report 4.8 million people were sold into sexual slavery in 2020[21] and in Australia, the number of sexual assaults reported were higher than any year on record, with 67% of homicides committed by men, a third being domestic violence cases. Public protests, surveillance cameras and legislation will not stop these numbers escalating. A shift in consciousness needs to occur within the collective psyche, through the reintroduction of social customs that ensure honorable conduct, particularly towards women and children, who are most negatively impacted by the current status quo.

We cannot shame, judge and vilify people for not acting honorably if we do not provide adequate social structures that model healthy human behavior and provide a framework to support it. We need to be taught how to be responsible with our sacred power for without adequate mentoring uninitiated people will continue to experience haphazard initiations into these powerful taboos and feel traumatized. To hear me speak about the three taboos, check out my video series, *Initiation: The Sacred Power of Blood, Sex* and

Death filmed in Bali, Indonesia, where the Dark Goddess is honored. It's listed in the resource section.

Reclaiming the Practice of the Red Tent

An ancient custom known as the *Red Tent* is one of the forums where young women learn about the power of sacred taboos in a safe space. How? They listen to women of all ages speak transparently about the experiences they are processing. The *Red Tent* is the most common *Grail* practice we see returning as part of a global grassroots movement. I am now one of many *Magdalenes* who initiate women of all ages into the practice of the *Red Tent*. I do this via an online training course that has trained women in over 44 countries. Again, listed in the resource section.

Traditionally, the *Red Tent* or *Moon Lodge* is where women would gather to explore the shadow aspects that surface within their psyche as the moon wanes to new moon. The *Red Tent* has been viewed by many as primarily a menstrual hut, a place of retreat women would go to bleed. However, it provides much more, including an ongoing practice to heal and integrate life experiences with the support of a community.

Monthly gatherings held in the *Red Tent* may include additional practices like meditation, sacred ceremony, healing and the consulting of oracles, but the central element is a sharing circle. Held during the darkest lunar phase to support women during their most challenging time of the month. For many, this coincides with their premenstrual or menstrual phase, a time of reflection and distillation.

The womb-like interior of the *Red Tent* provides an intentional space for a psychological death and rebirth. This is done through acknowledging the wisdom of the archetypal Dark Goddess who surfaces within the psyche during this time and assists with the conscious processing of taboos and painful experiences so they can be transmuted into wisdom. This is why the *Red Tent* was referred to as the place of 'Secret Women's Business', not a place that men weren't allowed so women could complain about men. This is behavior done by uninitiated women who, instead of exploring their dark side, scapegoat men for their suffering. An intentional 'women's only' space provides a concentrated dose of feminine nurturance and insight during a woman's most sensitive time of the month.

It was only later the *Red Tent* was viewed as a place of exile for menstruating women, who were seen by Patriarchy as 'unclean'. This was a distortion based on a fear of women's psychic power during their menses. The *Red Tent* was a custom in the earlier Goddess-worshiping cultures where women learned firsthand the gifts of authentic sisterhood as a source of mutual support.

Red Tents provided a childfree sanctuary for women to focus on their inner needs so they could cyclically shed their psycho-emotional skin, catalyzed by the shedding of their uterine lining, like a serpent. This cyclic practice of release and renewal grew their inner power. *Red Tents* also provided soul-centered education to understand and embrace womanhood from a mystic perspective. This is important for women of all ages, including those who never received a welcome to their womanhood. For without this threshold being formally acknowledged, part of a woman's psyche remains inhibited or injured, impacting her identity and expression. In the ancient world every young woman was welcomed to the *Red Tent* as a rite of passage when she became a woman. It was in the *Red Tent* pre-teens and teens learned how to understand their fertility cycle and how it and the lunar cycle influenced their moods, energy levels, creativity and libido. Without this sacred knowledge, many modern women feel like they're on an emotional roller coaster, disempowered by their lack of understanding to manage their changeable emotional states.

In pre-patriarchal Hebraic culture, they celebrated the power of a woman's voice when she entered puberty, referring to women as the 'daughter of the Voice'. The word *utterer* is derived from the word, *uterus*. Hence they were encouraged to speak their insights; 'the word of the womb'[22] during their menses when they were psychically expanded. This is why women were encouraged to practice using the power of their voice in the *Red Tent* by taking it in turns to speak and be heard. This practice increases a woman's personal power as it affirms that her insight, perspective and ideas are both valuable and worthy of acknowledgement. It's understandable that women who aren't initiated into the *Red Tent* struggle to speak up as advocates on their own behalf and assert their needs, ideas and insights.

Traditionally the *Red Tent* was also the place women birthed their babies, underwent rite of passage ceremonies for life transitions and received womb or yoni (vulva) massage to heal trauma stored within the most sacred parts of their bodies. Women who reached menopause were celebrated for their service as seers for the tribe during their cyclic descents in the *Red Tent*. This is why the *Red Tent* or *Moon Lodge* was considered the 'holy of holies'.

"In the native American tradition if you wanted to destroy a village you simply destroyed the Moon Lodge so it stands to reason the fastest way to restore our global village is to reinstate the tradition of the Moon Lodge"

Tanishka

Holy Blood Batman!

The *Magdalenes* were the women who presided over the sacred blood mysteries that were central to the practice of the *Red Tent*. They understood it was their womb's blood rites that initiated them through their major life transitions; menarche (first menses), pregnancy, peri-menopause and menopause. Patriarchy changed women's milestones to: debutante balls to announce a young woman's arrival on the marriage market, baby showers to receive material gifts for the baby, weddings and funerals - none of which honored the power of the womb. I speak about this in more detail in my Feminine Rites of Passage training listed in the resources section.

These blood rites did not involve the blood sacrifices of animals. Quite the opposite, they involved instruction to honor the sacred life-giving blood of the womb, *the Grail* cup. It's not surprising without this sacred knowledge, so many young women today view their holy blood as a curse or dreaded inconvenience.

The degree to which a woman has not processed Menarche; her initial rite of passage into womanhood, directly corresponds to her ability to make choices that honor her needs and her body. In other words, without this initiation to see and know her body as a sacred temple, she is more prone to desecrate her temple or sacrifice her needs. Despite many women reclaiming this tradition, the majority of women today remain uninitiated and treat their bodies without reverence. With men in uniforms collecting their holy blood in bins marked, 'toxic waste', who could blame them!

The shadow work done within the *Red Tent* awakened the codes of sacred feminine wisdom in their menses, making their *Graal* a powerful alchemical substance for healing, ceremony and initiation. The more cycles one had consciously traversed in *the Grail* tradition, the more revered their holy blood, due to the codes of cyclic wisdom it contained. The earliest Tantric text, the *Kaula Jnana Nirnaya* echoes this, listing the different names attributed to menstrual blood according to the different stages of a woman's life.

Unfortunately, it defines a woman's passage through time only by her relationship to men. For example, her first menses after being deflowered is called

Svayambhu, and the menses of a woman after she marries is called, *Svapushpa.* The continual deference to men suggests a distortion of the pre-patriarchal custom that honored the alchemical power of menses as a woman progressed through her life stages of maiden, mother, mage and crone. The many representations of the Black Madonna found in antiquity, such as graves and amulets featuring cowrie shells stained with red ochre, illustrate how widely menstruation was once revered as a time for worshiping the Dark Goddess as the inner guru. One descends to meet her for instruction when her blood spirals downward.

In Paleolithic and Neolithic cultures, the *Magdalenes* were respected as menstrual shamans who channeled the wisdom of the Dark Goddess and taught women how to embrace their menses as a sacred practice. Since women are most psychically open during menstruation, this was the ideal time for practicing the sacred arts of healing, visioning, channeling and manifestation. This is why patriarchs forbade menstruating women from temples, fearing their power would interfere with their ceremonial intent.

Distillers of Womb Wisdom

Just as distilling the essence of flowers concentrates their aroma into pungent oils, the *Magdalenes* distilled the strengths of the feminine. Not youthful beauty or fertility, the feminine traits most prized within patriarchy, but wisdom. And since the path to wisdom is often borne of suffering, many of those called to walk the path of *Magdalene* underwent challenging personal initiations to prepare them for their sacred service. Processing these experiences developed humility and compassion. This type of shamanic apprenticeship is the opposite of the scholarly approach we have been conditioned to aspire to. By way of contrast, the pursuit of knowledge and credentials, when not balanced by wisdom, can result in clinicians viewing those they serve with an air of detachment signaling an attitude of elitism.

Women initiated into *the Grail* learned to revere their bodies as sacred vessels and their wombs as the chalice of life, regardless of whether they gestated biological children, creative ideas, or insights. This meant they honored the ebb and flow of their energy levels on the observance of their cycles. In the two weeks leading up to ovulation, they did more active tasks, leaving sedentary tasks for the two weeks after ovulation, when their energy waned. Those no longer menstruating regulated their activities according to the waxing and waning of the moon. During new moon/menstruation they ceased domestic chores and nurtured their soul needs on the understanding this was when they were most inward, lethargic, sensitive and psychically expanded.

Without this understanding to manage the cyclic nature of feminine energy, many uninitiated women today judge themselves for not being linear like a man or machine and less changeable. Overriding our cyclic nature as women results in unexpressed tension being held in the cells and tissues of our wombs. This is the silent internal hysteria that manifests as 'women's problems'. During the 19th century, most of women's physical and mental health conditions were attributed to 'hysteria' - a word from the Greek word for womb. Victorian doctors treated hysteria with the earliest vibrators invented to relieve accumulated nervous tension.

Despite self-pleasure being more acceptable today than during the Victorian era, many women still feel inwardly hysterical due to the endemic misogyny within our culture that continues to cause an escalation of suffering and destruction. As fractals of the *Earth Mother*, women's wombs are sounding the alarm.

Hysterectomy is now the second most frequently performed surgical procedure (after cesarean section) for U.S. women who are of reproductive age according to the Center for Disease Control.[23] A study conducted in the year 2000 discovered 70% of hysterectomies performed in the U.S. were recommended inappropriately. This was my personal experience when a surgeon discovered a small fibroid in my womb when she removed my appendix. When I asked for a referral to a gynecologist to discuss treatment options, she responded, "I'm not going to waste the time of a gynecologist during COVID unless you're willing to have a hysterectomy." Fortunately, my local doctor was more accommodating, and after a scan showed it was only 16mm, I decided to treat it in a less invasive way with acupuncture. 60% of hysterectomies are recommended due to fibroids (benign tumors).[24] Fibroids are common in peri-menopausal women and usually resolve naturally after menopause. Without knowing this, women spend over 5 billion dollars annually on hysterectomies and take 6 weeks off paid work to recover[25] from this invasive surgery.

Meanwhile, the real cost to women may not be financial. According to a study published in the journal, *Neurology*, a hysterectomy can increase a woman's risk of developing dementia.[26] The Mayo Clinic reports women who had hysterectomies were more likely to develop a range of chronic conditions, including hypertension, obesity, cardiac arrhythmias, and coronary artery disease.[27] Bladder and bowel problems are also more common after hysterectomy and are usually permanent and progressive.[28] And yet, Hippocrates, considered 'the father of modern medicine', spoke of the womb as 'The animal within the animal' such was his reverence for its power. A theater nurse who attended my workshops said, "If women could see the powerful entity that is the womb, they would never remove it." I share this not to shame anyone who has had this procedure, but to raise awareness so more women can make informed choices and men can support them.

Embracing The Dark Mother Within

Without being taught a cyclic approach to self-care, it's not surprising women burn out and get sick rather than stop to attend to their needs. This is due to the cultural expectation a 'good woman' is available 24/7 to be caring and nurturing of others, even during her lowest ebb of the month. During this time, without adequate support, women are at risk of both self-harm and harm to those in their care. Should women lose control and erupt, they are wracked with remorse, which engenders an unconscious belief that they deserve to be punished.

Without acknowledging the archetypal Dark Mother and meeting her needs each month, this aspect inevitably becomes a destructive part of the psyche, undermining familial relationships. In the ancient world, the *Magdalenes* served as conscious embodiments of the archetypal Dark Mother. An aspect which was once revered as the Black Madonna, the sacred counterpart of the Divine Father.

Women who consciously descend to meet and integrate the lessons of this aspect embody her strengths; psychic power and wisdom. These are the women who are most able to identify what they've outgrown and release it, which accelerates their soul growth. For a woman to truly love and accept herself she needs to understand how the destroyer aspect of the Goddess is as necessary as the creative aspect. Such a woman transcends her fear of change, death and the unknown. This makes them ideal guides and spiritual midwives for people of all ages navigating their life transitions, including men.

CHAPTER 5

Crossing the Threshold:
The Quest Begins to Heal the King

As stated in *The Fisher King*, the land and her people are healed only when the king is healed. That's why the primary focus of this book is to address the wounds of the collective masculine. In this chapter, I share insights to empower men in every life stage so the inner hero can defeat his saboteur and fulfill his ultimate potential. For women, this offers greater understanding to love and support men but also how to discern a man's level of maturity and empowerment when considering whether a man as potential partner, friend or ally.

The Blame Game

As discussed, until recently, the collective feminine was blamed for the ills of the world. This was anchored with the Christian story of *Eve*, and the Greek story of *Pandora*. *Eve* and *Pandora*, as the archetypal maiden were scapegoated for the suffering of humanity. This mythos served as inspiration to justify prejudice towards the collective feminine. As a result, a misogynistic mindset was widely adopted for thousands of years, resulting in war crimes against women and the disempowerment of the collective feminine's identity and expression. War crimes that while widely acknowledged, have never been tried in a court of law and the agency that inflicted them, the Catholic church never held to account.

Since the women's liberation movement in the late 1960s, we have seen the pendulum swing the other way, with a cultural shift scapegoating the collective masculine; blaming men for the state of the world. This is why some men find the word *feminist* so triggering. I know, having been on the receiving end of hate from male internet trolls who targeted me for identifying as a feminist while doing a video about brotherly love. Within 24 hours, I received over 80 hate messages wishing harm to myself and my family, branding me as a femi-nazi. Since we are all comprised of masculine and feminine energies, investing in the scapegoating and subjugation of either gender is self-defeating. It's worth noting that the evil eye directed at men since the women's movement is a retaliation from the wounded feminine. While it's understandable the shadow feminine wields passive aggression to elevate their status as a victim, it just perpetuates a tit-for-tat cycle of war. The justification for misandry; fear of and prejudice towards the masculine, is fueled by the misconception that the white male is the uncontested victor of patriarchy. Such a judgment generates hate and stops us seeking further understanding. Whereas if we engage in further investigation, we can glean how men, including white men, have also suffered during patriarchy and release the misconception that men are to blame. The stats below support my claim. They are from Australia, a first-world country considered one of the best places in the world to live, especially if you're male. However, these figures tell another story…

- ❖ Suicide is the number one cause of death between men aged 15-45 yrs.

- ❖ In the male-dominated industry of construction, workers are 2 x more likely to suicide; 6 x more than 'on-site accidents'

- ❖ More than half of all Australian men say they can't rely on their friends for emotional support, leaving them vulnerable in a crises

- ❖ Beyond Blue, a mental health website, says men aged 30-60 lose friends

- ❖ Since 1999 more Australian soldiers have died by suicide than in war

- ❖ Suicide in men aged between 55-64 has risen to 60% in the last 10 years

Source: *Man Up* Documentary series ABC TV 2016

While these stats support my claim that white men suffer, I feel it essential to acknowledge indigenous Australians have the highest suicide rate in the world.

How Men Have Been Oppressed

Patriarchy is not simply a culture where men rule women. It is a social paradigm where the masculine traits and values are elevated, and the feminine traits and values are diminished and devalued. In such an unbalanced culture, everyone suffers...in different ways.

For women, whose feminine side is external, the oppression has been overt with a lack of external rights; such as lower pay rates and an expectation we do the lion's share of volunteer and domestic work, due to an unconscious belief women should work for free, out of the goodness of their hearts, asking nothing in return. This is not sustainable and reveals how 'the mother archetype' is projected on the collective feminine by the immature masculine (in both men and women). Women have also been denied a voice in decision-making. From the withholding of the vote, to a lack of equal representation in positions of authority. Those who do gain access to worldly power only do so if they repress their feminine traits and become masculine-dominant. Only then can they gain access to the power broker boy's club.

Whereas for men, whose feminine side is internal, the oppression has been covert. The more a man embodies feminine traits and values within a patriarchy, the more he is marginalized, discriminated against and persecuted. For example, men who were pacifists, refusing to sacrifice themselves as cannon fodder in the World Wars were bullied by men and women alike. Men who dared express their creativity were ostracized and targeted with homophobic hate crimes, regardless of their gender preference. Men who chose to serve in more feminine-dominated service professions; like social work, teaching, hospitality, nursing, disability and aged care, received low pay rates along with their female counterparts.

During patriarchy, men were only permitted to express their masculine side. This has created imbalance and dysfunction within the male psyche due to the suppression and shame surrounding feminine qualities. Wonderful qualities, such as vulnerability, compassion, sensitivity, empathy, nurturance and intuition. Qualities essential for good leadership, husbandry and fatherhood. Internally such repression manifests as self-loathing towards one's feminine side, perceiving it as unacceptable or weak. This leads to the repression of authentic feelings and emotions, except anger; the only socially acceptable emotion for men. This results in emotional dysregulation; outbursts of aggression towards themselves and others. It's this fear of being emotional that causes many men to shut down and become emotionally unavailable, to themselves and their loved ones. To sustain a state of disassociation from their innermost feelings, many men engage in compulsive distractions, such as work, sports, virtual realities, porn and substance abuse, all of which sabotage their wellbeing and relationships.

Before patriarchy young men were initiated into *the Grail* tradition, specifically to meet and integrate their feminine side. This is why women presided over *the Grail* rites. *The Grail* rites enabled a young man to mature so he didn't remain half a man, acting out in ways that would be destructive towards the feminine in himself, others and the *Earth Mother*. Without initiation into *the Grail* to truly civilize men, the ancients understood men would behave like monsters. It is fear of the monster within that undermines men's perception of themselves as acceptable and loveable. A fear that creates inner torment and sabotages intimacy.

The inner beast within the masculine psyche is portrayed in myth as the *Minotaur*, who is half-man/half-beast. Without the right support, it is understandable men struggle to integrate the primal masculine into their psyche as it is fear of their shadow self being exposed that keeps men emotionally and psychologically distant. They hide their shame in the shadows, like *The Elephant Man*, unable to truly commit and reveal the totality of their soul, keeping them from the love they crave.

Such self-sabotage stems from the belief that, at their core, they are unacceptable and unlovable. Without addressing this wound, men and masculine-dominant women compensate for their wound by trying to appear happy, confident, easy-going, strong and in control. Those whose wound is more pronounced may act out in more aggressive ways, punishing those who see their beast, to silence them with fear. Others may try to prove how much of a man they are by picking fights in a pub or choosing professions where they can assert their dominance over others, such as law enforcement and night club security.

So, What Makes a Man a King?

It's ironic that a king is a man who has integrated his feminine side, making him whole, stable and mature. A king is a man whose authority is his intuition. A man who is not yet a king psychologically and emotionally hasn't integrated the feminine half of his psyche so he tries to prove how much of a man he is by repressing his feminine side to appear more masculine, which he equates with strength. This makes him both unbalanced and unstable.

A king is a man who has found self-love, so he's not dependent on someone to affirm how loveable he is, a surrogate mother who will bolsters his self-image. A king is a man who has good self-care practices, so he doesn't need a mother-surrogate to take care of him. A king is a man who has individuated from his father and all external authority, so he knows his own mind and doesn't need external approval. A king is a man who has discovered his own gifts and talents and invests time honing and sharing them, instead of doing a job his heart isn't in.

The Grail assists men to make the transition from knight (youth) to king (adult), both emotionally and psychologically so they can enjoy interdependent unions with women, feminine-dominant men, or those who identify as non-binary or gender fluid. Without *the Grail,* immature men and masculine-dominant women swing between lover/destroyer; pursuing their love interests and then pushing them away due to the shame they feel about their emotional dependency. Without a balanced and whole sense of self, men and masculine-dominant women spiral when a relationship ends as they struggle to function without their 'other half'.

I speak more about the three levels of masculinity and femininity and how that plays out in relationships in my online program, *Conscious Relating* listed in the resources section.

Identifying the Immature Masculine

Those who have disowned the feminine within tend to go to great lengths to compensate for their fear of being seen as feminine. They do this by overtly asserting their masculine energy. This plays out in men and masculine-dominant women as displays of social posturing to assert machismo bravado, such as:

- ❖ A rigid posture with a deliberate swagger to their gait
- ❖ A refusal to dance in public, indicating a fear of letting go physically and looking like a fool by going with the flow
- ❖ Power dressing in conservative/butch clothes, wearing somber colors and dark glasses to appear unemotional and to be taken seriously in a 'man's world'
- ❖ Bulking up their appearance with gym workouts, protein powders and steroids to appear physically strong and intimidating
- ❖ Driving big vehicles to assert their dominance on the road

❖ Acquiring a large fortune and assets to wield worldly power

All of this compensatory behavior is like the defense mechanism of the puffer fish which, when scared, doubles in size to project a threatening display towards its perceived enemies. Yes, the elephant in the room is, the collective masculine is scared...of the feminine, in themselves and others. This is the root of misogyny, and until we address internalized misogyny, we won't see any decrease in misogyny directed outward as hate crimes against women and effeminate men. Address this, and it naturally follows women and feminine-dominant men will be honored as equals in all sectors of society. Healing this wound is how we create a world where the feminine traits are respected and embraced, creating a safe and balanced world for all.

Seeking the Bride Within: The Search for True Love

One of the universal occurrences the archetypal hero encounters in *The Hero's Journey* is a meeting with the

Goddess. The role of this 'special woman' is to serve as a catalyst for the hero's descent to become whole. How? First, a man or masculine-dominant woman meets a woman or feminine-dominant man who mirrors their unexpressed feminine. Naturally, they feel whole when they're with them, as if the other person completes them, so they fall in love with them.

For the sake of ease, I shall hereafter refer to the hero with male terminology and the Goddess with female terminology on the understanding both aspects exist within us all.

Due to the hero's immaturity, he loses his ideal woman; the archetypal 'Goddess' due to his underdeveloped feminine side rendering him unable meet her emotionally and psychologically. His grief takes him to the Underworld. Here the challenge for the hero is to embrace his own disowned feminine self.

This is illustrated in the myth of *Orpheus*, who journeys to the *Underworld* after he loses his Beloved, Eurydice. He is warned not to look back. If he focuses on love lost instead of self-love, he will lose his opportunity to experience true love. Similarly, in the archetypal *Hero's Journey*, the hero must seek the 'gift of the Goddess'; *the Grail* that will initiate him into kingship. The word *kingship* derives from the Sumerian culture, where kingship was identical with *kinship*, meaning 'blood relative'. This term[29] refers not just to familial kin; those who share genetic bloodlines, but to one's 'blood brothers and sisters'. Those who have also taken vows to honor the sacred blood; *the Grail.*

The archetypal Goddess is a fateful woman or feminine-dominant man who acts as an agent of the sacred feminine. Such a meeting acts as a catalyst for the hero to create the sacred marriage of opposites within. Without this fateful meeting, the hero would continue to operate out of his ego, governed by his rational mind that makes choices to ensure safety but limits growth. For example, limiting one's soul's expression by constructing a socially acceptable persona. This is done by conforming to external feedback, such as reading and responding to social cues and conditioning from one's family, community and culture.

A persona is not a solid foundation for one's personal identity, as it makes one dependent on constant positive feedback to bolster self-worth. When we operate out of a persona, we feel incomplete and inauthentic. This drives us to find someone who will love us for our true self, rather than our contrived persona. This external search is destined to fail until we take up the inner journey to find our rejected aspects and embrace them. Why? Life reflects our lessons. If we reject our inner self by refusing to go within, we attract people who also reject our true self. This is a painful process to constantly repeat.

In *the Grail* tradition, *Grail* knights would consciously undertake the *Descent of Orpheus* with a *Magdalene* as their guide. This initiation path was an equivalent to *the Descent of Ishtar*, undertaken by *Grail* maidens. *The Descent of Orpheus* introduced men to the seven masculine archetypes that govern the seven major energy centers, known as chakras. This process awakens the body's bio-electricity, known as *kundalini*, which raises one's level of consciousness. As the energy of each archetype is empowered, the meridian of energy within the corresponding energy center in the spinal cord is activated. This is why the *labyrinths* and *ziggurats* (stepped pyramids) had seven levels, one for each energy center representing each level of awareness. Completing the *Descent of Orpheus* prepared a man for his most challenging test, which he would confront during the annual rite of *The Holy Grail*.

The *Descent of Orpheus* was a process guided by a *Magdalene*; a woman who had awakened both her feminine and masculine meridians. She would assist heroes, step-by-step, to integrate their authentic masculine identity by piecing together the masculine aspects that comprised their masculine psyche. A practice illustrated by the Egyptian Goddess, *Isis* who assisted her beloved, *Osiris* to heal by assembling his severed parts.

Once heroes completed this initial descent journey of initiation they would return to meet and integrate the aspects that comprised their feminine half. In my experience it took 7 cycles assembling my feminine psyche before I was initiated into re-'membering' my masculine aspects. This process creates an integrated psyche, comprised of both feminine and masculine archetypal energies…an inner marriage.

These descent paths of *Orpheus* and *Ishtar* awaken self-love, the foundation for all healthy relationships. They support us to meet, understand and empower every aspect of ourselves and embody all of our strengths and be aware of our weaknesses. These conscious descent journeys catalyze an internal psychological shift from maiden to queen or knight to king, regardless of our chronological age.

In the ancient world, these initiation paths were the preparation for *Sacred Union*; a conscious partnership of two whole, sacred and sovereign beings. Without seeking the bride/groom within to create the inner marriage, it was understood a person remained half a man/woman which would cause them to desperately seek their 'other half' externally to feel whole. This lack of completeness creates a compulsive need for the other, which plays out as infatuation and love/sex addiction that can see crimes of passion committed if one half threatens to leave. I offer facilitation for both descent paths of initiation for men and women. Details in the resources section.

Crossing the Threshold

This chapter corresponds to the 5th stage of *The Hero's Journey*, where the hero commits wholeheartedly to their quest by stepping into the unknown. In our patriarchal culture, the only threshold crossing we acknowledge is the custom of the groom carrying the bride across the door of the honeymoon suite. Without understanding all the thresholds we encounter in life, it's inevitable men and women struggle to develop incrementally into their personal power and potential.

Since I spoke about the thresholds women traverse in the previous chapter, l will now explain the thresholds to the four chronological life stages for men. Life stages that are equivalent to the feminine life stages of maiden, mother, mage and crone.

As mentioned earlier, a woman's womb initiates her through her life stages with the onset of menstruation, pregnancy, peri-menopause and menopause. Since men aren't initiated by their bodies the way women are, the ancients understood how important it was to create equivalent initiation rites for men, on the understanding without subsequent initiations men would fail to mature and be an unconscious force for destruction, rather than creation. Today, without mentoring, support, and initiation to understand and embrace their life stages, many men live like *Peter Pan*, the boy who refused to grow up, that is until he meets his significant other, personified by Wendy, who shows him his shadow.

"Age is just a number. Maturity is a choice."

Harry Styles

Men's Initiation in to the Grail Tradition

As mentioned earlier, men were initiated into *the Grail* when they turned 21 and entered adulthood. However, this was not their first initiation. Boys were initiated into manhood by older men during their 14th year. This is half-way around their first Saturn return, Saturn being the planet that governs our chronological cycles. Hence its rings! Saturn evokes the archetypal energy of the satyr Pan, who is half man / half goat. This is why young men can incite 'panic' if their animal lust is unleashed without initiation!

The planet Saturn has a twenty-nine-year orbit, so at age 14, Saturn is opposite our natal Sun. (The position of the sun in our solar system when we were born.) Saturn is the planet of responsibility, so at age 14 when our natal degree of Saturn is opposite the planet Saturn, we rebel against parents, teachers or even the law as we feel an inner urge to individuate from authority. At this threshold, boys need to be welcomed by a circle of men who take responsibility for mentoring them through their next 7 year cycle. The sole purpose of this initial rite during puberty is to help boys individuate from their mother. If this is not done, a boy will not mature and may become a danger to his mother by behaving like a child in a man's body. He may also use and abuse women, like a child who thinks only of their own desires or he may project an unconscious expectation on to his partners to mother him.

The puberty rite for boys is not attended by women, except as part of a celebration upon their return. In a welcome to manhood initiation, boys are typically confronted with a challenge posed by the men to ensure they face their fears - usually a fear of the dark.

This is done by spending a night alone out in the wilderness. This is symbolic of their fear of the feminine principle; the wildness of nature and the unknown. This act of courage marks their childhood is over and prepares them psychologically for their next initiation, seven years later at age 21.

Fortunately, more men are now leading initiations to welcome boys into manhood which is a huge step forward in healing the endemic disempowerment handed down previously through the omission of this rite. As a parent, I have seen a marked difference in young men who have received this rite of passage. I suggest to parents considering the investment of such a ceremony to watch the comedy film, *Step Brothers* which is a painfully funny portrayal of the archetypal man-child who fails to make this inner transition.

Below are the four chronological life stages men encounter, consciously or unconsciously. The more a man understands the strengths he will gain in each life stage, the more he can embrace each one with confidence, releasing his attachment to his previous stage and identity, so he ages gracefully.

I provide more info about the equivalent life stages for women in my book, *Goddess Wisdom Made Easy* and in greater depth in my *Feminine Rites of Passage* training, both of which are listed in the resource section.

The 4 Stages of Manhood

Life Stage: Knight   Element: Fire   Age: 14-28

The first stage of manhood is the knight. This is where a man learns to balance his inner polarities of lover and warrior. From ages 14-21 in *the Grail* tradition he would train in the sacred art of war, learning to focus his energy and deflect the force of his opponent to defend and protect all that is sacred. This would be done under the tutelage of older men. He would also receive an education in how to court a woman and the sacred love arts.

At age 21, the third 7-year cycle begins shifting the focus from the solar plexus; the center of will, to the heart; the center of feeling. As mentioned earlier, this is when a young man would gain the 'key to the door'. This symbolized he had access to the mysteries and crossed the threshold into adulthood. The key being a symbol sacred to the archetypal wise woman, the gatekeeper to the mysteries.

At age 21, young men were initiated via a meeting with the Black Madonna, embodied by a *Magdalene*. This ensured they learned to respect the sacred power of the feminine and how to attune to the wisdom of their own heart. This respect would summon the courage to follow their conscience. Older men supported young men through this rite, modeling respect for the feminine and the importance of knowing one's place in the circle of life.

Without this understanding, young men today are more inclined to avoid taking responsibility for their actions and unconsciously destroy creation by dominating the feminine to prove their personal power as men. During patriarchy a youth's 21st was usually marked by getting drunk, an act of destruction. This is another inversion of a *Grail* rite. This unconscious rite of passage saw young men become unconscious through binge drinking rather than become conscious by drinking from the sacred cup of feminine wisdom.

As a *Grail* knight, a young man would learn to harness the power of the element of fire by examining his use of energy. This ensured he didn't become a risk to himself or others. During this initiation, he would commit to serve a cause, inspiring right action and honorable conduct. He would be taught to uphold the values of the sacred feminine and honor the sacred balance of life and death; light and shadow.

Participation in his first annual *Grail* rite ensured a youth acquired a greater sense of meaning and purpose, by committing to serve something greater than his personal ambitions. Ambitions that know no bounds if a man unconsciously seeks to prove his worth through personal accomplishment in an ego-driven quest for glory.

The Knight's Challenge: Facing Fear of Failure

During a youth's inaugural *Grail* initiation, he would face his fears about himself. Universal fears, such as the fear of failing should he dare strive to achieve his goals. He would also be encouraged to see and acknowledge his strengths and weaknesses in equal measure, supporting him to see himself in a balanced way, so he wouldn't act out of an unbalanced perception of either inferiority or superiority.

The Grail connected young men with the Earth to ensure they were humble. The word humble comes from the Latin, *hu*, meaning 'of the Earth'. The same root is found in the word, *humus*; decomposing matter that returns to the Earth. Someone who is humble has learned to surrender and accept their reality when life doesn't go according to plan. This enables them to cooperate with others and co-create with divine will if they've bowed their ego to a higher power. Without this internal shift, one perceives themselves as separate to the whole. This results in choices that don't consider the impact of their choices on all life forms.

Similarly, one who feels alone feels pressure to make their fortune to prove their worth and ensure security as a means of safety. This pressure can prove overwhelming and circumvent a man in the knight stage from trying something new, for fear of failure. Initiation into *the Grail* imbued young men with a 'down-to-Earth' attitude on the understanding failure is necessary for any learning process. This helped young men to be authentic, approachable and receptive; feminine qualities that attract people, increasing one's magnetism, growth, and success in all endeavors. Such an attitude comes from recognizing we all come from the Earth and return to her in the Great Wheel, so ultimately, our efforts must serve her. The dedication to commit one's soul to serve something greater removes the performance pressure of the ego. With these supports in place, young men could accelerate their growth in this phase, the Springtime of their life.

This is why the initiation to become a *Grail* knight involved youths taking vows to serve and protect the *Earth Mother* and women; considered her vessels. This call to action was not because the feminine was viewed as weak and in need of rescue. Quite the contrary, honoring the sacred feminine was seen as essential for life to prevail. Making this commitment gave young men a sacred purpose. This was the sacrament of *holy matrimony* which originally meant 'to be wedded to the Earth'. Only a youth who bowed his ego to serve in this way was considered a worthy candidate for *Sacred Union* with a woman.

Life Stage: King   Element: Earth   Age: 29-42

The entry to this threshold happens when a man experiences his Saturn return, when Saturn, the planet of cyclic wisdom, returns to the same place in the sky it was when he was born. It is then life's circumstances urge him to make a choice to commit to something for the long-term. Such as a partnership or a commitment to serve the mysteries in sacred service. This was when a man received his *stag night*. The male stag, unlike the female, sheds his antlers every year. This is why the stag is an icon for the sacred masculine. A man who embodies the sacred masculine sheds his past attachments to grow with the seasons, like *Kali*, the subterranean Goddess of time, death and rebirth.

Ever since 2012, iconography of the stag has become commonplace in pop culture, signifying a yearning for the return of the sacred *Stag King*. In the ancient world, his antlers were symbolic of a man who had awakened the *Shekinah or World Tree* within himself. As stated earlier, this is a mystical *Tree of Life* comprised of the seven activated energy centers that enabled the current of life force to flow up from the center of the Earth to activate one's consciousness. When we activate this inner tree, we can consciously traverse the three inner worlds; the Underworld, the Everyday World, and the Upper World. A man who activated his *Tree of Life* was grounded in union with the *Earth Mother*, giving him a stable foundation to foster the growth of children or creative projects. Hence the saying, 'putting down roots'.

The *Stag Night* is where our modern *Buck's Turn* or *Bachelor Party* originates from. Instead of it being a night of drunken debauchery and promiscuity where the shadow masculine sows his wild oats by attempting to do all the taboo exploration he fears he won't be able to do as a married man, this was a rite of passage where a young man was taught to embody the qualities of the sacred *Stag King*.

This activation of his power enabled him to feel confident to commit to the path of *Sacred Union*, should he choose a mate, without fearing a loss of personal power. Without a rite of passage to consciously cross this threshold, it's understandable many men avoid committing to a path of shared intimacy. However, if a man's potential has been nurtured in the Springtime of his life, it will bear fruit in this, his Summertime. This life phase is when a man expands his sphere of influence by having children or building his vision for a better world. He can only do that if he's learned to temper his ego in his previous life stage.

The King's Challenge: Facing Fear of Commitment

During a man's rite of passage into kingship, he would be called to confront his fear of commitment directly. Transcending this fear enabled him to progress to the next stage of his life, such as proposing to his Beloved or accepting the transition into fatherhood wholeheartedly. Below are some of the lesser fears that underpin a fear of commitment.

❖ **Fear of Making the Wrong Choice**. Someone who hasn't journeyed inwardly to face and integrate their disowned aspects won't trust themselves to make choices. In our youth, we like to explore our potential by keeping our options open, but as we mature, we need to commit to one course of action at a time, accepting that will mean letting go of other possibilities. If we don't know our true self, we fear making the wrong choice and limiting our potential.

❖ **Fear of Losing One's Identity.** If one doesn't truly know all aspects of themselves, they fear losing their identity due to their tendency to please others. Such behavior indicates their personal identity isn't fully formed and integrated.

❖ **Fear of Rejection.** A man who's operating from his constructed persona, rather than his authentic feelings, fears not 'being enough' to meet with approval or make someone happy. This is due to the distorted belief their true self is not acceptable or loveable.

❖ **Fear of Losing One's Personal Power.** A man who is basing his self-worth on what he does, rather than who he is, will feel disempowered. The more empowered his partner is, the more this fear will be evoked.

Women who sense their intelligence, talent and

ambitions trigger insecurity in their partners may subsequently 'play small' by downplaying their intellect, humor, talents and largess in order to gain acceptance, until their compromise becomes intolerable.

The more men confront these fears in this life stage, the more gracefully they will navigate the Pluto square natal Pluto transit that occurs between the ages 36-39. If they don't willingly confront these fears, Pluto, the ruler of the Underworld, will confront them with their unacknowledged shadow behavior in possibly brutal ways, as a wake-up call to change.

Life Stage: Magi   Element: Water.   Age: 42-60

At age 42, a man enters mid-life. During this phase, he experiences significant astrological transits that confront him with his deepest vulnerabilities. These include:

❖ Age 42-44, Neptune, the planet of watery depths, evokes a search for spiritual meaning to make sense of the deep feelings evoked by Neptune squaring one's natal Neptune.

❖ Age 44-45 Saturn opposite one's natal Sun evokes a complete restructuring of life, and for many, individuation from the system if they have awakened their intuition as their inner authority.

❖ Age 49-51 Chiron returning to its natal position evokes the biggest wound we've incarnated to heal. This drops us in our vulnerability so we can feel and heal old wounds.

❖ Age 40-42 Uranus, the planet of sudden realization and change opposes one's natal Sun. This evokes a sudden urge to break free from everything that inhibits the free expression of the soul.

These transits affect both men and women and often result in mid-life crises. In men, these midlife transits evoke the life stage of the magi. This is the term for a sacred magician - not to be confused with an illusionist who pulls rabbits out of hats! A magi focuses on inner alchemy, transmuting their shadow (ignorance) into light (awareness). This work of inner transformation is done through feeling the intensity of one's unresolved experiences, like a sword forged in a crucible of heat. Through this process, new insights are gleaned, by understanding how every experience has served their growth. This enables one to make peace with *Great Mystery* and experience grace through gratitude. As it is through acknowledging pain we develop compassion for ourselves and others.

If a man doesn't reflect on all he's journeyed and learned, applying his insights to heal himself during this life phase, he will become embittered and isolate himself. This is due to a fear of enduring further hurt and betrayal. This phase is when a man truly becomes responsible for his karma; that which he creates through his thoughts, words and deeds. This is done through observing one's harvest; what we've manifested in our external world. Since our waking world reflects our subconscious beliefs, the state of our reality flags the beliefs we need to transform. Taking responsibility for what we create empowers us to transcend the notion that we are a victim of circumstance, a perspective that creates dis-ease and a state of separation.

The Magi's Challenge: Fear of Change

Often it is at the commencement of this phase one where one's life is thrown into chaos. This may come through an unexpected life event such as divorce, job loss or illness. The ultimate challenge is to surrender and notice both synchronistic signs and blessings to strengthen trust in the benevolent Universe.

This phase corresponds to the season of Autumn/Fall when deciduous trees lose their leaves. This signifies the need to release what no longer offers growth and accept what is beyond one's control. In *the Grail* tradition men are encouraged to identify the lesson in their most painful losses in love and acknowledge their waning physical strength and virility. This is so they can experience the gifts that come through the release of attachments. In this phase, a man must become like the element of water; he must go with the flow, release the old, feel deeply and reflect on his choices. This is when a man must acknowledge his fear of experiencing his human frailty and being seen in his vulnerability. This is when his identity is tested beyond the roles that previously defined him and he must develop greater self-care to heal.

Life Stage: Sage   Element: Air   Age: 60+

This is when a man becomes an elder if he has done the preparatory work in his previous life stages by embracing the lessons of his transits. For a true elder is a man who has consciously journeyed the cycles and embodied the lessons learned so he can mentor others through their trials.

Such a man holds great power within himself. He commands respect, without demanding it. Without *the Grail* helping men navigate these transits, instead of true elders we see many frail old men who are cynical and disempowered. Fortunately, there are many younger men now seeking personal growth to change this trajectory.

The sage phase is when a man develops higher thought; known as feminine intuition. Having integrated his opposite within, he embodies positive feminine traits, like patience and wisdom. This is done through distilling past experiences into insight. Through understanding, he can return to a state of trust in the Divine plan and feel like he did as an innocent young child. In this phase, he comes home to his true nature; one who is awed and humbled by the magnificence of the benevolent Universe, like the archetypal magical child. If a man doesn't come full circle in his life, his inner child/teenager remains wounded and dominant. When a man champions the return of his magical inner child, he risks looking like a fool, making him truly available to love and the magic of life.

The Sage's Challenge: Fear of Death

This is the fourth rite of passage when a man must learn how to completely surrender to the power of the Cosmic feminine, the infinite void of *Great Mystery*; the void. This prepares him for his elder years which requires the greatest humbling of his ego. This is when a man is challenged to just 'be', embracing stillness like the season of Winter instead of compulsively doing. This is a challenge for the masculine polarity that derives empowerment through taking action.

During the shift into the sage stage, a man must confront his fear of not being externally validated. This can evoke his deepest insecurities upon retirement from a career that provided both identity and self-worth. This is when a man must develop the feminine qualities of receptivity, trust and surrender. It is a time to acknowledge what he's learned and how he can serve future generations with his experiential wisdom.

Sound Familiar?

Some of you may recognize some of these aspects from the book, *King, Warrior, Magician, Lover* by Robert Moore and Douglas Gillette inspired by the work of Carl Jung…especially if you've attended men's circles with *The Mankind Project*. I hope the contribution of the sacred feminine perspective, connecting these aspects to the cycles that men traverse, will make their relevance clearer. Cyclic wisdom helps us make sense of our time here on Earth. This is why the Hindu Dark Goddess, *Kali Ma*, was considered 'The Goddess of Time, Seasons, Periods and Cycles'. Her name is the root for the word, *calendar* (Kalindar).

I would like to make it clear that men are not limited to expressing these corresponding aspects in each of these specific life phases. Like the feminine life stages of maiden, mother, mage and crone, the cycles of time evoke these four aspects, not just chronologically, but during the seasons. Men in *the Grail* tradition were taught to honor and embody these four aspects as they journeyed the seasonal wheel to help them cope with change. This helped them to mature into well-rounded individuals...men for all seasons. It is important to illustrate how these aspects serve as a map for navigating men's life stages rather than as the archetypes that comprise a man's psyche, as this perspective limits men from the full spectrum of their soul's expression which is found through embodying the 7 masculine archetypes that govern the seven energy centers.

For an overview of the seven masculine archetypes, check out my book, *Creating Sacred Union Within* or my *Rainbow Warrior* course listed in the resources section.

CHAPTER 6

Tests, Allies, and Enemies:
The Round Table

T he *Grail* tradition taught success was not the attainment of a single goal by a solo man. Success was measured by one's perseverance and commitment to serve an ideal and was achieved through collaboration. Like the credo, 'All for one and one for all!' made famous by the story of *The Three Musketeers. The Grail* tradition taught that a man was only as strong as his inner circle and that good leadership was always dependent on the support of true fellowship. Without this, a man was not held accountable for his actions. This is why legendary *Grail* kings, *Arthur* and *Yeshua,* had the support of an inner circle of brothers. So too, in this chapter we'll discover the benefits the hero receives when he meets a band of brothers who form a 'ring of fellowship' to assist him in his quest.

The practice of gathering in a sacred circle of brotherhood was a key element of *the Grail* as within the construct of a circle, every man is considered equal, as all present are equally seen and heard. This is why indigenous cultures gathered in circle for tribal council. (Which is nothing like the distorted portrayal seen in the reality show, *Survivor*). In the sacred practice of sitting in circle, every man earns both self-respect and respect from his peers by publicly questioning himself and acknowledging the effects of his choices and actions. This is what is needed for authentic and ethical leadership in men and women, and why corruption and abuses of power have been rampant without this ancient practice that promotes ethical behavior. *The Grail* also taught chivalry, not just towards women but also men as an embodiment of brotherly love.

"We must live together as brothers or perish together as fools."

Martin Luther King Jr

It's significant the origins of the wounds of *The Fisher King* are due to his inability to comprehend the concept of brotherhood. The story goes, one day, in his youth, *The Fisher King*, dressed in armor, encountered a foreign knight coming towards him on the path. He responded to this sight by lowering his visor and attacking the other knight, killing him without enquiring as to his intentions. The other knight retaliated in self-defense, slashing *The Fisher King* in the groin as he fell to his death. Later *The Fisher King* discovered the other knight, a Muslim, was also seeking *the Grail* and his quest had been inspired by a vision of the cross*; a symbol of *the Grail*.

It's worth noting, this was not the patriarchal cross symbolizing crucifixion, but the earlier 'even cross' which features in all indigenous traditions, representing the equal, balanced union of Earth Mother and Sky Father that creates 'Heaven on Earth'. The vertical line represents the path of Spirit and the horizontal line represents the diameter of the Earth. The word diameter originates from Demeter, the Greek name for the Earth Mother. The original cross, also known as Wotan's Cross to the Norse was replaced by the patriarchs with the uneven cross, which tilted the emphasis up towards the Sky Father, giving him greater dominion over the Earth.

Had *The Fisher King* paused to consider the possibility that the other man could be an ally, rather than an enemy, he would have saved himself an injury and gained a brother to share his adventure. It is also significant that, despite the other man's apparent differences, they were seeking the same thing. Hence the saying, 'You can't judge a book by its cover'.

To feel uplifted and inspired by true stories of brotherly love where men learn to 'love thy enemy', I recommend watching the films, *The Railway Man* and *The Water Diviner*. Likewise, to watch a moving true story of brotherly/sisterly love I highly recommend watching the film, *Best of Enemies*. These films are deeply moving as it's rare for us to witness portrayals of brotherly love. Why? Men have been conditioned to view other men, especially foreigners, as potential threats. This anchors a fear-based mindset where one anticipates competition rather than perceiving possible opportunities for collaboration. Such a mindset promotes scarcity consciousness, the belief one must fight to meet their needs on the basis there's not enough to go around. This engenders division amongst men and leaves them isolated, lacking real support.

In a patriarchal culture men fear homophobic abuse if they openly show affection for another man. This is more pronounced in Western cultures. The message men receive is they can only display physical and verbal affection for one another after they've first engaged in shared acts of violence. This is why the crowd roars in our modern gladiatorial arenas - sports stadiums, when teammates embrace at the end of their ritualistic battle. No wonder many men hunger for the touch of other men and indulge in anonymous sex in parks, toilet blocks and bath houses. Why? Brotherly love is taboo, and yet brotherly love is a key ingredient to healing the wounded masculine.

Women have also been conditioned to view each other as potential threats. This distrust is mostly directed at single women, on the assumption they can't be trusted around partnered men. Fortunately, thanks to the fast-growing number of women's circles, this attitude is changing. Today, if you search the term, *sisterhood* you see images of sisterly love amongst women who are not sisters by birth. These are often women who have experienced sisterhood in sacred women's practices. Meanwhile, many uninitiated women continue to behave like 'mean girls', regardless of their age. This is usually passive-aggressive behavior, such as gossiping and social exclusion.

The Lost Boys

In Australia, the colloquial term we have for brotherhood is *mateship*. My observation is that this is very different to brotherhood, as mates usually keep conversation to a surface level, so as not to make the vibe awkward. This means there are many topics considered taboo and avoided. Typically mates share activities and discuss external events like politics and sports, but not their innermost thoughts and feelings. In these friendships, men may feel social pressure to maintain a certain level of bravado to offset underlying homophobia. This breeds unconscious power dynamics where the alpha male of the group dominates, often using humor to ridicule and lower the status of his male counterparts. To avoid being at the bottom of the pecking order, everyone present may engage in similar behavior. This does not create a safe space to share one's inner landscape, let alone admit to feelings of vulnerability. The culture of *mateship* often centers around alcohol as a lubricant to alleviate social anxiety.[30] While alcohol initially raises serotonin levels, resulting in relaxation and good vibes, the more we imbibe, the more dysregulated our emotions become, which can result in volatile behavior.

This type of relating is reminiscent of *The Lost Boys* in the story of *Peter Pan*. Men who behave like boys, and like Peter, are rebelling against life and the dark father, characterized by Captain Hook. They do this by refusing to grow up. Rather than confront their issues directly, they engage in escapist and often destructive behavior, illustrated in the film, *Jackass*. Without initiation into manhood and ongoing support to face themselves honestly in a spirit of brotherhood, we see men of all ages act out as the 'angry young man' or 'rebel without a cause'. This is because young men who aren't initiated into the cycles of life and death inevitably become a force for destruction. Today we see young men seeking out initiation in unconscious ways. Such as passing a marijuana bong around a lounge room, instead of a talking stick...or daring friends to steal something to prove their courage as a sign of their manhood to gain acceptance from peers. Instead of shrugging it off with an apathetic 'boys will be boys' attitude, we need to implement social structures to change this picture.

"We initiate the boys so they don't burn down the village."

African proverb

The Power of Circle

Gathering in social space is very different to gathering in an intentional sacred space. Why? When we gather in a circle with a clear intention, we create a positive vortex, a current that generates energy as a force for transformation. This is because a circle has no beginning and no end, so within that configuration, energy spirals and generates intensity. Since the energy is focused on whomever is speaking, this directs intensity evoking that which is unresolved and seeks resolution and integration through acknowledgement. Whereas in social settings, one has to compete to be heard and the energy scatters and dissipates.

The circle is an ancient and universal symbol for unity and wholeness, so it stands to reason that when we abandon the practice of sitting in circle, we become disconnected and experience a sense of separation. After all, when we unplug from the bright lights and distractions of urban life and 'go bush', it's what we naturally do, build a fire and sit around it - in a circle. People have sat around fires for millennia to tell stories, sing songs, offer prayers and listen to each other speak, all of which provides connection and support. In traditional cultures, circles were also used as a construct to resolve conflicts and make decisions for the common good.

That is, before the advent of TV. When tell-a-vision was introduced, we were programmed with corporate propaganda. Within a generation, many stopped sitting around a dinner table to share their day. The introduction of TV into most homes contributed significantly to the huge rise in divorce, family breakdown and obesity. Why? Television places viewers in a passive mode of behavior, unlike circle, which encourages the equal active participation of everyone.

When we sit in a circle we can't avoid connecting. As we face each other, we face ourselves, because as each person speaks they reflect aspects of our common experience which heals through providing validation.

Healing Through Brotherly Love

The idea of sitting in a circle and speaking about one's feelings sounds about as enticing as a root canal for most men. This is because the experience is foreign, and the ego tends to fear, devalue and dismiss what it has no point of reference for. To be honest, men's circles aren't suited to every man. Those whose psyches are fractured from trauma and have not yet begun their journey of personal growth and healing usually need to start with one-on-one therapy sessions to build trust and safety before attending a circle. Why? Exposing wounds that have never been faced with a group of strangers is initially too overwhelming. However, as we progress and become more comfortable with the process of exploring our wounds, with a trusted therapist, healer, or guide, we benefit from the support of authentic, ongoing connections with others who are navigating similar challenges. This reduces any sense of stigma and feelings of isolation.

Circles create a safe container for sharing the lived experiences of the human shadow, our dark side. Known as 'shadow work', this involves acknowledging the parts of ourselves we fear are unacceptable and unlovable. This is simple, but profoundly powerful, both for the individual and the group. As each person shares their innermost truth, they validate the unspoken thoughts and feelings of others, reflecting the universality of our human wounds. This is how we heal shame, the most toxic emotional state that undermines our wellbeing on all levels.

Sharing our most closely guarded secrets also creates trust and deep bonds of brotherhood amongst men and sisterhood amongst women. The Catholic Church, the religion created by the Roman Empire, replaced this tradition with the confessional, a private booth where in exchange for confessing your sins, you were assigned penance, usually in isolation to beg for forgiveness from a higher power. Trying to achieve purity to gain acceptance anchors shame, fear, and rejection of one's shadow rather than integration. This exacerbates a split in the psyche, so the disowned aspects act out in inappropriate and unhealthy ways.

Today many mental health and rehabilitation programs include sharing circles on the understanding that connection is the most effective cure for addiction[31] with scientifically proven benefits.[32] What's missing is the awareness of how the natural cycles influence our thoughts and feelings. Such awareness would result in support circles scheduled at specific times when people are most at risk of self-harm and destructive behaviors, such as just before the new moon and over the month of Winter Solstice.

Another reason men may resist the idea of attending a men's circle is because a circle is a feminine construct. Watch little girls at recess, and they sit in a circle to eat their lunch and share their experiences. Watch young boys, and they'll use their free time to play a game to pit their wits or strengths against one another. It's for this reason I've found the dynamic of a female facilitator can dissolve the unspoken pressure of competition amongst men in circle. While I used to dissuade women from facilitating men's circles on the basis it would be emasculating for men, I now facilitate circles for men and have found this dynamic helps men to feel safe enough to share their psycho-emotional experiences, their feminine side, as it removes the pressure to appear masculine.

It is my understanding that it was the more experienced *Magdalenes* who facilitated men's circles to prepare men for their annual *Grail* rite. These were women who had personally journeyed many cycles and initiated many women through their cycles. I base this on my experience. My work initiating men began 25 years after I first initiated women, at age 50, the age a woman was said to 'attain her power' in the native American tradition. The circles I facilitate for men are to support men through *the Grail* practices; *The Descent of Orpheus* and *The Hero's Journey*. The latter I refer to as the *12 Suns* as it aligns with the solar wheel, the equivalent initiation path of the *13 Moons* for women.

I have found journeying with men around the solar wheel and women around the lunar wheel that this enables them to see the strengths and weaknesses of each zodiac sign within themselves. For men, aligning with the sun empowers their masculine essence and identity. For women, aligning with the moon empowers their feminine essence and identity. The discrepancy in the number of cycles is because there are 12 solar months and 13 lunar months in a calendar year.

I believe this is why the famous 13th seat at *Arthur's* round table was reserved for one who was said to be pure of heart. This was the seat reserved for the one who offered mystic insight to assist the men with their trials around the 12 signs of the zodiac. The 13th seat was not to represent Judas Iscariot as patriarchal writers suggest. 13 is the number that has always been associated with the sacred feminine because of the 13 lunar cycles in a year.

The Labors of Hercules

The word, *labor* is synonymous with birth…doing the work to create. *The Grail* practice of the *12 Suns* supports men step-by-step in a spirit of brotherhood to birth the inner hero who lays dormant within by journeying the solar wheel together. This is a practice I was intuitively guided to create by combining the cyclic journey of the 12 *Labors of Hercules* with the 12 stages of *The Hero's Journey*. As stated earlier, when we combine myth and astrology, magic happens!

This process of remembering began, unbeknownst to me at the time, in my early twenties when I saw a copy of the book, *The Labors of Hercules* by Alice Bailey on the bookshelf at my accountant's office and I felt compelled to buy a copy. A theosophical author and mystic, Bailey was the first to connect the 12 labors of Hercules with the sun's transit around the zodiac. Decades later, in 2013 I was guided to turn this into a circle practice for men.

The initiation path of the *12 Suns* awakens the solar hero, the holy son (Sun), as the archetypal World Savior. The idea that only one man, such as *Yeshua*, fulfills this role for all men, leaves the collective masculine passive and waiting for a savior to rescue them. This diminishes the latent potential of the true Christos, the crystalline man in all men.

Yeshua is but one example of a man who awakened the solar logos; the sacred masculine essence, as did King *Arthur*. They serve as inspiration to show it can be done with the right support. That being the support of a circle of brothers and a *Magdalene* to guide them through their 12 labors. It is by no mistake *King Arthur* had 12 knights seated at the round table, and Jesus had 12 disciples. This is also why court juries once consisted of 12 men. In fact, *King Arthur* appears for the first time in the writings of a Welsh historian named *Nennius,* who cited a list of his 12 battles. The round table was not just a round piece of furniture but a euphemism for the wheel of 12 zodiac signs that men once journeyed in circle. A sacred practice that afforded mutual support to fulfill their potential as heroes; sacred warriors. For without both a mentor and brotherly support, they would surely fail.

The Dark Brotherhoods

The sacred practice of gathering in circle and taking turns to speak teaches us how to share power, as each person is afforded equal right to speak and be heard. Without these sacred practices, dark fraternities have filled the void. Secret brotherhoods whose ceremonies inverted *the Grail* rites, using them as a means to seek power, instead of love. These dark brotherhoods welcomed young men from dynastic bloodlines, those they viewed as having the potential to generate wealth and wield power and influence. Meeting in frat houses in Ivy League colleges, these elite boy's clubs require members to demonstrate their allegiance through taking part in depraved acts that can then be used as blackmail. Compliance is rewarded with the bestowing of greater power and influence in the world.

In these social circles, young men have their spirit broken through extreme abuse when they come of age to ensure compliance when they're invited into the circle of trust in the dark brotherhoods. Often the father is complicit or the main perpetrator, the opposite of a positive role model. This is the extreme betrayal of a child by an ego-driven father who accepts the Devil's bargain, to fulfill their own ambitions. In lower socio-economic classes, the child's sacrifice by the father may play out in varying ways, such as a father imposing his ambitions on his children. This was portrayed powerfully in the film, *Dead Poets Society*.

We have been told it is human behavior that when a boy comes of age, tensions will inevitably rise between a father and his son for supremacy until there is a showdown. This is simply the dynamic that has been anchored within the group mind with teaching parables like that of the biblical *Abraham*, who God called upon to kill his son to prove his loyalty. This is a very dangerous message as it justifies such an atrocity as the will of God, implying it is not just acceptable, but noble! As a result, parents have been compliant in sacrificing their sons to war. Wars they believed were noble causes to uphold an ideal or serve God. In actuality, they were the exact opposite; orchestrated blood sacrifices by the ruling elite whose demonic allegiance was fed by the horrors of war as it elicits the lowest expression of human nature. This may be shocking to consider, but we will not have peace on Earth simply by writing it in *Christmas* cards! It is only by acknowledging this shadow truth that we can bring such distortions into the light of day to heal them. I am passionate about reinstating *the Grail* as I know it has the power to diminish this covert culture by anchoring an honor code amongst men that insures against abuses of power.

Chivalry is Not Dead

Below are the 12 tenets of the honor code agreed to by those who were knighted in *the Grail* tradition.

The 12 Rules of the Knights of the 4 Table.[33]

- ❖ To not lay down arms
- ❖ To seek wonders
- ❖ To defend the defenseless
- ❖ To not hurt anyone
- ❖ To refrain from attacking each other
- ❖ To fight for the country's safety
- ❖ To give one's life for the country
- ❖ To only seek honor

- ❖ To not break faith
- ❖ To practice religion with great effort
- ❖ To be hospitable to everyone according to ability
- ❖ To be honest about their experiences, whether honorable or disgraceful

Without an honor code providing clear guidelines for acceptable behavior given to young men, it's become culturally acceptable for young men to behave badly, especially towards women. This is evident in the number of court rulings that excuse young men charged with sexual assault based on promising sports careers. This is exacerbated by the recurring incidents of sexual assault towards young women perpetrated by male athletes, politicians and celebrities whose status and wealth results in an assumption they're 'above the law'. Unfortunately, this is all too often proven right, indicating the societal bias. While we need to ensure consequences fit the crime, we need to prevent such grievances by re-introducing the tradition of chivalry towards the feminine.

Allies and Enemies

The Grail instructed young men and women to cultivate brotherly/sisterly love, rather than simply viewing their own gender as potential competitors and the opposite gender as potential conquests. This is why people hunt for a lover on dating apps and lack the skills needed to form healthy relationships. In our dualistic; love/hate approach people swing between idealizing their latest love interest to fighting 'till death do them part' in the divorce courts.

Without compassion and mutual respect between the sexes, we have no solid foundation for healthy communities, families or partnerships. By establishing friendships that are psychologically and emotionally intimate, we can better understand the opposite gender. Rather than project onto our opposite our deepest fears and desires and scapegoat them with our unresolved wounds.

CHAPTER 7

Approach to the Inmost Cave:
Meeting with the Goddess

At the seventh stage of *the Grail* quest the hero prepares for the daunting task of meeting their match. In our war-based culture, Hollywood portrays this as a showdown between the hero and an arch-villain or nemesis. Meanwhile in reality, this is more likely to manifest as a potential new partner, rather than *Dr Evil*.

The more we've explored, developed and integrated the opposite polarity within our psyche, the easier our mating dance will progress. Whereas, if we have not developed the opposite gender polarity within, we will most likely struggle to make the approach. This results in suffering the slings and arrows of unrequited love from afar. To prevent such a tragedy, in this chapter we'll explore the tests encountered in romantic/courtly love. Including how to identify and master those lessons to win the heart of one who is true.

The chance meeting with a love interest usually appears after one has passed an initiation of self-love, as this is what increases our wattage and attracts love. In *the Grail* tradition, self-love was developed for men, through *The Descent of Orpheus* and the ongoing practice of the *12 Suns*, supported by brotherly love. This equipped the hero for success in romantic love. Without initiation to master these preparatory lessons, it's little wonder we have a culture where many feel demoralized by the dating scene and jaded about relationships.

> *"Those marriages generally abound most with love and constancy that are preceded by a long courtship."*
>
> **Joseph Addison**

Courtly Love: A Lost Tradition

The Grail resurfaced during courtly love in Europe, which was then adopted by the noble class in Britain, Ireland, Wales and Scotland. Courtly love, like *the Grail*, honored the feminine as a vessel for the divine. During this time, the legendary *King Arthur* inspired men to be chivalrous toward the feminine, indicating he was a man who had learned to revere the sacred feminine. In our modern culture chivalry may not be dead, but it's certainly not thriving. That's understandable without initiation into the love arts and instruction on courtly love as a precursor to consummation.

Courtly love is most often associated with the Arthurian legend of England. However, it originated in the south of France in the 11th century with troubadours and poets who were inspired by the mystical love poetry of Persia that they'd encountered during the crusades.[34] The romanticism of this time offered welcome relief from the austere works of the puritanical Middle Ages.

Honoring the feminine as a muse for sacred love inspired reverence for women after hundreds of years of persecution, led by the Roman Catholic church. Romantic balladeers and bards celebrated the noble qualities of women as the spark that ignites a courtly lover's passion. This ushered in a new era of poetry, song and storytelling that portrayed love as the force that endures despite seemingly insurmountable obstacles and opposition.

As stated earlier it was due to the oppressive tradition of patriarchal marriage that served as a social structure to form alliances to seal acquisitions of wealth, title and property, that this new arts movement was enthusiastically embraced. As it gave a voice for the romantic of young nobles who felt trapped by their familial duties and societal expectations. Like the reality shows of the day, the courts embraced the romantic literature that reflected the personal intrigues occupying their conversations. Most centered around tales of unrequited love, a trend that continues today with songs on commercial radio parading yearning and loss as true love. It is my understanding that Arthurian romances such as

Tristan and Yseult once served as teaching parables before being reinterpreted through the lens of patriarchy. For folktales and fairytales were traditionally used to illustrate the fate of our soul choices. They were passed down via the oral tradition to ensure the meaning was correctly conveyed. When *the Grail* parables were published and preserved as works of early literature in the 12th century, their meaning was misinterpreted and their distortion widely disseminated.

Archetypal Lessons in Love

If we view tales of courtly love as symbolic parables, instead of literal events, we gain a deeper understanding of our lessons in love. This was how they were intended to be utilized, rather than serve as mere entertainment. The tales of love popularized during the Arthurian period emerged from the mystic tradition of the Middle East where the sacred feminine was once exalted and direct union with the divine sought through sacred practices. This is why the love poetry of Persia spoke of union with the divine, rather than profane love. This meaning was lost in translation to many in the West as the church taught union with the divine was earned through punishment and blind obedience. In addition to persecuting those who spoke of self-realization, as heretics, the doctrines introduced by the Roman Empire taught their subjects to abstain from any expression of Earthly love, seeing it as 'giving in' to the temptation of evil. Through the eyes of the church, only a sexually chaste woman could be viewed as a vessel of the Divine, hence the Christian concept of the Virgin Mother. This ideology promoted the ideal of celibacy, even in marriage on the basis that the ideal love object was unattainable. This created an obsession with a fantasy rather than love as an embodied reality. The more one experienced feelings of forbidden desire, the more guilty they felt and the more forgiveness was sought in a codependent cycle of psycho-emotional abuse with the cult of Rome. This left parishioners immature and disempowered.

If we stay stuck in the mindset of youth, we never mature beyond the emotional drama of young lovers. Instead, we persist with a narcissistic urge to attract others to validate how beautiful and loveable we are. This is what drives us to unconsciously use looks or charm to enchant others with our projected persona. At this level of psycho-emotional maturity, we fixate on securing a love interest's attention, affection and approval, while neglecting our own needs.

The Grail provided a template to escape this destructive pattern; we know it today as the *Tarot*. The Tarot, is an oracle that encoded *Grail* teachings to ensure they weren't lost to future generations. The Tarot first appeared in the West in the 1200s and was introduced by the *Templars*, the *Saracens*, and the gypsies who came from the East.[35] It then quickly spread throughout the royal courts of Europe. I suspect the Tarot was introduced as a means to assist people to transcend their self-negating behavior and seek a higher expression of love. When we consider the popularity of the Tarot during this time amongst the aristocrats we can appreciate that the term, *courtly love* referred, not simply to the romantic affairs of the social set of the royal court, but to the lessons portrayed in the court cards of the Tarot. While the Tarot has recently experienced a resurgence in

Sir Galahad Passes by the Land
by Edwin Austin Abbey

KNIGHT of CUPS.

popularity, the majority of people are more familiar with its derivative, the common card deck used for competition, gambling and casting illusion. However, the playing deck still retains the numerical symbolism of the natural cycles that *the Grail* teaches. There are 4 suits and 4 seasons. There are 12 court cards and 12 solar cycles in a year and there are 13 cards in every suit and 13 lunar cycles in a year.[103]

The court cards in each suit of the Tarot serve as archetypes that detail the maturity that develops as we master the material, mental, emotional and energetic realms. It is the *Suit of Cups* (*the Grail*) that teaches us how to master our emotional lessons so we have the capacity to equally give and receive love. This is why *the Knight of Cups* shows an image of a *Grail* knight - a young man on a white steed representing purity of intent. *Sir Galahad*, the knight of the round table who was said to be successful in attaining *the Grail*, was also portrayed on a white horse, wearing the robes of the *Red Knight*, symbolizing the sacred blood of the feminine and the red path of sacred feminine wisdom.

The Seat Perilous by Edwin Austin Abbey

Sir Galahad was said to be so pure of heart he could occupy the 13th, 'empty chair' known as the *Seat Perilous* at *Arthur's* round table, reserved for one who was considered so pure of heart, they would suffer the pain of death should they be proven false.

The Knight of Cups is the embodiment of an earnest youth who seeks to understand the true meaning of love. As such, he is willing to invest the time to seek *the Grail*, the feminine wisdom needed to mature psychologically and emotionally. It is through initiation into the mysteries of the sacred feminine he learns to fill his own cup to eventually become the *King of Cups*, a man who is whole, having integrated his feminine side. This ensures he's emotionally mature enough to offer love instead of just seeking to fill his cup, like a child.

Like many uninitiated men, the knight extends a goblet, assuming he has a gift of love to give because of his sincere intent. But if he has not done the inner work; that being the descent within to find his true self, his offer of love will be empty, like his cup, so he'll drain partners with his need for validation, unable to offer them true emotional support. Such a man may put his love interest on a pedestal and worship them, often from afar, where he feels safe, like Lancelot, who held a torch for *Lady Guinevere*.

In today's world, that may be enacted via a virtual romance, long-distance relationship or an unspoken infatuation. These scenarios are often an unconscious way of avoiding intimacy, to avoid the fear of rejection. Such is the torment of one who has not been initiated into *the Grail* so let's identify the 4 court cards that illustrate how equipped we are to meet our Beloved and take the journey of true love.

Stage One: The Page of Cups

The first figure we embody is the page, who is as emotionally mature as a child. The myth of *Narcissus* describes the *Page of Cups*. Someone who is so focused on meeting their own emotional needs, like a child, they are oblivious to the needs of others. Those operating at this level of psycho-emotional maturity unconsciously seek out partners who will

prioritize their needs, like a surrogate parent. Should their partner focus on their needs, they will escalate their needs by creating drama to demand their significant other's undivided attention.

When their partner expresses dissatisfaction with their behavior, they will explode with anger or implode with passive aggression, to punish them rather than examine their own behavior. Lacking the capacity to process their own emotions, they may use substances to self-soothe, like a baby with a bottle, rather than take responsibility for healing their wounds. Essentially someone operating at this level is 'all take and no give' but oblivious to their own destructive patterns of behavior. In the mating dance, they may seek to bond by sharing their painful childhood experiences to gain sympathy.

We master this stage when we realize that other's needs are just as important as our own and we assume self-responsibility by taking steps to directly meet our needs, instead of unconsciously expecting others to. This often coincides with us beginning the work of personal growth and healing; looking at our emotional wounds, instead of blaming our parents and seeing ourselves as a victim.

The card, the *Page of Cups* features a young child holding a goblet, symbolizing *the Grail*. There are turbulent waters behind him. This indicates we must take responsibility for healing our childhood wounds, if we are to find emotional calm as a precursor to finding true love. This means finding soul-centered mentors, therapists or healers who we feel safe enough to expose our wound to, so we can gently begin the work of psycho-emotional healing.

Stage Two: The Knight of Cups

The second figure we encounter and embody is *the Knight of Cups*, who is emotionally as mature as a youth. This card depicts someone who seeks attention to prove how loveable they are. They may spend a lot of time preening to make themselves appear more attractive, as they base their lovability on their appearance. This approach attracts superficial encounters. Why? Just like a teenager, they're so busy constructing an impressive persona to enchant their desired love interest they withhold their innermost thoughts and feelings. This leads to feeling unseen and unloved for who they are inside.

At this level of emotional awareness, one thinks happiness depends on finding the one true love so they compulsively hunt their prey in bars, clubs, on dating apps or singles events. Often relationships don't make it past the honeymoon stage when it becomes apparent their love interest isn't their perfect ideal...or their own wounds inevitably surface undermining the perfect persona they've worked hard to project. If one stays stuck in this phase, they can end up feeling jaded and bitter about love.

Driven by a lack of self-love, they crave loving validation. This is what underpins love-addiction; seeking a regular fix of attention and affection to boost their poor self-image. This makes commitment to one person a challenge as they constantly seek attention, flirting with others who have the same need for validation or they may avoid commitment altogether, so they're free to enjoy the thrill of the chase.

When we're as immature emotionally as a youth, we confuse love with desire, thinking we love those we feel attracted to. This is not a feeling of love from the heart. This is a lower desire based on emotional need and physical attraction. At this stage of awareness, we may see ourselves as 'a lover, not a fighter' but fail to see the emotional trauma we cause ourselves and others. In the mating dance, we may parade our perceived assets or share our achievements to impress others, fearing we are not enough, just as we are.

We master this stage when we seek *the Grail*, as this helps us identify our shadow behavior so we can mature and stop sabotaging our efforts to find love. I'm referring specifically to *the Grail* initiations; *The Descent of Ishtar* and *The Descent of Orpheus* that help us accept and appreciate all the facets of our womanhood/manhood, in both their light and shadow aspects. Only when we've learned to accept and love ourselves, warts and all, do we stop trying to project an image of perfection which is both unattainable and deceptive.

The Tarot card, *the Knight of Cups* shows a knight holding a goblet, symbolizing *the Grail*. The knight is on land signaling he is not yet comfortable with the element of water that represents emotion. He is wearing armor, highlighting his challenge is to transition from a mindset of war (separation) to love (union). We do this by confronting the conflict within to heal self-loathing and criticism. This frees us from needing to find someone externally to prove how loveable we are.

Stage Three: The Queen of Cups

This is the stage when instead of seeking someone to love us, we focus on giving love. If this urge isn't balanced by self-love, we may hopelessly devote ourselves to someone and self-sacrifice our needs on the assumption this is love,

QUEEN of CUPS.

rather than see it as codependency. At this stage of the journey, we have to learn to attune to our feelings to identify our needs so we can maintain our emotional equilibrium by actively meeting our needs, rather than being constantly distracted by the emotional needs of others. This can be a challenge for women within a Patriarchy who are conditioned to earn love through acts of service, rather than know they are worthy of receiving love for who they are.

This shift to focus on our own process usually occurs when we stop looking externally for love and learn to give generously to ourselves. Love is a verb, so love requires us to take action. Filling our own cup through acts of self-care reduces the compulsive yearning to seek someone to fill our cup. We often enter the queen stage after we've had our fill of broken hearts. A catalyst that sees us abandon the search for true love and instead embody the love we previously sought from others. Only then do we become emotionally available to ourselves instead of rejecting ourselves in a search for a significant other.

At this stage, instead of actively trying to hide our flaws to project a flawless persona to prospective partners we may willingly share our shadow traits as an invitation to connect authentically. This establishes a foundation of trust and psycho-emotional intimacy as a precursor to physical intimacy. It also indicates a level of self-responsibility for personal healing and caretaking of our needs. We master this stage when we seek to understand and embody the opposite within. This occurs when we understand the potential partners that we attract mirror the maturity of our inner bride or groom. If we don't truly see and honor ourselves, neither will anyone else. As stated previously, this awareness is anchored via a subsequent descent journey of initiation to create the 'inner marriage' by understanding and empowering the archetypes of the opposite gender within. This promotes a foundation of inner balance so we can enter into a harmonious dance with our opposite. The real challenge in this stage is to give up trying to be seen and understood by our opposite. So long as this need drives us in an attempt to heal the lack of validation and love we felt growing up, we will keep attracting and choosing partners who can't truly see and appreciate us.

The card, The *Queen of Cups* shows a woman sitting on a throne holding a goblet, symbolizing *the Grail*. She is seated on land, next to calm water. She's someone who has learned to balance their ego and soul; the feminine and masculine polarities within so she signifies someone who has found enough self-love to discern who is capable of love and who isn't.

Stage Four: The King of Cups

The card, The *King of Cups* shows a man who is

KING of CUPS.

comfortable with his feelings. He has learned how to swim, rather than drown in emotion, by accessing his soul as a guide to navigate his feelings. Having found the bride within, he is emotionally sovereign. He's no longer seeking his 'other half' to feel whole and complete. He is emotionally available to himself and others. The king represents mastery of one's emotions. Not through subjugation; seeing emotions as spiritually inferior and something to transcend or overcome, but via reverence. He understands emotions surface as an invitation to go within and explore the depths, to become wise through self-awareness. Like a ship's captain, the *King of Cups* is a figure who has learned how to read and navigate the waves of emotion, rather than fear them.

Such a man has mastered the art of being truly available emotionally to the present moment, without judgment. This means he can allow emotion to surface and be expressed, even intensely in the present moment. Like a waterfall, he can allow his emotions to flow unbounded. This ensures his vessel and intuition is 'crystal clear' like the archetypal *Christos*.

Such a person has a deep respect for emotional vulnerability and the courage it takes to express it, so they will never shame another for expressing emotion. This gives them the ability to hold space for others, with compassion, offering emotional support, as needed, without imposing solutions as unsolicited advice.

The *King of Cups* takes time to sit with the element of water and reflect. This lessens the chance of emotional drama as he takes the time to ponder lessons learned to avoid repeating dysfunctional patterns. Whether male or female, this is someone who has learned to embody the *Queen of Cups*, the feminine part of themselves, so they do not fear the power of the feminine externally. As a result, they will neither avoid or dominate the feminine, in themselves or others. In the mating dance, they will equally share their strengths and shadow traits, maintaining a balance of intimacy and autonomy to create an interdependent dynamic.

To master this stage, one is typically initiated through an experience of deep grief. Through this deep internal journey, they find acceptance and a new perspective. Having learned the value of the grieving process, they take the time necessary to grieve all endings rather than seek a new love interest to avoid processing their past. They are someone who has learned to forgive and feel gratitude for lessons learned. Like the element of water, they go with the flow, trusting the process, knowing change is inevitable and the universe is benevolent. This enables grace on the understanding that what is occurring is always happening 'for them', rather than 'to them'. Such an attitude makes it easier to identify the blessings and personal lessons in challenging situations.

The Grail Parable of Lancelot and Guinevere

Like *Tristan and Yseult*, I suspect the romance of *Lancelot and Guinevere* was employed as a teaching parable to mentor youths through their lessons in love. Why? It's a parable that echoes the lessons portrayed in the Tarot's *Suit of Cups. Lancelot* embodies *the Knight of Cups*, a man who embodies the pathos of unrequited love. His lack of self-awareness and self-love keeps him yearning for the love of the external feminine, while neglecting his own inner feminine.

We know this because he holds *King Arthur* and *Queen Guinevere* in such high esteem. This suggests he doesn't feel himself to be their equal, signaling low self-esteem. Instead of falling for a woman who is truly available to him, such as someone who is single, he falls for a woman who embodies the qualities of the *Queen of Cups*. This indicates his desire to win the favor of an emotionally mature woman. This is an unconscious bid to earn the love of a mother figure. This signals an unresolved mother complex; fearing he is not enough to please a mature woman. Unaware of this unhealed wound, he concludes he is unworthy of being truly loved. This results in him being attracted to women who are not emotionally available.

Lancelot strives to do and say what he thinks will please the object of his affection, rather than be his authentic self. Such efforts further disempower him as they reinforce his need for feminine approval. From the perspective of feminine wisdom, Lancelot's choices serve as a warning to men…to avoid feeling powerless in love, they must find self-love by seeking the feminine within.

Without the perspective of feminine wisdom, the tale of *Lancelot and Guinevere* has been viewed as a great romance, glorified for its tension and drama. This is to see it through the lens of the immature ego, a sexual attraction between a younger man and a married woman who represents the temptation of forbidden fruit. She's a coveted prize, a challenge for the knight to land as the ultimate conquest to prove his male power.

From this perspective, one assumes *Queen Guinevere* loves the king but isn't sexually fulfilled by him, so she's tempted by lust for *Lancelot*, a younger man. In the mystic tradition, the archetypal *Queen of Cups* is loyal in love and not drawn in by a young man who flatters her ego with attention. As a Queen, she is sovereign, so she doesn't need external validation or recognition and would not compromise her love for *Arthur*. For *Arthur* is a *King of Cups*, twice the man the knight, *Lancelot* is, having integrated his inner feminine to become whole.

The assumption *King Arthur* is impotent reflects how older men in a patriarchy are disempowered, like the archetypal *Fisher King*. A disempowerment that originates from their refusal to seek *the Grail*. Within Patriarchy older men are viewed as frail and impotent, rather than wise and compassionate. Such a pessimistic expectation feeds a fear of being usurped by younger, more virile men. This is why older men who are emotionally and psychologically immature seek young women to prove their virility.

A mature man such as *King Arthur*, who embodies the *King of Cups*, wouldn't feel threatened by a younger man with looks and charm being near his wife. He would feel secure in his attractiveness to his wife, knowing she values him for more than his appearance. He would also trust her because of her character, borne of learned lessons in love. Such a man would pity *Lancelot* as a dysfunctional figure of pathos, a young man who cannot love someone who is emotionally available because of his lack of self-love that plays out as hopeless devotion to the Queen.

As a *Grail*-initiated man, *King Arthur* would know any union between two individuals at the psychological stages of Knight and Queen would be fated to fail. For the Knight would always feel inadequate, as a man who has not found his inner riches, leading him to seek constant external approval. He would also know a Queen is a woman of substance who has found self-love. As such, she resides in her heart as a sovereign being who needs no external validation, so she is not tempted by flattery. He would also know that should such a woman enter into an intimate relationship with an emotionally immature man, she would find the relationship unfulfilling.

Why? She has journeyed within to see more of her soul, making her a larger being. If she were to settle for such a union, she may be tempted to diminish herself, so as not to trigger his fear of inadequacy. Only an emotionally immature woman (or feminine-dominant man) is flattered by the attention of an immature man (or masculine-dominant woman). Whereas, a mature person possesses the wisdom needed to discern the maturity of a potential partner.

Just as a man needs to prepare for intimacy by developing his inner feminine, who takes responsibility for his self-care, a woman needs to develop her inner masculine, to ensure disciplined discernment with prospective partners. This is what it means for a woman or feminine-dominant man to have their 'good king' on board... an inner father figure who ensures one's value is known and honored. Equally, a man or masculine-dominant woman needs their 'good queen' on board. This ensures they won't betray their core values to impress or gain acceptance from a woman or feminine-dominant man.

When these inner counterparts are not developed, the immature feminine typically nurtures her partner to reassure and empower him at a cost to her own needs, while the immature masculine places his love interest on a pedestal, provoking feelings of inadequacy. Ultimately, the test for a woman or feminine-dominant man is to face their fear of being alone, instead of hoping their immature partner will step up to meet them in the heart. Similarly, the ultimate test for a man or masculine-dominant woman is to face their fear of being unacceptable so they can relate to women and feminine-dominant men as equal and not sabotage themselves due to a fear of being unworthy.

With Love, Everything Grows

Love is considerate, kind, and honoring of oneself and others. Without the healing power of love in our lives, we wither. Equally, when we are truly appreciated and cherished, we blossom. You can tell someone is well-loved by their gait, their posture, their centered demeanor and their glow. Similarly, you can tell if someone is unloved, for they will be neurotic, scattered, physically burdened and their inner light diminished. Self-love ensures self-honoring choices are made and healthy boundaries established and upheld. A lack of self-love results in compromises and betrayals of oneself and mixed messages to others.

So now we have identified how to prepare for the opportunity of meeting our true love by doing the work of healing and personal growth. It's time to prepare the inner hero to face his greatest fear; looking like a fool for love! This requires coaching—something many men (and masculine-dominant women) have not received since it is sorely lacking in our culture.

They're Out of My League

A disempowered man or masculine-dominant woman will often perceive a potential love interest as being 'out of their league'. If immature, this sense of inadequacy will be based on how sexually attractive the love interest is, as immature relationships are based more on physical attraction. To improve their chances they will tend to focus on enhancing their looks or financial status to woo their intended lover. Whereas as one matures, they value more internal characteristics, like wisdom, humor and a positive mindset. The more mature we are, the more we empower ourselves with awareness on the understanding this is what is most valuable. The more we master the stages outlined in the *Suit of Cups*, the more empowered we are to discern who is a 'good match', capable of truly meeting us. Similarly, a male (or masculine-dominant woman) who has done the inner work will have more confidence to initiate a courtship and a female (or feminine-dominant man) who does the inner work will have the self-esteem to wait for a proposal of courtship befitting their value.

This is key, as it is the dynamics of the mating dance that determine the ongoing relationship dynamics. Whoever leads the mating dance will embody the masculine polarity, so if you're a woman (or feminine-dominant man) who wants to attract someone who leads with an empowered masculine energy, indicate your receptivity but wait for them to initiate the first date. If a man (or masculine-dominant woman) lacks the confidence to actively pursue you, they will continue to be passive in all decisions, keeping you in a masculine role.

If you're a man (or masculine-dominant woman) who is passive in making the first move, for fear of rejection, know this increases your chance of attracting a woman (or feminine-dominant man) who may unconsciously seek to dominate you due to a fear of being dominated by the masculine. To avoid the destructive cycle of 'karma drama' it's essential we observe the early signs and take responsibility for our part in the mating dance.

People show us who they are at the outset. It's up to us whether we take notice or overlook the warning signs and repeat the old dance, only to wonder why we keep experiencing a similar dynamic with subsequent partners. To discover whether you're feminine or masculine-dominant and why you attract the partners you do, check out my *Conscious Relating* online program in the resource section.

Reinstating Sacred Love in a Tinder-Obsessed World

Without *the Grail*, courtly love survives predominantly today in works of art and literature, with the exception of religious sects who enforce a strict moral code. As a result, modern romance is now void of any real courtship, with dating apps like *Tinder* promoting hookups for sexual gratification as the norm. Teen girls recently surveyed report boys expect sex before kissing and many experience rape or sexual assault as their first sexual experience.

The escalation in sexual assault has risen markedly since pornography became available online and not surprisingly, the largest consumers of porn are 12-year-old boys, those starting their journey of discovery in human sexuality. With the content of porn sites becoming increasingly violent in a competitive marketplace where addicts seek greater thrills via taboos that grant greater stimulus, boys are emulating portrayals of young women (and feminine-dominant men) being raped, beaten and choked as their introduction to sex.

This creates a disturbing expectation that sex is violent and more about power than love. Meanwhile, a growing number of older men are investing in dungeons to torture women (and feminine-dominant men) to emulate their dark, virtual escapades in an unconscious effort to assert their male power by denigrating the feminine. Yes, the pendulum has swung from imposing prudent ignorance and strict morality onto our youth to over-exposing them to sexual perversions borne of a wounded psyche at an inappropriately young age. To stop the cycle of abuse we need to heal the psyche of the collective, instead of merely condemning the abusers.

The current status quo is a dangerous foundation for the future of human relating. It's an escalation of the gender war that needs to be acknowledged as a state of emergency with widespread restoration of rites of passage essential to stop the violence that's happening on all levels, not just physical, to the innocent. We cannot blame our youth if we do not intervene as elders to show them another path, such as an education in the sacred love arts to pierce the delusions cast by porn and inspire mutually honoring patterns of relating. Only then will our youth be inspired by love rather than power. We need to reinstate priestess women instructing young men on the art of sacred love and courtship because in their absence we have seen a dangerous reversal where male yogis and Tantriks exploit and assault naïve young women. On a positive note, I'm also aware of well-meaning men openly answering boys' questions about sex as part of their welcome to manhood initiations. However, without older men being initiated into the sacred love arts, they pass on advice that lacks a true understanding of what it means to be a great lover.

Why? Men cannot speak with any direct knowledge of the feminine experience of sex, and you cannot teach what you don't know. This is why in advanced ancient civilizations like Mesopotamia, Egypt and indigenous cultures it was priestess women who schooled young men in the art of lovemaking. They taught men how to play a woman as a sacred instrument, known as a *Yantra* in Tantra.

Without adequate instruction, an immature man will focus on breasts like a child seeking comfort from his mother. A woman's genitals will simply be an entry point for his immediate gratification, without comprehending physiologically it takes 45 mins of stimulation for the vulva to become fully aroused and ready for penetration, so she feels tight, hot and wet. In other words, if she's not beside herself with pleasure begging you to enter her, wait!

A few years ago, I discovered those considered 'sex experts' lacked any mystic comprehension of sex. Jet-lagged in Bali and needing to stay awake until sunset to adjust to the local time zone I accepted an invitation to attend a free workshop on self-pleasure and anal massage offered by a lovely brother who attended the local morning dance meditation. He held a masters in Sexology so I was surprised to learn he had no concept of accessing multi-dimensional trance states through self-pleasure. This indicated to me that traditional training institutions focus solely on physiology and psychology.

Love is the ultimate aphrodisiac so focusing on sex without love is missing the point entirely. Initiation into *the Grail* mysteries ensures young men and women value soul connection as the key ingredient for transcendent sexual experiences.

In my book, *Creating Sacred Union in Partnerships*, I share a conscious courtship template; 'The 7 Dates at the 7 Gates' that promotes soul connection on all levels. It does this with a simple 7-step process to connect from the crown first - our spiritual center, then down to the base, our physical body. This supports us to create unions not merely based on lust that fuse us at our lowest expression as a foundation for relating. For what often follows is a gradual disappointment as you realize the other is incapable of meeting you on all levels. This template provides a simple framework to get to know all aspects of each other before becoming energetically enmeshed through the act of sexual union. This also better equips us to discern who can match us on all levels, creating a solid foundation for soul-fulfilling relationships.

Money Can't Buy Love

As stated earlier in a patriarchal culture, a wealthy man is considered a 'good catch' on the marriage market by immature women seeking material security. A man who is physically good-looking is also considered a hot prospect for dating. Whereas emotional and psychological maturity is less likely to make the top 10 criteria young women use to discern the eligibility of 'matches' on their dating apps.

This is why we're accustomed to seeing the pairing of an older man with a younger woman within a Patriarchy...from network news desks to high society weddings. Why? A man who has established himself financially can buy the affection of an immature woman, who trades her looks and freedom for material security. This is a Devil's bargain for both parties as they compromise their chance of a truly soul-fulfilling love to appease their ego desires. The unspoken expectation is; she will be content with the lifestyle provided so she won't challenge him to grow emotionally or psychologically.

Our concept of *wedlock* is, however, changing. During Patriarchy it was introduced as a legally binding contract to trace the ownership of women and their assets and heirs from father to son. This was what taking on a 'sir'-name signified. Now we have couples using double-barrel surnames to honor both matrilineal and patrilineal parentage, however this gets tricky for subsequent entries on the family tree! Still in most Christian wedding ceremonies, the father gives away the bride signifying she was his property and is now the property and responsibility of her husband. While Jewish ceremonies do honor the role of the mother in the handover, if you're Orthodox and choose to leave the marriage and the religion, your children are considered the property of your husband and his faith.[36]

Today the average wedding costs $30,000. A price tag one can attribute to the immature maiden's quest to create the perfect fairytale ending to her childhood. This is enabled by those in the wedding industry who prey upon the insecurities of immature brides-to-be who are trying to prove they are 'the fairest in the land'. Understandably this increases the anxiety for commitment-phobic immature men tenfold. It is a hotbed of anxiety exploited by reality TV shows like *The Bachelor* and *Married at First Sight* whose audiences attempt to bolster their own low self-esteem by watching evasive, irresponsible and reckless behavior that results in meltdowns, all in the name of love. Without rites of passage, sharing circles and initiation into the love arts to support enduring relationships, many add $30,000 for the price of the average divorce soon after.

"It is the act of bowing to the feminine that reveals the crown

of a man's head, so she may crown him king."

Tanishka

The Proposal: Transcending Power for Love

The custom of the bridegroom proposing on bended knee to his intended has been derived from *the Grail* tradition where men acknowledged their Beloved as their *kingmaker*. Traditionally, a *kingmaker* was a woman who had completed her *Descent of Ishtar* and made the inner shift from maiden to queen. She was the 'fateful woman' the hero met on his path who inspired him to be a better man. She did this by only consenting to enter union with him on the condition he take an equivalent descent to truly know his own heart and mind. For without this his immaturity would sabotage their union. A woman (or feminine-dominant man) who is rebuked for insisting she be honored has the confidence to tell immature suitors they must forfeit her company.

This dynamic was depicted beautifully in the film, *As Good As it Gets*, starring Jack Nicholson and Helen Hunt. This re-enactment illustrates a woman will be treated according to what she allows as acceptable behavior. The more self-love she has found, the more she will have the self-esteem to set self-honoring boundaries. Ultimately a man's love for his 'fateful woman' will inspire him to transcend his fear and risk looking like a fool to express his love…making true love possible, so everyone wins.

Immature men will attempt to woo like Prince Charming, promising the world but not honoring their word with their deeds. So a woman (or feminine-dominant man) must learn to discern a man's (or masculine-dominant woman's) level of maturity, so as to not be complicit in dishonoring themselves. A woman (or feminine-dominant man) who has enough self-esteem to set and uphold self-honoring boundaries acts as a catalyst for a man's (or masculine-dominant woman's) personal growth. How? A woman (or feminine- dominant man) who doesn't give themselves away readily ensures a man must prove himself worthy of 'her' heart. He builds trust through right action, proving 'his' intentions are honorable via noble choices. Since it takes time for a man to reveal his true nature, a courtship process is far more reliable and less costly than a prenuptial agreement.

Without *the Grail* to support men in understanding and embodying the qualities most prized by the mature feminine, the immature masculine strives to prove their value to 'her' by increasing their net worth. Many make the mistake of neglecting their partners emotionally and psychologically in their ardent pursuit of money and success. Why? The patriarchal concept of buying a diamond ring to prove a man's love anchors the distortion that 'money maketh the man'. The truth is, a man who invests time and energy in his soul education becomes irresistible to women as he's developed a greater capacity to embody and express love.

Crouching down on a bended knee as an act of submission has long been associated with chivalrous knights, true 'gentle' men who were initiated into the ways of *the Grail*. Such a gesture demonstrates a man's willingness to humble his immature ego before the wisdom of the feminine. Such a soul has learned to traverse the depths in order to ascend. This willingness to humble one's ego is what signifies a man's internal shift from knight to king. It symbolizes he's no longer the *puer aeternus* meaning 'eternal boy', running from the feminine for fear of domination or rejection. This gesture is the act of a man who understands and values his true love will always speak the truth, even if it is hard to hear. For it is inevitable she will help him grow by pointing out his immature ways. Bowing to her grace signifies he is psychologically and emotionally ready and available to journey the path of true love with his opposite. He understands her motive is love and growth rather than suspecting she harbors an agenda to dominate him. The latter is a projection of the immature male ego. If a man persists with that fear-based projection, he will destroy her love.

One might question whether this sets up a dynamic where the feminine dominates the masculine if the union is entered into with an act of subjugation by the masculine. My understanding is that in the male/female sex act, the masculine penetrates the feminine, even in homoerotic unions. The masculine imposes 'his' will upon the feminine, and 'she' submits herself completely. Our anatomy dictates this dynamic, with the female genitalia being receptive and the masculine genitalia protruding and active. When a man leads by example, submitting his ego by bending down he demonstrates to her that she's safe to surrender herself completely. Personally, I like the practice of each party mutually bowing to the other upon meeting or prior to lovemaking. Such as the Polynesian tradition of the *hongi*, 'touching noses' - a greeting where each bows their head, touching at the third eye, the center of the wisdom; the seat of the soul or bowing in a prayer salutation, as is the custom in Eastern cultures.

How the Grail Promotes Soul Union

A relationship between two *Grail* initiates is a soul union. This is entered into by those who have undertaken a perilous inner journey to seek their soul. It makes sense they are attracted to those who have also taken 'the road less traveled'. This preparation is what makes a soul-fulfilling union possible. The 'fateful woman' in a man's life who embodies the Goddess is a woman whose true beauty lies in the wisdom of her soul. This is the opposite of what men are conditioned to seek and value in a Patriarchy. Men are programmed to value women primarily for their looks and youth. This is why our ego-based culture grooms women to focus solely on perfecting their outer appearance.

Similarly, women are programmed to value men primarily for their material wealth and status. This is why men are groomed to achieve wealth and collect status symbols like expensive cars to attract a mate. This destructive conditioning creates tumultuous unions where the egos are dominant. Based on an initial sexual attraction, they lack the substance to endure and fulfill the soul. For love to survive beyond the initial spark of sexual attraction, we need to understand the cycles that govern us and how they affect our patterns of relating.

She is Changeable Like the Moon

The first phase of any love match is known as 'the honeymoon phase'. This refers to the love bubble of young romance when we want to spend most of our time with our new love interest. This usually involves a lot of sex and bonding in the lower energy centers. Both parties project upon the new love interest, their fantasy of the ideal partner. This is usually short-lived as our inevitable humanness surfaces and cracks the mirror of enchantment.

The custom of a 'honeymoon' was once part of *the Grail* tradition, albeit a far cry from what it means today. Nowadays the term, 'honeymoon' conjures images of newlyweds on holiday in a tropical destination with the best suite in the hotel enjoying candlelit dinners, cocktails and enough sex to go home with a UTI...basically, a lavish extravagance costing a month's wage. In the ancient world, the purpose of a honeymoon was for a man to meet every face of the Goddess in his bride during her 28 day lunar cycle for only then would he truly know her. For just as the sun is constant, the moon is changeable.

This is why men's moods are usually more constant on a day-to-day basis, as the masculine is governed by the ebb and flow of the sun's light and transits. The sun spends a month in each zodiac sign and only loses its light gradually once a year.

Conversely, women are ruled by the moon, which changes astrological signs every two and a half days and loses light for half of every month. For a man to truly appreciate and love a woman, he must understand the changing nature of a woman. Without this understanding, many uninitiated men view women with judgment, suspecting women of emotional manipulation due to their changing moods. If we view a woman's monthly cycle from the perspective of the rational mind, it would appear like the Chinese yin/yang symbol, an ever-turning cycle of light and dark.

Chinese Yin Yang symbol

Yes, two weeks after a woman's menses until ovulation, she's on the upswing, feeling more light, bright, confident, optimistic, social - with stamina and strength to multitask like a banshee. Then in the two weeks after ovulation until her menses, she's on the downward trajectory, feeling increasingly heavy, dark, unsure, pessimistic and reclusive with less energy and physical strength. The more a man understands this, the more he can extend consideration, empathy and support, rather than view her as a psycho who can't be trusted. This cycle is more pronounced in fertile women due to their changing hormone levels, which intensify when a woman is pregnant.

Women who are no longer fertile cycle in the same way, just less intensely, with the new moon being akin to their menses and the full moon, being the equivalent of their ovulation phase. If we view this

monthly cycle from the soul's perspective, instead of a black and white cycle it would appear as a color wheel indicating the subtleties of the full spectrum women journey emotionally and psychologically within a lunar month. It's helpful for men in intimate relationships with biological women to know what day of their cycle their partner is on so they can gauge their psycho-emotional temperature. Such a visual aid enables greater understanding and compassion all round…(pun intended). *Grail* initiated men learn the art of true husbandry through gaining an education in the cycles, which includes the fertility and lunar cycles that govern the feminine.

"The Course of True Love Never Did Run Smooth"

William Shakespeare

Understanding What Women Want

This is the age-old question synonymous with *the Grail* that men have pondered. It's understandable that without instruction to understand the cycles of the feminine, most men struggle to answer this riddle. Why? A woman's answer will differ on any given day due to her changing nature so a man is more empowered to court a woman if he understands the many faces of the feminine and how to woo them. Without *the Grail* teachings to guide men, it's understandable most men feel ill-equipped to navigate the changing nature of women. This fear is what underpins derogatory jokes about women during 'that time of the month' such as this misogynistic slur I heard as a little girl: 'How can you trust something that bleeds once a month but doesn't die?'

Such cultural misogyny conveys our societal lack of understanding about the cyclic nature of women and how women's hormones and the lunar cycle impacts their moods, energy levels, creativity, psychic sensitivity and libido. This ignorance exists amongst both men and women and contributes to tension and conflict experienced between the sexes in intimate relationships. The more couples understand these phases and navigate them, the more the path of love can run smoothly!

Today the majority of women are oblivious to their cyclic needs and feel shame about their changing moods. A woman who hasn't been initiated into *the Grail* will be more emotionally erratic with intense high's and low's due to her inability to manage her emotional states with understanding and compassion. Whereas a woman who's aware of her ever-changing nature will honor each in turn and radiate her full spectrum of inner beauty.

Without understanding and wisdom, love isn't possible as the two go hand in hand. This is why in the ancient world the cyclic wisdom of *the Grail* was an integral preparation for *Sacred Union*. Like the adage, 'knowledge is power', the more a man understands women, the more empowered he feels relating to them. This is why, traditionally, men in their *Grail* kingship rite, would learn about the four faces of the Goddess they would meet during their bride's monthly cycle, so they could appreciate the gift in each phase. Such an introduction creates a sense of curiosity, rather than fear and resistance borne of ignorance. To that end, here are the four aspects a man will meet in his female partner in a lunar month, along with a thumbnail guide to 'what women want' during each week of their cycle. This is also helpful info for homosexual men to gain greater insight into their mothers, sisters, daughters, friends and work colleagues.

Phase One: First Quarter - The Virgin Bride

First Quarter Moon

This face of the Goddess is the archetypal maiden, a youthful woman who embodies hope and the return of Spring. She emerges in the first week of a woman's cycle after her menses ends.

For post-menopausal women, this is after the new moon, when the darkest lunar phase ends. The maiden phase is when a woman feels reborn, energetic, expansive, social and optimistic. This is due to the increase in her estrogen levels which also amplifies the allure of her magnetic feminine appeal.

This is the time of the month she wants to have fun, try new things and explore new places. If a man negates her invitations to 'lighten up' by doing something fun together, she may feel trapped, bored and dissatisfied with her partner. Whereas if he surprises her with a mystery date or flowers at this time, she'll melt and fall in love with him all over again. If a woman is immature, during this time of the month she may flirt with others, overspend or break agreements to please herself in the moment without considering others.

From a pre-patriarchal perspective, the virgin phase evokes the sovereign woman, a woman who is independent but open to exploring connection with her opposite. When this aspect is empowered women, regardless of their relationship status, romance themselves by buying flowers, pampering themselves and taking long walks on the beach. They know their happiness is not dependent on being chosen by a man to validate their self-worth. This confidence comes from devoting time to exploring their potential.

Patriarchy diminished the maiden aspect to a naive and immature girl; a princess who unconsciously seeks to be rescued and validated by a man's attention. The shadow embodiment of this aspect is rife, with maidens competing to prove their sexual attractiveness on social media via staged poses, camera filters, a ton of cosmetics, butchery parading as cosmetic enhancement and self-loathing manifested as eating disorders. This is the opposite of the maiden's true beauty, which is her playful, spontaneous, natural and inspiring demeanor, regardless of her age.

The word *bride* comes from the ancient name *Bridie*, a derivative of *Brigid*, the Celtic Goddess of new beginnings. *Brigid* is a fire Goddess, a source of inspiration. Reconnecting with and honoring this face of the Goddess is what 'keeps the spark alive in a marriage' but search the origin of the word, *bride* on Wikipedia and you'll see its origins are attributed to the European word, *bru* meaning 'to cook, brew and make broth' - the Patriarchal expectation of a daughter-in-law.[37]

Today brides wear a veil, on their wedding day in an unconscious attempt to mimic the sovereign priestess; a magical woman who once earned the right to wear the veil. The veil was a sacred article of clothing that distinguished a woman who had journeyed beyond the veils of illusion. Such women were revered as keepers of sacred knowledge and vessels for the healing energies of the Goddess. The veil signified a woman who had undertaken *The Descent of Ishtar* to unveil all 7 aspects of the Goddess within and awaken her *kundalini* or *Shakti*, meaning 'Goddess essence'. Only when a woman unveiled the 7 aspects of the sacred feminine was she ready to unveil her true self for her Beloved. This was the original symbolism of the 'unveiling of the bride' custom that has since been lost. It was once a great honor to be wedded to a woman who embodied the regenerative powers of the Goddess. This is why young men underwent an equivalent initiation to meet the 7 aspects of their masculine psyche in *The Descent of Orpheus* to ensure they were ready for the challenge of ongoing initiation, that union with the cyclic Goddess evoked.

Phase Two: Full Moon - The Maternal Queen

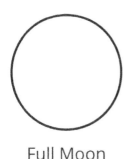

Full Moon

This face of the Goddess is the archetypal mother, the face of Summer representing the zenith of the light when good times are shared with loved ones. This is when a woman feels patient, kind, nurturing, generous and sensual. This is when a woman is said to be, 'full of the milk of human kindness'. It is the phase when women are most likely to ovulate and secrete the highest amount of estrogen so their breasts become fuller until an egg is released from one of their ovaries. For post-menopausal women, this is akin to the week of the full moon.

The mother phase is a woman's most creative time of the cycle when she is most likely to encourage others to fulfill their unexpressed potential. At this time in a woman's cycle, she will feel most loved if her partner does his share of housework, without being asked or if he takes their kids to do something so she can nurture herself. During this phase *Grail*-initiated men acknowledge, with gratitude, the bounty she provides. This is an ideal time to co-host a shared meal with friends, family or community as it's when she has the energy to give. This is also a fortuitous time to focus on joint plans, make love and be generous with cuddles, tactile affection and offers of creature comforts, such as cups of tea, warm baths and foot rubs. If a woman is immature, she may be extremely codependent at this time of the month, facilitating her partner's personal growth as her priority project. This dynamic emasculates her male counterpart, causing him to push back like a teenager in an unconscious effort to assert his autonomy and power.

Women who insist on mothering their partners increase the risk of breast cancer which can be an alarm to alert them that their pattern of intimate relating is not sustainable.

Phase Three: Last Quarter - The Enchanting Mage

Last Quarter Moon

This face of the Goddess is the archetypal Amazon; a woman's second maidenhood. This is when a woman feels most discerning, autonomous, self-reliant and focused on her own healing process. This lunar phase evokes the matriarch, a woman in her Autumn season, whose energy is waning like the moon's light, causing her to withdraw and conserve her energy, regardless of her chronological age.

This phase is akin to a fertile woman's luteal phase when her body starts producing progesterone, as well as estrogen. In a woman's life-cycle, this is when she enters peri-menopause. For a post-menopausal woman, this is akin to last quarter moon. Physical symptoms for a fertile woman can include headaches, acne, bloating and breast tenderness at this time of the month. This is also when a woman's sensitivity is increased emotionally, psychologically and energetically and when her subtle senses; her clairvoyance, clairsentience, clairaudience, precognition and intuition are more honed.

During this time a woman is less likely to tolerate situations that feel dishonoring. She's also more likely to assert her needs and state her boundaries. This is the phase when a woman evaluates her harvest and reflects on what she needs to do differently to ensure a better outcome. It is when she reflects on her past experiences and lessons learned and evaluates if her choices reflect her values. In this phase, a woman needs space to process. Men who understand this can encourage their partners to take time apart to journal, have healings and spend time in sisterhood /brotherhood to gain perspective. If a woman is immature, without this introspection she may be hypercritical of her mate and scapegoat him. This is a potentially testing week for relationships.

Phase Four: New Moon - The Wise Crone

New Moon

This face of the Goddess is the archetypal wise mystic. This is when a woman feels most inward, vulnerable, psychic, quiet, tired and sensitive. This lunar phase evokes the elder woman; a woman whose energy is inward. This is her Winter season; the week of menstruation for fertile women, when they appear older as the blood drains from their faces and wombs, causing them to feel heavy, dense and slow. Psychologically and emotionally, they feel more internal as their sacred blood spirals down, taking their consciousness deep within.

For post-menopausal women, this is the final week of the lunar cycle, starting at the last quarter moon. This is when a woman becomes aware of what lies beneath. This is when she acknowledges the need for endings and prioritizes her needs to caretake her sensitivity. When consciously embraced, the Crone phase helps distill one's inner power through meditation, contemplation and insight. This focus ensures one can intuitively access pearls of wisdom.

When men understand a woman's acute sensitivity at this time, they can be mindful of the impact of their behavior...such as not making excessive noise with power tools at 7am or startling her with sudden, erratic entrances if she's deep in thought. A chivalrous man will do his best to shield her from the harshness of the outside world. If he does, her gratitude will be immense.

Saying the Princess from the Tower

Once a man has rescued his 'damsel in distress' - his own inner feminine whose been locked away for fear of him being thought 'less than a man'...he's better equipped to accept the faces of the feminine he'd previously devalued or rejected in women. In today's culture, that's usually the mage and the crone; the more mature feminine aspects. These are the aspects every woman embodies as the moon wanes to her lowest ebb. The mage and crone are also evoked within the fertility cycle, from ovulation to menstruation. During this time, a woman's outer beauty fades, but her inner beauty shines. Only a man who has awakened his soul can appreciate and embrace the deeper and darker aspects of a woman.

The film *Shrek* echoed this *Grail* teaching with *Fiona*, the female lead shapeshifting into an ogre at night, symbolizing the dark feminine. At the start of the film *Fiona* is locked away, on the belief she will incite fear and no one will love her. Similarly, *Shrek* hides in his swamp, fearing he is unlovable because of his lower nature. Only through accepting what they both fear is unacceptable in themselves are they available to recognize true beauty; the beauty of the soul. *Shrek* won hearts worldwide with its message of true love. It showed us true love is only possible when we see and appreciate both the light and shadow aspects in ourselves and others. Aspects that are revealed by the ebb and flow of the natural cycles, such as the turning of day into night. The film, *Shrek* echoed the message of *the Grail* parable, *Gawain and Lady Ragnall* that reveals how *King Arthur's* nephew, *Gawain* helps him solve the age-old riddle, 'What do women want?' I deconstruct this parable in my book, *Creating Sacred Union in Partnerships* listed in the resources section.

CHAPTER 8

The Stag King:
Reclaiming the Origins of
Christmas

W elcome to chapter eight! Eight is the number of infinite power that is available to us when we surrender our will 'to infinity and beyond' to quote *Buzz Lightyear* from the film, *Toy Story*. Number eight is the infinity symbol...but we have to shift our perspective to see it. *In The Hero's Journey*, the eighth stage is the crisis moment mid-way when the hero is faced with an all-important choice. His choice indicates whether his ego or soul will reign supreme. Such a dilemma requires we confront our inner demons, acknowledging the power we've given to our fears and desires. Without this showdown, we remain a slave to them.

In the mystic tradition, this stage was referred to as *The Dark Night of the Soul.* It is a dangerous time for the hero as a death will occur, one way or another. Either the death of their greatest dream or the death of their greatest illusion. The path to navigate that choice is a labyrinth. This signifies we must go deep and consciously traverse the neural pathways of our subconscious.

Despite conventional thinking, a labyrinth is not a maze, featuring many confusing paths and choices…this is a trick of the mind. A labyrinth is one continuous path, so the only failure is giving up. The word, *labyrinth* is associated etymologically with the Minoan, *labrys*, a double-sided axe that was the symbol of the mother Goddess in ancient Crete.[38] It signified the mother Goddess would behead the ego of those who dared enter the

labyrinth. To enter the labyrinth was to enter her realm, the Underworld, previously revered as 'the womb of the Great Mother' where souls would descend to be reborn. This is why her ax is double-sided, like her labia; the gateway portal of death and rebirth.

This is also why Neolithic Goddess-worshiping cultures all built labyrinths as walking meditations to support this inner journey.

Labyrinths have been found in India, Greece, France, Turkey, Ireland, England, Norway and America[39] - countries whose cultures are diverse but all once honored the teachings of the sacred feminine.

Traditionally one enters a physical labyrinth with a question; an all-important choice. Walking the labyrinth helps us observe fears that surface as we symbolically traverse our neural pathways. Once in the center, the querent stops to meditate, surrendering their question up to highest will. Insights are often received intuitively as the initiate commences their walk out of the labyrinth.

In pre-patriarchal times, priestesses assisted male heroes to navigate their inner labyrinth. Today, we see mythic heroes like *Thor* on the silver screen escaping the *Underworld* single-handed but originally it was the Norse priestess, *Hel* who assisted *Thor* out of the labyrinth.

Hollywood casts *Hel* as *Thor's* enemy who he must defeat. Such distortions anchor the belief men should be able to navigate the dark without the help of feminine wisdom or alternatively, perceive women as the enemy, rather than an ally. *Thor* wasn't the only mythic hero who was guided out of the *Underworld* by a priestess. *Theseus*, the Greek hero was guided out of the labyrinth by the priestess, *Ariadne* so he wasn't destroyed by the *Minotaur*. As mentioned previously, the *Minotaur* was a being who was half man/half beast, representing a man's lower nature that will sabotage him if he doesn't seek feminine guidance. *Ariadne* provided *Theseus* with a sword to slay the *Minotaur* and a thread to follow his way out of the dark.

Due to such cultural conditioning the majority of men don't seek feminine guidance so they remain trapped in the labyrinth of their psyche, depressed and unable to process past painful experiences. This is what keeps a man from discovering his true purpose and undermines his self-worth. A man without a purpose is at risk of suicidal ideations. For one who doesn't take the inner journey to discover their soul gifts is unable to shine their light in the world. Frustrated, they implode like a dark star, spiraling destructively like a black hole, taking those closest down with them.

Men need the support of a feminine guide to develop the mystic abilities needed to navigate the darkness within, the realm of the feminine. Without a guide to midwife an ego-death, many men give up hope and take their life. The Tarot card, *The Hanged Man*, illustrates this archetypal lesson. It depicts a man

THE HANGED MAN.

hanging upside down from a tree. This was a custom practiced by both the Celts and the native Americans (who hung from a large rock instead of a tree) to facilitate a 180-degree shift in perspective. By looking at the expanse of the sky, an initiate would turn their thoughts towards the big picture of the Cosmos to contemplate

their place in the universe, rather than be distracted by the constant activity of their mundane world. Turning upside down is what a fetus does prior to birth. It's also how bats sleep, an animal that's symbolic of gestation and rebirth.

Without mystic initiation, too many men are hanging themselves to end their suffering. The World Health Organization statistics for June 2021 show more people die worldwide by suicide than war, homicide, HIV, breast cancer or malaria. One in 100 deaths are suicides and men are twice as likely to take their own life than women.[40] As high as those stats are, they don't portray the extent of men who are suicidal. The silent majority of men are killing themselves slowly by enacting a death wish with destructive choices that negatively impact themselves and those closest to them.

The Rebirth of the Holy Sun God

As stated previously, Winter Solstice is the most challenging time of year for men since masculine energy is amplified by the strength of the solar light of the sun. When the sun's light is at its lowest ebb, men are more prone to struggle with darker thoughts and emotional states. Why? Winter Solstice is the most inward and feminine time on the seasonal wheel so men who are at war with the feminine within are more prone to feel eclipsed by self-loathing and act out in destructive ways, escalating the risk of injury, illness, depression and suicide.

Known as *Yule* in *the Grail* tradition, this seasonal 'holy' day was acknowledged as a man's equivalent to menstruation; a psychological death phase when his unhealed aspects would loom large to be healed. This is also when all a man has outgrown becomes apparent, urging him to release what no longer serves his highest growth. The *Holy Grail* was a rite of passage ceremony for men held annually to support men with this process, held over the nine darkest days of the Winter Solstice. It was facilitated by the local *Magdalene* and her *Grail* maidens and considered essential for men's wellbeing and the wellbeing of the collective. Today, without men observing this rite, we see men unconsciously become a 'force for destruction' at a cost to themselves, their loved ones and the world. Without participation in the annual *Holy Grail* rite, the wounded feminine in uninitiated men results in patterns of self-sabotage and poor self-care which undermines their health, relationships, purpose and potential, evidenced by the life-expectancy rates for men which are lower than women's worldwide.[41]

Sir Gawain, the knight most renowned for being successful in his quest for *the Grail*, was said to 'strengthen and wane with the cycles of the sun'. This trait was common amongst the heroes of Welsh legends that inspired many of *the Grail* poems. The character of *Gawain* was said to have derived from the Welsh hero, *Gwalchmei* who was closely associated with *King Arthur*.[42]

The Great Deceiver and The Return of the Sacred King

As we approach the end of the Piscean Age, those attuned to the old age are awaiting the second coming of the *Messiah*. Meanwhile, those more attuned to the new age; the Aquarian Age view this prophesied return symbolically. Instead of waiting for an external savior they're seeking to develop their 'Christ consciousness' within, the clear consciousness of the Christos; the crystalline soul.

The latter seems more congruent with the original teachings of *Yeshua* as the Dead Sea Scrolls; the early Biblical texts omitted from the Roman Bible and discovered in 1947, reveal *Yeshua* taught people to attune to the guru and kingdom within the heart rather than defer to external authority. Inspired by his example, many are now taking responsibility for their own enlightenment rather than waiting passively to be saved, like a helpless child by a good father figure.

It is my understanding *Yeshua* was persecuted for practicing and disseminating *the Grail* after the Roman Empire conquered those who practiced *the Grail* and forbade it. Why? *The Grail* posed a direct threat to the power of Rome as the empire relied on manpower to implement their war campaigns. Men who took allegiance to serve the Earth through acts of love would not betray their vows to assist the war machine of the empire to amass its power at a cost to the Earth and her people. This is why the Roman Empire sought to make an example of *Yeshua* and then reinvented his public image, portraying him as the one and only World Savior.

This was a direct inversion of *the Grail* teaching that every man is here to awaken the savior within. It's a bitter irony that Rome traded on his popularity, misrepresented him and subverted his legacy to serve their own ends. Why? A man who fails to awaken the savior within remains disempowered. Such a man will seek approval from an external authority, making him more inclined to compete with other men to advance his status in the ranks of a hierarchy. Since men seek to serve something greater than themselves to give their life meaning and purpose, the empire replaced the earlier custom of pledging allegiance to the *Earth Mother*, to the Fatherland of Rome, appointing *Yeshua* as their sacred male figurehead.

"The most powerful thing in the hands of the oppressor are the minds of the oppressed."

Steve Biko

What is held as most sacred within a society wields the most power as this is what motivates people to act. This is why *the Grail* was outlawed, appropriated and inverted to create the religious cult of Rome; Christianity. While the doctrine of the state of Rome encouraged the singing of 'Onward Christian soldiers' *the Grail* had previously sought to uphold peace.

This was instilled annually via *The Holy Grail* rite that enabled men to serve love, not war in a spirit of brotherhood. This practice supported men to bow their ego through acknowledging the wisdom and power of the divine intelligence inherent in the cycles of nature. Men who participated were celebrated as an embodiment of the living God. Sacred sons, considered noble men due to their willingness to descend psychologically and emotionally to face their deepest fears and insecurities during the sun's shortest day, the Winter Solstice.

All the ancient Gods were said to be born at the Winter Solstice, illustrating how widespread *the Grail* was prior to the rise of Rome whose army conquered a quarter of the globe. Gods such as *Dionysus* and *Adonis* in ancient Greece, *Osirus* and *Baal* in ancient Egypt, *Mythra* in Persia and *Tammuz* in Mesopotamia. This previously had referred to the birth of the God-consciousness within a man, constituting his 'second birth' - his soul rebirth. It is from here the Christian term, 'born again', was appropriated to signify one who accepted 'Jesus, the Christ' as their savior, surrendering to him rather than Divine Will. In the pre-Christian mystic tradition, the men who surrendered to a higher power to experience a 'second birth' were celebrated as the archetypal 'Dying God'.

The Roman Empire took this theme to create a patriarchal 'Festival of the Dying God' that commemorated the crucifixion of Jesus. Whilst the ancients celebrated the sacrifice of the immature male ego to awaken the divine potential in all men, the Roman Empire appointed one man as 'the son of God', ordering subjects to worship him alone as the *World Savior* and honor his sacrifice with loyalty to their doctrine. The religion of Rome taught men to earn approval from an external *Father God* by slaying their brothers in a spirit of competition to glorify the power of the empire. The legacy of this distortion has enslaved the group mind for two thousand years with guilt, one of the most dense and toxic of human emotions.

The original 'Festival of the Dying God' was celebrated at the Autumn Equinox, the gateway to the dark months when the solar light fades, initiating men to confront their dark side. Those unwilling to undergo the mystic initiation to acknowledge and integrate their unconscious and unhealed aspects were considered a potential danger to society. Whereas those who were willing to take the inner journey were celebrated for their act of heroism.

This was appropriated into the Christian festival of *Easter*, which celebrated fertility with the moon hare and decorated eggs, representing new beginnings. These were appropriated into the *Easter Bunny* and *Easter eggs* despite them having no relevance to the Christian mass that celebrated the empire's crucifixion of *Yeshua* as a sacrifice for humanity.

The True Origins of Christmas

Just as *Easter* was formerly *Eostre*, *Christmas* was originally the festival of *Yule*. This was the seasonal gate when *The Holy Grail*, considered the holiest festival in the ancient world, was observed. What we know today as the 'silent and holy night' originally referred to the Winter Solstice; the longest, darkest night in the seasonal wheel. *The Holy Grail* midwifed the 'virgin birth' of the *solar hero* so the *World Savior* who lay dormant within the heart of every man could be reborn. This rite was distorted into *Christmas*, meaning 'Christ Mass' - a church service to honor the Christed One'. Before the Roman church, the ancients would burn an oil lamp in their window to signify they were observing this holy festival. *Yuletide Greetings* was a blessing to wish someone safe passage through their annual psychological death and rebirth.

By identifying how the distortion of *the Grail* has disempowered the collective male psyche, we can liberate the collective masculine by piercing the illusions of Empiric conditioning that have kept us blind. Ironically the book of *Revelations* in the *Bible* warns us we would encounter *The Great Deceiver*. This is a blatant attempt to pre-empt the truth-tellers who would inevitably surface at the end of the Age to reveal the lie perpetuated on humanity, encouraging the faithful to scapegoat them as the 'anti-Christ'.

The Oak King and the Holly King

The rise of the Roman Empire made it impossible to practice *The Holy Grail* as men were enlisted in war campaigns during the Winter months on the basis they could attend their fields during the warmer months. Having men commit acts of war to amass empiric power leveraged the dark months as a time to amplify the shadow masculine and this prevented men from turning inward to contemplate, mature and grow wise. This also impacted men's ability to form close bonds with their wives and children.

Prior to Rome, *The Holy Grail* prepared men for *Sacred Union*. This is why it was referred to as the *Stag Night*, when the men would meet in the forest to awaken the 'good king of the forest'. That being a man who embodied the sacred masculine and would act on behalf of the Earth, women and children.

Such men inspire trust and appreciation from initiated women who know themselves to be fractals of the *Earth Mother*, connected to every sister by their cycle and every child by their heart. When men stay silent, complicit with those who violate the Earth and her people, trust is broken.

The *Oak King* and *Holly King* were two aspects of *Cernunnos*, the ancient Celtic 'Lord of the forest', known colloquially as 'The Green Man'. 'The Green Man' is often depicted with oak or holly leaves crowning his face, suggesting he is one with the Earth. Alternatively, he is portrayed as a wild stag, symbolizing the sacred masculine. Like all *Grail* parables, the story of the *Oak King* and the *Holly King* illustrated how the cycles of nature initiate us to grow wise.

At Summer Solstice, the kind and wise aspect of the *Oak King* was said to suffer a wound, causing his energy to wane like the Sun. Due to his waning energy, he could not win against the dark forces of the Holly King, who reigned from Summer Solstice to Winter Solstice. Instead, he had to wait until the Winter Solstice, when the new annual cycle would commence heralding the return of the light. As then, his energy would strengthen.

Yule was when the wise, kind elder; the *Oak King* returned. Unlike holly, which grows quickly, an oak takes a long time to grow into maturity. This is why oak was the tree favored for wands and staffs used in sacred rites. The *Oak King* was the archetypal 'good king' whose wisdom grew through weathering the cycles. Hence he was portrayed as a wise old man, revered and loved by his people. The *Oak King* defeats the dark Lord, the *Holly King* when *the Grail* is sought in earnest by good men.

This folktale indicates the importance of divine timing; comprehending the impact the greater cycles have on our energy levels, psyche and the sustainability of our world. By aligning with the ebb and flow of nature, victory and wisdom are assured. Like other *Grail* parables, this tale recognizes both aspects, the light and the dark exist within the natural man. When the *Oak King* takes the crown, he is permitted to wed the Springtime maiden. It's interesting the Springtime maiden is referred to as *Cerridwen*, the crone Goddess indicating she is also the one Goddess, as cyclic and changeable as he, the God is.

Why We Deck the Halls with Holly

The ancients honored both the light and the dark equally on the understanding both served a purpose and were necessary for the life cycle to prevail. On the longest day; Summer Solstice, our ancestors would thank the 'Sun God' for the lighter months of Spring and Summer and acknowledge the arrival of the Holly King. Just as the leaves of the plant holly are sharp to touch and bear red berries that are poisonous to eat, the *Holly King* signified the dark side of the masculine who would rule for six months while the sun's light was waning. If the men didn't seek the wisdom of *the Grail* mid-Winter, the *Holly King* would continue his reign and destroy all the Goddess created. It's significant we have been held in a dark enchantment by the distorted illusions of *Holly-wood*. Although recently we have witnessed the public fall of 'Hollywood royalty' as their Devil's bargains and shadow behavior have been exposed. It was in reference to the *Holly King* a sprig of holly decorated the plum pudding and it was set alight! Halls were decked with holly was to celebrate the end of the reign of the *Holly King*. I also can't help but wonder if *The Holy Grail* was originally called 'The Holly *Grail*' since it signifies the death of the holly king and the end of his cycle.

The Dark Origins of Saint Nicholas and Santa Claus

Christianity appropriated the wise old *Oak King* into *Saint Nicholas*. Named after the Turkish bishop, *Nikolas*, who was said to have enslaved the *Devil*. *Nikolas* would travel door to door to see if children had been bad or good, while the *Devil* would drop candy down the chimney to reward those who complied with their authority figures. This anchored the betrayal of the wild self in exchange for the Devil's bargain from a young age. This concept was undoubtedly taken from the hearth gods who were previously said to come down the chimney, wearing red. In the latter version, if a child could recite a *Bible* verse, they got candy. If they couldn't recite a verse or behaved 'badly' this indicated their mind couldn't be indoctrinated and their wild spirit broken by the rod...in which case, *Ruprecht*, his *Devil* servant, would whip the child or take them away in his sack! For a great comedic portrayal of a 'Devilish imp' by the name of *Ruprecht*, I recommend watching Steve Martin in the film, *Dirty Rotten Scoundrels*.

19th century writer Theodore Stom describes the whippings given to children as 'sadomasochistic rites' enacted by a Bishop who visited homes in a dark-hooded robe. The concept of *Santa* flying through the sky in a sleigh was thought by some to be inspired by the Norse God, *Odin* who was said to 'travel the sky' deciding who would die and who would prosper, accompanied by a horned goat, symbolic of *Pan*, the nature God who was demonized in the Christian concept of the *Devil*. Here we see the origins of the 'naughty and nice list', anchoring the Christian polarization of good and evil.

Others claim the inspiration for the 'flying reindeer' came from an earlier Nordic mythos where it was the ancient *Deer Mother* who drew the sleigh of the *Sun Goddess* at the Winter Solstice. Her regenerative powers were said to gestate and rebirth the Sun mid-Winter. Her antlers were frequently depicted as the *Tree of Life*, carrying birds, the sun, moon and stars. In the Latvian and Lithuanian cultures the Goddess flew across the heavens in a sleigh pulled by horned reindeer and threw pebbles of amber (symbolizing the sun) into chimneys.[43] While others claim this appropriation stems from the Siberian shamanic tradition where caribou and shamans ingested psychotropic *Amanita* mushrooms. The shamans dressed in the colors of the mushrooms, which are red and white and entered homes via the chimney, due to snow obstructing the front door.[44]

The story, *The Night Before Xmas*, changed *Saint Nicholas* into a magical, loving figure. Originally penned as a poem in 1823 titled, *A Visit From St.Nicholas* by an unknown author, it was Clement Clarke Moore who later claimed authorship in 1837[45] Moore was not the original author. He simply rewrote the poem into a story for his children. He is therefore, the author, attributed as the one who recast the horned devil servant into *'jolly Saint Nic'*, the man who enslaved the eight stag deers. Thanks to him, by 1880 *Saint Nic* was a folk hero.

Today the patriarchal *Santa* anchors the message that a good father figure buys affection with a sack or sleigh of gifts. Santa is portrayed as the CEO of an enterprise that uses the slave labor of childlike minions to project an image of abundance and generosity. Unlike the *Oak King* whose initiates would return from *the Grail* rites in the forest embodying the kind, wise and loving father, *Santa* was like the distant patriarchal *Sky Father* God, *Zeus*. *Santa* showed up once a year to parent with rewards or punishment, taking all the credit for the tireless work done by the unsung Mrs. Clause aka Mum who created the magic of *Christmas* with home-made gifts, cards, decorations and baked goods. No wonder we culturally accept the idea of Dads only being 'hands-on' in the holidays.

Perhaps even more significant was the fact the patriarchal festive father enslaved the archetypal stag to do his bidding, driving his sleigh. Where once the stag was revered as the 'wild man of the forest', representing the primal power of a man's soul that's found in the wild places of Mother Nature...*Santa* literally 'reigns in' the wild masculine and whips him as his slavedriver. While the original message instilled during the *Yuletide Grail* rite was; to be a good father, a man had to face his fears to become loving and wise, the patriarchal distortion portrayed the distant alpha male as the 'good father'. In the latter version, a man was valued more for his wealth than his heart. Those considered 'noble' were those who inherited wealth rather than those who possessed true valor. The patriarchal aristocracy hunted the stag to mount his head as a trophy instead of embodying the traits of the *Stag King*. Similarly, amongst the gentry classes it's commonplace to hunt and capture a trophy wife, a woman who is for show, rather than develop the strengths of one's inner feminine to attract a woman of substance.

The killing of a stag deer is an assertion of male power through an act of dominance over the alpha male of the forest. Not a fair contest given only one contender is armed. I suspect the origins of this barbaric custom may represent a ritual defeat of the archetypal wild man by those who sought dominion over the Earth-worshiping tribes. I find it symbolic that instead of seeking to become like the stag, a symbol of authentic male power, through initiation into *the Grail*, they take life for personal glory in an attempt to prove their manhood.

Where The Wild Things Are

The Stag King; the archetypal 'Green Man' survived in folklore as Jack in the Green, the *Green Knight*, Puck and Robin Goodfellow, better known as Robin Hood. Male figures who lived by their wits in the forest, heroes of the people because of their ability to outwit the corrupt authorities and serve the people. In 1977 folk-rock duo, *Jethro Tull* released a song called, *Jack In the Green* on the album, *Songs From the Wood*.[46] As I write this chapter, Hollywood is promoting a film called, *The Green Knight*, based on a medieval portrayal of the archetypal Green Man. The *Green Knight* is a character who featured in the 14th-century poem, *Sir Gawain* and the *Green Knight*. Based on a man by the name of Bertilak de Hautdesert, who *Morgan Le Fey*, aka *Morgana, High Priestess* of the

Avalon mystery school, was said to have transformed into The Green Man.

This theme is congruent with the mid-Winter *Grail* rites presided over by the reigning *High Priestess*, who sought to awaken the *Oak King* aspect within men by beheading their egos.[47] In true Hollywood form, in this latest offering, the *High Priestess* is again (yawn!) portrayed as evil, rather than wise. She transforms a man into the *Green Knight*, not to empower his soul, but to scare another woman to death! Yet again, another *Grail* parable is perpetuated as a distortion, being repackaged and sold with special effects and gratuitous violence to the collective masculine. Fortunately, there are others acknowledging the true origins of *Christmas*. Check out *Annie Lennox's* version of *God Rest Ye Merry Gentlemen* where she leads people back to the *Green Man* in the video clip. Below is the story of *Gawain and the Green Knight* from the perspective of the sacred feminine.

Gawain and the Green Knight

The story opens on *Christmas* Day when *King Arthur* is holding court. The poem states, 'As he waits for an adventure to arrive, a *green knight* comes riding in.' The knight is not like other men. He has a magical appearance - his skin is green in color and his stature is grander than most. He is the ancient God of the nature realm. He is *Cern*, the *Green Man*, who is one with the *Earth Mother*, indicated by his appearance as part man/part oak, a tree considered the wisest in the land.

The stranger to the court declares a challenge to every man present. He invites any one of them who dares, to chop off his head, on the condition that in a year's time, they allow him to return the favor of beheading. The only one to accept the challenge is *Gawain, King Arthur's* nephew. He swings his sword and cuts the *Green Knight's* head clean off his shoulders. The *Green Knight* responds by picking up his head and to everyone's surprise, continues speaking from his severed head, reiterating the terms of their agreement. A year later, *Gawain* sets out to find the *Green Knight* to honor his word. *Gawain* ends up lost in the forest but is given refuge by *Sir Bertilak de Hautdesert* and his wife. Gawain is told to keep his wife company for three days and give to his host whatever he gains from her. On each of these three days, the host's wife is joined by the *High Priestess* of *Avalon, Morgana*. The attendance of the spiritual authority of the land as a witness indicates this is some kind of test of *Gawain's* character. On the first two days, the host's wife kisses *Gawain* on the cheek, and when *Gawain's* host returns at the day's end, *Gawain* kisses him on the cheek, faithfully conveying what had occurred in his absence. On the third day, the host's wife gives *Gawain* her green girdle to protect him from being slain by her husband. *Gawain* conceals this gift, offering his host three kisses instead.

When *Gawain* arrives at the green chapel the next day, he discovers the *Green Knight* is in fact his host, *Sir Bertilak de Hautdesert*. *Gawain* bows his head humbly, ready for the fall of his axe. The *Green Knight* swings his ax deliberately missing on his first two attempts to reward *Gawain* for his honesty on the first two days. On the third swing, he gently nicks *Gawain's* neck to remind him of the moment his integrity faltered due to his fear of potential consequences.

Off With His Head!

The painting from the original manuscript shows the *Green Knight* holding a severed head in his hand. This image represents the dominant ego-mind that he has defeated. This beheading of the male ego by the sacred feminine is the theme of both *The Holy Grail* rite and the parable, *Sir Gawain and the Green*

*Gawain and the Green Knight.
Artist Unknown*

Knight.[48] A tale which illustrates the meaning behind the ritual performed in *the Grail* knighting ceremony. In this ceremony, conducted during a man's first attendance at the mid-Winter *Holy Grail* rite, each new initiate would be invited to take a vow after correctly answering a riddle posed by the *High Priestess*. The initiate *Grail* knight would then kneel before her, bowing his head in submission. In honor of the parable of *Gawain*, the initiate would receive the touch of her sword on the neck as a symbolic beheading of his rational mind[49] with the sword of truth, *Excalibur*.

Kangra painting of Kali.
Artist Unknown

This is why it became a custom to behead one's enemy and return with it to prove the threat of the untamed male ego that wreaked havoc on the innocent was over. It's also why *Grail* legends featured a man's head being served on a platter, representing the severing of the destructive lower mind when not balanced with the wisdom of the heart.

Here we see the same symbolism in the Hindu tradition with images of the Dark Mother Goddess,

Kali Ma, shown holding the severed head of a man, while wearing the skulls of men whose ego she has slain while dancing on their graves.

The Accolade
by Edmund Blair Leighton

In *The Accolade* painted in 1908 by Edmund Blair Leighton, we see *Lady Guinevere* and *Sir Lancelot* enacting this ancient *Grail* ceremony. It may be significant that it is *Guinevere* and not *Morgana* performing this rite, as it was originally performed by the *High Priestess*, a representative of the *Earth Mother*. Perhaps this painting depicts how this rite was appropriated to reward allegiance to the ruler of the empire, the reigning monarch. Alternatively, this may be an acknowledgement that it was folklore no one could rule Wales without, the blessing of the first lady of Wales, *Gwenhwyfar*, who was said to exist 'so long as there was surf to pound against the rocky shore'. Renowned for her wisdom and judgment she was an agent of the Goddess.

The Dragon Woman

As stated earlier, *The Holy Grail* rite was a man's 'meeting with the dragon'. An expression synonymous with folktales that depicted brave men seeking fire-breathing dragons to prove their valor and win the hand of a fair maiden. These parables alluded to a young man's meeting with the power of the dragon; kundalini, the 'sacred fire' or bio-electricity of the Earth via a priestess who served as a conduit; *The Dragon Woman.* Today, the term, 'Dragon Woman' is a derogatory term used to describe powerful women who disempowered men find intimidating. Without understanding the function of a Dragon Woman, she's been misrepresented and ridiculed. One such portrayal is the character of the *Queen of Hearts* in the book, *Alice in Wonderland*. Here we see a woman with no redeeming features who shrieks, 'Off with his head' simply to amuse herself.

Pre-patriarchy, a 'Dragon Woman' referred to a woman who had accessed her 'dragon power' or 'serpent power' through being 'one with the Earth'. This refers to the inner *star fire*, known in Sanskrit as *kundalini*; the life force that lays dormant within the base of the spine until it is awakened through sacred initiation.

In Sumerian literature, *Ninkhursag* was celebrated as the *Serpent Lady*, the *Grail*/Dragon 'Queen of the Ring Lords'. Her womb became famous within *Grail*, Dragon, Fairy, and Ring culture....and was the inspiration for Tolkien's *Lord of the Rings* trilogy.[50]

A *Dragon Woman* was a senior *Magdalene* who had learned to draw upon the 'dragon lines', the energy meridians of the *Earth Mother*, to raise her 'dragon power' through her body and direct it in ceremony to activate spiritual awakening in others. To 'face the dragon' was to confront the face of the dark mother aspect of the Goddess who would call out the shadow of the aspirant; the aspects they were unaware of in themselves. Her presence would evoke a man's subconscious fear of the destroyer aspect of the feminine, so he could understand and transcend the power it had over him.

"Nothing in life is to be feared. It is only to be understood."

Marie Curie

Men were told to 'seek the dragon' to be considered worthy of union. If a man didn't confront his deepest fears about himself and recognize his destructive unconscious thoughts and behaviors, he would destroy his partner physically, emotionally or psychologically when she called out his shadow during her dark time of the month. Alternatively, he would avoid intimacy with the feminine and fear commitment. For without awareness of his shadow, he would remain a boy, like *Peter Pan* blaming others for his self-created drama.

The Roman patriarchs appropriated this custom by manufacturing a legend to suit their agenda. They introduced the figure of *Saint George*, the son of a Roman officer, who was a Roman soldier celebrated for slaying pagans, symbolized by the dragon, a symbol of the sacred feminine. His image was put on

Roman coins as an aspiration figure. To complete the inversion of truth, he was portrayed wearing the 'red cross', the symbol of the earlier *Grail* knights. Today if you search the meaning of the flag of England you'll see the symbolism attributed to the story of *Saint George*.

Saint George. Artist Unknown.

A similar tale created by the Roman Empire as propaganda to undermine the pre-Christian mystic tradition was that of *Saint Patrick*, credited with driving all serpents out of Ireland. The serpent being another symbol synonymous with the power of the sacred feminine. Fast forward to today, and men of legend are constantly portrayed slaying physical dragons, conveying the message; a hero proves his courage by destroying nature to face his fear of physical death. This is another inversion of *the Grail* tradition where a man who sought the dragon did battle humbly with the dragon within rather than slaughtering life to prove his might as a man. Today the mystic power of the sacred feminine is still portrayed as evil, with Hollywood continuing to perpetuate this prejudice...

"The most powerful witches are here amongst us. They're here

to destroy us. You must fight."

The Last Witch Hunter

Even in the modern interpretation of *The Hero's Journey*, we are taught that men must beware the potential enemy that is *Woman as Temptress*, suggesting a significant woman will try to convince the hero to abandon his quest. More often than not, it is a man's uninitiated friends who seek to entice him to deny the call to adventure. Like the saying, misery loves company...a lost boy doesn't have to question his own 'refusal of the call' if his friends join him - avoiding their fears by avoiding challenges through seeking distraction and escapism. Again this anchors an expectation of 'women as the enemy' or a distraction to a man's true purpose, rather than the catalyst for the hero's transformation.

The Yule Log and the 12 Days of Christmas

The saying, 'he was cut down in his prime' refers to *the Grail* custom of the *Yule log*. The *Yule log* represented the phallic God; the *Green Man*. For this purpose, a tree would be carefully selected for its grand size and permission requested from the tree dryad for its willing participation as a sacrifice for the annual rite. It was then ceremonially cut down and decorated as a Maypole; a phallic symbol of male fertility in the Spring before it was dried in preparation for *The Holy Grail*. There it burned for a total of 12 days as a source of light for the men to keep their spirits bright through their darkest night. Each day of this custom represented the 12 solar months encountered in *The Hero's Journey* to awaken the savior within so men would throw 12 offerings of gratitude into the sacred fire. These offerings represented the gifts they'd gained during their 12 stages of *The Hero's Journey*. Patriarchy commercialized this tradition with the song, *The 12 Days of Christmas*, which speaks of a man proving his love by buying his sweetheart 12 gifts. The burning of the Yule log offered a focus for deep contemplation on the need for endings while signifying the burning away of karma from the previous year. Interestingly, the ancient tradition of the sacred fire and the cycle of the *Oak King* and *Holly King* was absorbed into the Christian tradition with oak fires being burned at Midsummer up until Victorian times.[51]

In Europe, women would bake log cakes eaten at the *Yuletide* feast in honor of the tree spirit that sacrificed its life for the rite. Meanwhile, today, one can buy log cakes all year-round in supermarkets, and Maypoles are void of any sacred meaning. Yes, excited to attend the erecting of the Beltane Maypole in a Bavarian village in 2019, I was soon disheartened to glean it was merely an excuse for the men to drink beer in the morning while the women and children cheered their physical strength. The Maypole was reduced to a mere civic pillar displaying marketing plaques for local businesses.

What's In a Date?

December 25 became significant when the Roman Empire made it the first day of their 12 day *Christmas* festival. Why? Previously, December 25 was the day *The Holy Grail* rite ended and the festivities of *Yule* began in the northern hemisphere. It wasn't until the 4th century that the church of Rome started saying this was the time of *Jesus Christ* to win over their pagan populace. Many Christians would be surprised to learn that the church was the last to celebrate *Christmas*. They did this through Sunday school programs enticing children with sweets to celebrate the birth of *Jesus Christ*. This was also how the church embraced Halloween, which was originally a day to honor the ancestors and is now more about gore, horror and scavenging sweets. Before *Christmas* became synonymous with expensive gifts to prove one's love, December 25 was when the menfolk would return home from the forest to their loved ones who had kept a vigil of light and prayer with candles and carols to honor their bravery until their safe return. Homes would be decorated with dried slices of oranges and lemons reminiscent of the sun and the men would be welcomed with mulled wine to symbolize the *Graal* and baked goods. Women and children would celebrate the return of their husbands, fathers and sons, for embodying the 'good king' as noble knights who sought *the Grail*. This is why the tale of *Gawain and the Green Knight* opens on December 25, *Christmas* Day; when feasting began to celebrate the return of the *Green Man*. This is why the *Green Man* enters the court of *Arthur*, a *Grail* King and invites the men to meet him 'in the green chapel' the forest, in a year to face their fear of ego-beheading. This tale was a call to remember the ancient rite to ensure it was honored, despite the appropriation of *the Grail* rite into a Christ mass.

"Even the darkest night will end and the sun will rise"

Victor Hugo

CHAPTER 9

Seizing the Sword:
Excalibur and Magical Gifts

H aving passed the 'Supreme Ordeal' the hero is now bestowed with secret treasures long hidden from himself and the world. With these gifts he is invincible! But before we reveal the gifts that grant the hero secret powers, in this chapter we're going to examine our relationship with magic and the power of sacred ceremony.

Sighting a raven signals magic is afoot. Considered the totemic ally of the *Lady of Avalon*; the *High Priestess* of the mystery school most associated with *the Grail*, ravens are the bird of the *Underworld*, invoked for prophecy. Feared by the uninitiated as a harbinger of death, they're a carrion bird that picks the bones of those whose spirit has passed. So too, when we are willing to dissect the remnants of past choices, we awaken the spirit medicine of raven. This manifests as a shift in perception that gifts us 'eyes to see and ears to hear' the unseen world, which is symbolic. This is done through recognizing patterns and synchronistic messages from the Spirit world, so we can join the dots to see the big picture and better navigate the mystery of life. This awareness awakens the inner mystic who makes sense of the chaos and our own fateful tale so we can feel grateful for our trials, knowing they were necessary.

"Wear gratitude like a cloak and it will feed every corner of

your life."

Rumi

In this, the 9th stage of *The Hero's Journey: Seizing the Sword*, we rediscover the magical perspective we had as a child, before our 'loss of innocence' that saw us become increasingly cynical. This earlier time is when we were soul-dominant, relating unself-consciously to all life-forms, including those in the subtle realms. The return of this perspective is the reward we gain for surrendering ourselves to Highest Will during our darkest night. This is a gift more precious than anything money could buy. This is the gift of 'second sight' - the ability to perceive the inner meaning of what we experience in the outer world.

This is what awakens our supernatural skills, such as knowing if someone is lying, sensing what will work and what won't, intuiting trends before they happen and the ability to 'read between the lines' to glean the true significance of everything that transpires. This is when life becomes mythic, and we feel excited and inspired to be the central figure in our own epic adventure! We are liberated from the limited perception of the 3D *Muggle* world to the awareness of the multi-dimensional magical world that coexists, but is hidden to the uninitiated. This is why raven, the bird of the *Underworld* is synonymous with shapeshifters; those who can transform themselves.

In *the Grail* tradition, initiates would befriend the *Underworld* as 'The Special World' a place of possibility, potential and magic. Those who were uninitiated would fear it as the abyss where one experiences only loss and death. *The Special World* awakens the inner magi who consciously manifests their thoughts into reality by knowing when and how to seed their intentions in alignment with the natural cycles. In *the Grail* tradition, men would seed their intentions for the coming year in the first few days after the Winter Solstice. So, the descent to the *Underworld* was essential for men to not just awaken their inner hero but also to embody the strengths of the 4 phases of manhood, that correspond to the seasons.

This diagram shows how the male psyche develops as

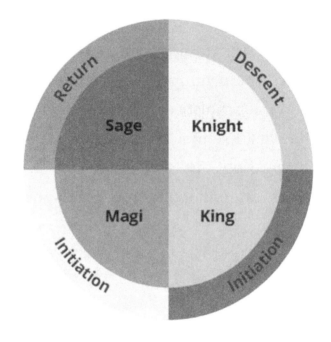

the hero completes each quadrant of *The Hero's Journey*. If a man lacks belief in himself, he will remain stuck as the knight experiencing a 'failure to launch' due to his fear of commitment. If he takes the conscious journey to descend and explore his wounds and perceived weaknesses, he will shift into the king phase. If he experiences the death of his ego, shattering his previous identity and worldview in 'The Supreme Ordeal' he will emerge as the magi. If he applies that awareness to navigate his way back to a state of complete trust, to serve all with the gifts gained, he will return victorious as the sage…one who has come full circle and returned to a state of innocence; trusting in Divine Will.

The Prodigal Son

This is what it means to return home as the *prodigal son*. During the Age of Empires, the concept of a *prodigal son* became associated with the triumphant return of a young man who had fought in a battle to achieve a great victory or won public acclaim. Usually, such feats were achieved through acts of daring and physical courage. What we don't usually associate with a *prodigal son* is a man whose questioning mind has led him into the internal abyss to experience crippling self-doubt, depression and social isolation to then emerge with a new perspective. This is the true meaning of the tale which *Yeshua* shared as part of his teachings and demonstrates the core teaching of *The Holy Grail* rite. That being, one has to become lost to find themselves. I see this tale as another *Grail* parable. See for yourself…

The Tale of The Prodigal Son

There was once a man with two sons. The older son stayed with his father to help run their estate, while the younger son requested his inheritance early and used the funds to travel to foreign lands. Being a youth, he spent the money indulging his ego; drinking, gambling and paying for prostitutes. When his money ran out, a famine struck the land, so he took a job as a swineherd to survive.

His living conditions were worse than those of the pigs he tended. This caused him to ponder the world he had left so long ago and see it in a new light. He recalled how well his father had treated his farmhands and his conscience urged him to swallow his pride and return home, asking his father for a job. After the long journey home, exhausted, he arrived at the front gate, unsure of how he'd be received.

Seeing him from a distance, his father rushed down the long dirt road at the bottom of the hill to embrace his son, kissing him and welcoming him home with tears in his eyes. His father called for a celebration, which his older son questioned, asking what his brother had done to deserve such a welcome, given his selfish actions. His father replied, "A celebration is fitting when a son returns from the dead".

This celebration is the true meaning of the origins of *Christmas, The Holy Grail*. It is to celebrate one who has safely returned from their perilous descent to the *Underworld*, exploring their dark side to return, a changed man after the humbling of their ego. In the Biblical version of this story, the focus is instead placed on the father's capacity to forgive his son. However, this casts the *prodigal son* as a sinner, shaming his choices that resulted in the loss of money rather than affirming what he found, which was far more valuable than material wealth.

The Magical Gifts Bestowed on the Prodigal Son

Let's now explore the specific treasures the hero receives when he has passed his 'Supreme Ordeal'. These are not material gifts, but special skills that assist him to be successful in every area of his life. Perhaps even more importantly, they enable his release from the inner torment of the *Underworld* so he may return to enjoy the *Everyday World* with a more mature, clear and solid sense of self. This is what it means to be a 'self-made man'. A term, Patriarchy associated with acquiring external status symbols as a measure of material success. The irony is, the treasures a man needs to secure his release from the darkness within are often the opposite of what he seeks. This is why it takes a guide to assist him to identify and value the inner gold he has overlooked as since these magical gifts are not tangible they are often dismissed as worthless, just as the immature masculine dismisses all things feminine as not worthy of his time, attention and energy.

Before I reveal the gifts men receive as they emerge from the labyrinth in *The Holy Grail* rite, I will share how they acquire them. Each gift represents the medicine of the raw elements that together comprise the creative power of the *Earth Mother*. This is why in order to acquire them; men must first become one with the *Earth Mother*.

The Wheel of Eight

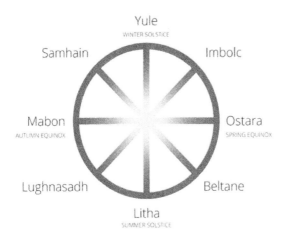

Earlier I mentioned men would wed themselves to the Earth by taking vows to serve the *Earth Mother* as part of their initial *Holy Grail* initiation. This prepared men for *Sacred Union* with a Grail initiated woman. *The Holy Grail* rite conducted at Winter Solstice was part of a series of initiations that aligned with the seasonal vortices, known as the *Wheel of Eight*. *The Wheel of Eight* was the initiation path to embody one's union with the *Earth Mother*, enacted by both singles and couples.

The *Wheel of Eight* was a descent journey of initiation that began at the Autumn Equinox, known in *Tantra* as 'the dark wedding'. This is the seasonal gate that heralds the start of 'the Fall' into the dark months. From this time, unhealed psycho-emotional wounds are more easily triggered due to the waning solar light. This influence can cast a shadow of doubt within our minds, resulting in darker moods. This is why *Grail* initiates were supported through the dark months with seasonal festivals that assisted them to identify, observe and integrate the lessons of the dark seasonal vortices of Autumn Equinox, *Samhain* (Halloween) and *Yule*, the Winter Solstice. Having this support promoted social sustainability through ceremonies that midwifed people through the lessons being evoked by the seasonal vortices. Lessons that directly impacted their relationships. These ceremonies helped people to embody the sacred balance needed to anchor 'Heaven on Earth'. They included ritual enactments of the seasonal myths which served as teaching parables. These festivities were later appropriated to create the Christian mystery plays for the Patriarchal holy days.

In the practice of the *Wheel of Eight*, couples would descend the seasonal wheel together as a path of shared personal growth. This involved an agreement to acknowledge their shadow traits as they surfaced on the understanding their partner would serve as a mirror and reflect/evoke what was unhealed in their psyche. This encouraged both parties to take responsibility for healing their wounds rather than project their rejected aspects onto their partner.

Without supportive structures like the *Wheel of Eight* to navigate relationships, we see modern couples struggling through the dark months, wrestling with their shadow and scapegoating their partners, destroying love and trust. In the ancient world, this practice supported the archetypes of the inner king/queen who reside in the heart and ensure love thrives. These are the aspects who are mature enough to face the shadow in themselves and help us accept ourselves and our partner, warts and all, instead of trading them in for a new model in search of perfection. Since nothing evokes one's wounds and unintegrated aspects like intimacy, men who dared enter the covenant of *Sacred Union* with a woman who embodied the Goddess were deified as mythic heroes and worshiped as Gods.

In ancient Greece, at the Autumn Equinox, *Grail* initiates would imbibe *Kykeon*, a ritual drink. This symbolized their willingness to drink the 'elixir of death' offered by the dark Goddess to become wise. This is where the saying, 'the land of milk and honey' originates, as this drink would take participants beyond the veil of death to the *Eleusinian Fields*. *Kykeon* was a herbal brew consisting of goat's milk and honey and psychotropic visioning plants.[52] Plants that expanded the consciousness of initiates, so when they watched the ritual plays performed in ceremony, the Gods and Goddesses, played by priests and priestesses in masks, came to life. This opened one's receptivity to receive direct transmissions to pierce their consciousness.

This type of ritual theater survives today in Bali, Indonesia where the locals imbibe hallucinogenic brews in ceremonies that aren't open to tourists. While it might seem pretty 'out there' from a 3D mindset to mix what mainstream society would perceive as church and drugs, it makes sense that without addressing our human need for ritual and altered states of consciousness to make sense of the mystery of life, people today risk their mental health by seeking this experience in secular ways. Like going to  rock concerts loaded up on cocktails of synthetic drugs comprised of toxic chemicals.

Similarly, *The Holy Grail* involved a sacred elixir - hence the image of the cup that's synonymous with *the Grail*. This was a mulled wine brewed with sacred herbs and the magical properties of the menses of the *High Priestess*. This was the original *Sangria*. It contained *Graal*, the holy blood of the womb of the *Magdalene* whose alchemical codes distilled her cyclic wisdom and would assist the initiate with an ego-death to awaken the codes of the mystic within, when imbibed with an open heart.

In the Celtic tradition, this ritual drink was known as *mead*, a honeyed wine of the Faery Queen. It was fed to Celtic kings to assist them in becoming Gods. Given we live in a time of phobias about the transmission of pathogens I had my menses made into a homeopathic essence in a laboratory specifically for use in ceremony. It contains no physical trace of my *Graal* but as a vibrational remedy is highly effective. In Mesopotamia the menses of a *High Priestess* was referred to as, 'gold of the Gods' and the 'vehicle of light' revered as the ultimate source of manifestation and the flow of eternal wisdom.[53] In the Tantric tradition, this custom of awakening an initiate via an energetic transmission of *Shakti*, meaning 'Goddess essence' was known as *Shaktipat*. In India, this was originally done by *Dakinis*; priestesses of the dark mother, *Kali Ma*. They would place a red dot of ochre signifying menses on the third eye of initiates. Patriarchy appropriated this symbolism of the *bindu* to identify a woman as the property of her husband. Today we see Westerners wearing *bindis* as a Boho fashion accessory with no idea it signifies a menstrual initiation into the mysteries. This rite was later appropriated by male gurus who touch the third eye of initiates to transmit *kundalini* energy. In the West we see a similar custom done by male pastors in evangelical Christian revival meetings, where parishioners appear to fall dead as they receive the blessing of the *Holy Spirit* with a touch to the forehead.

Understandably, ingesting menses may sound repugnant to a 3D Western mind, given the two thousand years of indoctrination we've had anchoring a perception of the holy blood of the womb as dirty and unmentionable. However, the ancients revered the alchemical properties of bodily fluids rather than perceiving their bodies as dirty. They understood the *Graal* is so full of life force it could be used as a miraculous healing elixir, like stem cells. Today scientists are discovering how powerful menses is, healing cuts in record time and reversing the effects of aging. This vitality is why the 'wise blood' was revered as the most precious substance on Earth, an elixir of youth, used for healing and sacred initiation.

The remnants of this custom we see in the *Tantric*, *Gnostic* and *Pagan* traditions. This is also why 'blood red' has long been considered a royal color associated with good fortune in many cultures, paired with gold, representing union with the Sun. China celebrates *Lunar New Year* with red decorations, and uses red in their homes and temples to bless them with vitality, fertility and abundance. This is also why all around the world, sacred objects and graves have been found stained with red ochre to imitate the sacred blood. This is also why women in the East decorate themselves with the red pigment of Henna and paint their toenails red. Traditionally this was done to embody the power of the Goddess in ceremonies, such as weddings.

In the West, the power of the feminine was diminished by dressing the bride in white, the color associated with innocence rather than the power of creative fertility. Similarly, the sacred custom of the *Henna Night* was diluted into the secular *Hen's night*, signifying one who is married off is no longer considered a 'spring chicken', but an 'old chook'. Without Our Holy Rites, we struggle to become whole.

Given how popular *the Grail* was prior to the dominion of the Roman Empire, the earlier mystic tradition had to be incorporated as the basis for the new religion to ensure any level of acceptance. With the true meaning distorted these sacred customs became an instrument of war, used to sever people from their ancestral cultural practices and identity. While the original *Grail* rites of passage empowered the individual, the patriarchal versions empowered the church's authority over the individual.

So instead of rites that marked one's entrance into adulthood by empowering one's identity as a man/woman with teachings to empower every facet of the masculine and feminine psyche and guidance to navigate the cycles, the church imposed their own 'coming of age' ceremonies. Such as *Holy Communion* undertaken by children, who swear allegiance to the religious institution of the empire. The Roman Catholic rite of *Holy Communion* is a direct appropriation of *The Holy Grail* rite once undertaken by 21 year old men; those who are old enough to make an informed choice. It is inspired by *the Grail* rite *Yeshua* re-enacted at *The Last Supper* before his crucifixion where he, *Mari* and his disciples drank from the *Graal* cup, renewing their vows to serve the Earth, come what may...knowing his arrest was imminent.

Two thousand years later, agents of the Roman Catholic church still teach children to mark the cross of torture on their bodies. This custom constitutes an energetic branding and dedication of one's life force to power the cult of Rome. It does this by marking and affirming one's energy field to the symbol of the Church of Rome, a crucifixion cross, a symbol of sufferance. The repetition of this act affirms their body is owned by the Roman cult. Similarly, wearing the patriarchal distortion of the cross as a tattoo or jewelry is also a form of branding oneself, just as a rancher brands a herd of animals as their property. People are now so oblivious to this tactic they allow themselves to be branded by corporations, wearing logos to declare their allegiance.

This ritual abuse perpetrated on unsuspecting congregations is due to the fear of magic instilled by the church of Rome. Their superstitious fear campaigns resulted in a 'dumbing down' of the populace regarding the conscious use of energy. Where Mysticism had previously empowered people to use energy wisely, the church persecuted those who had knowledge of the mystic arts, so they could wield power through their knowledge of the occult. As a result, today most people are unaware they are complicit in charging up magical sigils that invoke power for those who use and abuse them.

This is because the mark of the cross mimics the *Mark of Cain* referred to in the *Bible* as a symbol of protection the patriarchal Father God placed on the forehead of *Cain*. *Cain* was reportedly the older son of *Adam* and *Eve* who killed his brother, *Abel*. This is an appropriation of the mark of the *Red Cross* made on the foreheads of the men who entered into the sacrament of matrimony with the *Earth Mother* during *The Holy Grail* rite. Originally this mark was made with the *Graal*, the holy blood of the Mother, affording a *Grail* knight her protection in exchange for his pledge to defend and uphold the sacredness of all life.

"The Sumerian Gra-al, which biblical tradition calls the Mark of Cain, was an emblem dignified as the Cup of the Waters, or the Rosi-Crucis (the Dew Cup), and it was identified in all records (including those of Egypt, Phoenicia and the Hebrew annals) as being an upright, centered red cross within a circle. Throughout the ages it was developed and embellished, but it has always remained essentially the same and is recognized as being the original symbol of the Holy Grail."[54]

Interestingly, the symbol of the even *red cross* is today synonymous with the aid agency, the *Red Cross*. While publicly they do acts of philanthropy, like all cabal entities this may well serve as a cover for covert activities. For this association has married the sacred symbol of *the Grail*, the *Red Cross* indicating union with the *Earth Mother* to one of sacrificial bloodshed synonymous with war and the taking of blood. I find it curious, the *Red Cross* website directs people to report those who use the symbol of the *Red Cross*.

The secret society, the Freemasons, also appropriated and distorted *The Holy Grail*. Initiates undertaking the 33rd degree are asked to drink from a human skull and pledge their total allegiance to the cult under threat of their own sacrifice by citing this oath.

"May this wine I now drink become a deadly poison to me…should I ever knowingly or willfully violate my oath."(55)

Here again we see the need for men to swear their allegiance to something greater than themselves in order to find meaning and purpose. Without *the Grail* fulfilling this intrinsic need, dark impersonations inevitably result, disempowering those who surrender their autonomy to that which isn't pure of heart.

Similarly, today we see children, proud citizens and soldiers swearing their allegiance to their nation's flag; the heraldry of the empire that governs them. Under closer scrutiny, by searching entries on securities commissions, one can discover the true identity of their nation is in fact, a private corporation parading as a public institution so swearing allegiance to a nation's flag is another way of charging up an emblem of the ruling elite - another impersonation of the allegiance once sworn to *the Grail*.

Flag of England

The flag of England bore the red cross of *the Grail* on a white background. This represented the union of *Mother Earth* and *Father Sky*. Where once people pledged their heart to serve a noble ideal, now they instead unwittingly energetically charge something

Union Jack; Flag of the British Empire

far less noble. Below you can see how this ancient emblem was assimilated into the Union Jack, the heraldry of the British Empire.

The Covenant of Holy Matrimony

Today when we speak of *Matrimony* it's assumed we're referring to a marriage between two consenting adults. However, as previously mentioned, *Holy Matrimony* was a *Grail* rite that was appropriated with its meaning distorted. The Latin root, *matri* means 'mother' and *mony* refers to 'a status, role or function', such as a ceremony. So, as the name suggests, *Holy Matrimony* was entered into by those willing to honor the sacred rites of the Mother.

The rites of the Mother promoted growth, both personal growth and the growth of the clan. The focus of these rites was to prepare people to enter into *Sacred Union* as a container for loving creation, be that physical children or creative acts inspired by love. This is why, upon reaching the marrying age of 21, men sought *the Grail* by preparing their psyche with a marriage to the *Earth Mother*. They entered into this sacred covenant with the Earth by pledging their allegiance to serve her. This act wedded them to the land. In the Polynesian tradition, descended from ancient Lemuria, where people lived harmoniously with the Earth, young men are taught to perform *Hakas*. To the uninitiated who see the New Zealand rugby team perform a *Haka* before a match, this looks like a display of male power intended to intimidate the opposition, and perhaps to those who perform it without understanding its true power, it is. However, when done with the right intent for a purpose more significant than winning a ball game, the *Haka* is a sacred warrior dance that summons the power of the Earth by re-stating one's commitment to serve her. Here is one *Haka* translated from the Maori people of New Zealand known in their mother tongue as *Aotearoa* meaning 'Land of the long white cloud'.

"We are the children of Aotearoa.
We stand proud,
We stand strong,
We seek the path to success.
We carry our legacy for future generations, We are the land,
The land is us, here we belong,
We will rise to the challenge. Always."

The most significant line in that *Haka* is, *We are the land*. This signifies the sacred covenant of *Sacred Union* has been entered into with the *Earth Mother*. Like many women, watching the *Haka* moves me to tears. Not as a display in a sports arena, but when enacted to mark a milestone. Such as the YouTube videos where it's performed at the airport to welcome kin home or at weddings as a declaration to the bride that the groom will defend and protect all that is sacred. It moves me, as I suspect it moves the brides to tears, as it represents the deepest wish of the feminine. Having spent my formative years as a child in New Zealand, I was lucky enough to return 40 years after I left suddenly as a 7-year-old and be gifted the opportunity to witness 100+ high school students; male and female, black and white, perform a *Haka* with such conviction and heart it brought me undone. What a welcome home!

Who Does the Grail Serve?

In the film, *What Women Want*, starring Helen Hunt and Mel Gibson they claim Freud died at age 83 plagued by the age-old question, 'What do women want?' This is a riddle as synonymous with *the Grail* as the question, 'Who does *the Grail* serve?' Why? These were the questions men who sought *the Grail* would have to answer correctly to be honored as a *Grail* knight. If not answered correctly, they would not be offered *the Grail* chalice during the rite of *Holy Matrimony*. If a youth accepted the invitation to drink from the symbolic 'cup of death' this act would be pledge his allegiance to serve the *Earth Mother*. As *the Grail* chalice was the sacred cup that represented her creative power to bring forth life that was within the womb of all women. Such an act signified a man's willingness to surrender his ego to serve the life-giving essence of the feminine. If he could answer her riddles and drink from her cup he earned the right to invoke her power, as needed. In order to invoke her power, he first had to understand how to honor her creative elements. This instruction was done over four days. One day to honor each of the four directions that comprise her body and power to create. When a man knows how to wield this creative power, he no longer feels inferior to the power women have to create life in their wombs.

The Circle of Life

Learning to honor the four directions is what indigenous cultures call the shamanic teachings of the Circle of Life. The sacred cross of the *Earth Mother* is known by many names; the *Medicine Wheel* to the native Americans, the *Creation Circle* to Indigenous

Australians, *Wotan's Cross* to the Norse, and *The Pentagram* to the Celts. While this sacred knowledge has been awakening since the Aquarian cusp in the 1960's, many are surprisingly unaware that the power of the circle must be invoked in accordance with the magnetic spin of one's hemisphere. Without this understanding, no real creative power is invoked or raised. In other words, if you're in Australia you can't invoke the elements in the same order as someone in the UK or US. I explain this in more detail in my book, *Goddess Wisdom Made Easy* listed in the resources section.

In the rite of *The Holy Grail*, men would spiral inwards prior to the Winter Solstice by reflecting on what they needed to release to each of the 4 directions. The first 4 days of *The Holy Grail* rite focused on acknowledging the ways one had dishonored each element. This would incrementally humble the ego, preparing the men to surrender to the fifth element of Ether (Spirit) on the day of the Solstice.

When a man seeks to embody all the elements positively, deferring to the *Earth Mother* as his teacher, he is liberated from looking to his partner for direction. This frees a man from the unconscious need for a mother surrogate. For a man to truly individuate from his mother and not seek mothering in his partnerships, he needs to awaken all of his feminine gifts; those awakened in *The Holy Grail* rite. This is what empowers men to function well autonomously, without needing a woman to perform feminine functions on their behalf, such as processing their thoughts and feelings. The degree to which a man develops these gifts determines how well he weathers the dark months; the feminine half of the year.

After the deconstruction of 'the year that was' in the first 4 days of *The Holy Grail* rite, the men were ready to surrender to *Great Mystery*, the void of pure potential on the Winter Solstice. They would then spiral out from their Winter chrysalis like a fern, by honoring each of the four directions with intentions for the coming year. The native American equivalent of this ceremony is the *Act of Power*. In this ceremony one fashions death arrows that represent what they're releasing to the ceremonial fire, before creating life arrows that they bind prayer bundles to, representing their intentions for the coming year. The patriarchal religions outlawed these sacred Earth teachings, preaching that these traditions and any other form of sacred expression was the work of the Devil. Without this wisdom it's little wonder people have struggled to walk in balance and create sustainable lives.

The act of wedding the Earth through practical application awakens the archetype of *Cernunnos*, the *Green Man*. *Cernunnos* is a custodian of Eden, the Earthly Garden of the mother. He is a demi-God, a universal entity who resides in the macrocosm of the collective and within the psyche of every individual, regardless of their physical gender. He is an aspect who is returning after he was lost during the Industrial Age. He is the embodiment of a man who understands the cycles and seeks to live in alignment with them. He does this by honoring the lessons of each element evoked by our journey around the Seasons.

By learning how to express each element creatively, rather than destructively, each *Grail* initiate could set clear intentions to ensure he walked in right relationship with each of the elemental forces in the coming year. This humility was the key to invoking their power and guidance as needed. This was done through surrendering one's body as a vessel to wield energy in service to the greater good. Only through the act of surrender could one awaken the magical gifts of the feminine.

The Magical Gifts Bestowed on The Prodigal Son

Just as the 7 dwarves in *Snow White* descend to find the precious gems found within the darkness of the Earth, *Grail* knights were encouraged to mine the depths of their psyche to find the inner riches of their soul. Without *the Grail*, many modern men (and masculine-dominant women) compensate by seeking external riches. Whereas *Grail* initiates, receive magical gifts when they harness the power of each element, like a character in a video game who collects tokens when they master a level of skill.

These magical gifts, and the steps to attain them are encoded in the suits of the Tarot that represent the 4 Earthly elements. Unlike many video games that reward killing as an achievement, the magical gifts outlined below are rewarded to the degree one has attained levels of self-mastery over their ego.

Air: The Sword of Excalibur

The magical sword of truth, *Excalibur*, is shown as the first card in the Tarot's Suit of Swords, the Ace. In divination, this card signifies growth on the mental plane via new paradigms of thought that pierce old illusory beliefs that have limited our perception. During patriarchy, a sword was a motif synonymous with war, not higher thinking. Why? Men were taught to brandish a broadsword to slay their enemies as a soldier; a pawn in the Empire's battles, rather than take up the fight with the enemy within.

Pre-patriarchy, a sacred warrior would turn his attention inward to battle his lower mind that anticipates conflict with all that is unknown; foreign. This is how war is perpetuated, from ignorance, so a sacred warrior was taught to question his own thinking, so as to not create unnecessary conflict with others.

The element of Air corresponds to the mental plane and the lessons we encounter in the realm of thought. Air is what carries thought forms around the planet and via the wind, Wi-Fi and our spoken word. All change starts with a single thought, so our thoughts are the seeds that manifest as our reality, like a dandelion being blown to the winds. If we operate on autopilot, never questioning our beliefs, we unconsciously create a reality according to what we were taught to expect. Whereas the more we observe our thoughts and question our beliefs, the more we consciously manifest our soul's desires.

If we haven't individuated from our childhood conditioning, our mind is not our own, so it is more easily clouded by the influence of others. This can result in forming judgments without due consideration. This results in cynicism; a closed mind. This inhibits us from discerning truth from illusion. *Excalibur* symbolizes the inner 'sword of truth' that we must learn to develop to know our truth to avoid getting hooked into a battle of wits and wills, trying to impose our truth on others.

When we struggle with clarity of mind, we lack the single focus needed to actualize our ideas. *Excalibur*, originally known as *Caliburn*[56] was fashioned by *Morgana*, the *High Priestess* of *Avalon*, and said to have magical properties. It was famously gifted to *King Arthur* to ensure he never lost a battle. *Excalibur* is depicted as being encrusted with precious gems, signifying the colored energy centers within the spinal cord that, when activated, open a channel from our crown to our heart so we can receive intuitive messages at the speed of light from the quantum field of infinite intelligence. This ability is why ancient mystics and saints were depicted in art with halos. The light around their head indicated their ability to access the 'mind of God'. This enabled one to know in an instant whether something was true or false. This is why one who possessed the protection of *Excalibur* would never lose a battle, as they would be divinely guided by higher truth. This is the blessing bestowed on the bearer of the sacred sword.

Excalibur represents the awakening of intuition, a feminine gift able to be accessed by both men and women who develop the ability to be receptive. This enables one to walk the middle path of peace, known as *Sushumna* in the Yogic tradition, without polarizing into mental constructs of right and wrong that form limiting judgments and prevent one from true learning. When our mind is balanced, we're able to see both sides of an issue, so we can resolve conflict instead of instigating it.

Meanwhile, one who is ego-dominant is so filled with preconceived ideas, asserting what they know, they are not receptive to receiving flashes of insight. Whereas those who awaken their intuition have learned how to harness their lower mind, rather than be enslaved to its incessant chatter and need for stimulus. We are enslaved to the lower mind when we attach to our rational thoughts as our identity. When we develop the intuitive witness, who observes our internal dialogue, we can discern the inner voice of the lower mind from transmissions from higher intelligence, as each has a distinctly different frequency, like AM talk radio compared with FM.

In-tuition is the ability to access guidance from the *guru*, meaning 'teacher within'. We do this by attuning our attention within and asking a question of the Universe and noticing, with a sense of curiosity, the answer we receive internally as a knowing. Like the saying, 'Ask and it is given'. Since intuition is a subtle sense, it's easier to notice this gentle knowing within our heart when we've learned to still our rational mind as the mind's thoughts are louder and more demanding, like a child. Intuition is like a muscle. The more we seek to utilize this ability, the stronger it gets. Eventually, it becomes second nature to notice our initial intuitive response to everything we experience. This makes it much easier to make choices based on *gnosis*; inner knowing. This is a much more reliable guidance system than rationally weighing up the facts as 'pro's and con's'. Why? The higher mind has access to the big picture as intuition comes from the ultimate supercomputer; the quantum field of divine intelligence. Whereas, our rational mind has a limited perspective based only on what it knows.

Since intuitive thought travels at the speed of light; 670,616,629 mph, it's a much faster navigation tool! While intuition has become a buzzword amongst ethical entrepreneurs, *Psychology Today* dismisses it as 'the ability to notice patterns'.[57] This indicates the inability of the rational mind to grasp intuition without a direct experience of it.

Fire: The Tree of Life

The *Tree of Life* is a motif we see in every philosophical tradition around the world; the Celtic *Tree of Life*

depicted its branches and roots forming a full circle. Known as *Yggdrasil*, the *World Tree* in the Norse tradition and the *Shekinah*, the sacred feminine principle in the Hebraic tradition that formed the basis for the *Kabbalistic Tree* it was also known in Hinduism as 'the chakra system'. More recently the *Tree of Life* has been portrayed as the 'Mother Tree' in the film, *Avatar*. The *Tree of Life*, like *Excalibur*, is internal. When activated within our energy system, it connects the three inner worlds of consciousness. Those three worlds are:

- ❖ The *Upper World* of conscious awareness, where we perceive reality from a mythic, archetypal and symbolic perspective to identify our *lessons*.
- ❖ The *Everyday World*, where we learn through the consequences of our choices and actions.
- ❖ The *Underworld*, the place of our subconscious, where we store our deeply rooted beliefs.

We learn to climb this inner tree by awakening the energy centers within that act as vortices of perception, known as 'the eyes of God'.

A seeker who journeys deep into their subconscious to explore the roots of their everyday behavior awakens the inner *Tree of Life*. This inner gardening work prepares the soil for planting new seeds of awareness as it frees up latent energy that's stagnant with unprocessed thoughts and experiences. This enables one to access a back-up supply of life force known as *Shakti*, *kundalini* or 'Serpent/Dragon Power' the essence of the Goddess. Only one who has journeyed to the depths and become one with the *Earth Mother* will access her sacred creative fire.

This is why *Grail*-initiated men wore stag antlers during the Spring rites of *Beltane*. The antlers of the stag resemble the branches of the *Tree of Life*. Just as a tree's branches only grow as tall as their roots go deep, a man was considered only capable of greatness if he had invested time and energy in deepening his foundations. The wearing of antlers signified a man was a conduit for the energy of the sacred masculine, one who would do no harm, as he shed his antlers each year to mature and grow wise, like the *Stag King*. This is why in the tale of *Gawain and the Green Knight*, the *Green Knight* resembles a tree and he asks *Gawain* to meet him in the forest, the landscape of the Earthy feminine, where the stag roams free. So too, the Celtic,

European and Scandinavian forests were once synonymous with *the Grail*...hence the folklore of wise women residing in the forest who practiced herb lore and divination and assisted those who braved the wild places, both internally and externally. With the advent of Patriarchy, storytellers like *The Brothers Grimm* portrayed wise women who lived in the forest as evil hags who stole and ate children, anchoring cultural misogyny; the fear of the feminine in the very young.

In the Tarot, the *Tree of Life* is depicted in the Ace of

Wands, which shows a branch, budding with new life. A branch signifies a magic wand, meaning one who is plugged into 'The Force' within the Earth like a tree, has the power to create. When we activate the energy centers that comprise the inner *Tree of Life* we appear lit up like a *'Christmas* tree' as we

367

possess the charisma that inspires people to co-create with us. This is the light of true leadership.

The '*Christmas* tree' is an appropriation of the *Yuletide* 'evergreen tree' a pine tree celebrated for retaining its life force year round when deciduous trees lose their leaves. It was a reminder the inner *Tree of Life* was ever-present and eternal, despite the demise of the outer world during the dark months. So too, those who have awakened the inner *Tree of Life* are connected to the light above and below, so they find times of chaos and transition easier than others.

Traditionally the *Yule* 'evergreen tree' would be decorated with ribbons tied to the tree as prayers, candles, representing the light of Spirit and apples, the fruit of wisdom, sacred to the Goddess. The 'evergreen tree' was a symbol of hope during mid-Winter when everything was dark, including our temperament. Today's '*Christmas* tree' features artificial lights and factory-made decorations, and is even erected mid-Summer in the Southern hemisphere!

How did this happen? Monkey see, monkey do! Just as *Royal Doulton* devised a marketing strategy where they gifted sets of fine bone china to royal families on the understanding the higher classes would buy their product to emulate the royals and the middle and lower classes would collect one piece at a time to emulate the upper classes…when Queen Victoria was shown standing next to a 'Christmas tree' within a year, most of the US followed suit. In 1843 Charles Dickens' book, *A Christmas Carol*, made the concept of a 'Christmas tree' irresistible to families. In 1897 this custom migrated to the US as Charles Dickens packed theaters reading his story aloud. By 1890 all states voted to make *Christmas* a legal holiday.

Today, the only real function of the 'Christmas Tree' is somewhere to place material gifts. Whereas, in the ancient world, the *Tree of Life* gifted one the everlasting gifts of hindsight, foresight and clear sight in the present to create a good fate. This came with the ability to traverse the inner 3 worlds and glean the past, present and future simultaneously like the crone Goddess who is shown with the 3 faces of maiden, mother and crone. The ghost of past, present and future in the tale, *A Christmas Carol* by Charles Dickens was perhaps an attempt to recapture this original meaning. We see this echoed in the film, *It's a Wonderful Life*; which sees a man mid-Winter struggling with suicidal ideations, reach out to a higher power, fearing his life is of no value. This 1945 cinematic classic highlights multiple *Grail* themes examining the value of our choices, legacy and the spirit of true community. Themes that speak so strongly that many watch this film every year as a Xmas tradition.

Water: The Cup of Compassion

The chalice is the most well-known symbol of *the Grail*. It has multiple meanings. As previously discussed, *the Grail* cup is symbolic of the womb that distills the wisdom of the cycles and offers an initiation to meet the hidden aspects within the psyche. It also symbolizes

370

the cup within the heart that 'runneth over', depicted in the Tarot's *Ace of Cups*.

This is the cup of eternal love, the wellspring of self-love we discover when we surrender our devotional heart to the Divine. Drinking from this cup shifts our perception; how we see ourselves, others and the world around us - from the critical mind to the compassionate heart. This enables us to see and appreciate the inherent perfection and blessing in everything. This is how we heal self-loathing, by cultivating self-acceptance, so it blossoms into self-appreciation and eventually, self-love. We experience a state of self-love when we see ourselves as a reflection of the Divine.

Only through cultivating self-love can we develop the capacity to truly love others. This is why initiates of *the Grail* would be encouraged to connect with their 'feeling function' to access the will of the heart. Patriarchy conditioned men to shut down their feelings. This led to a betrayal of the heart, causing suffering and disempowerment. Whereas when we're guided by our heart's conscience, we serve Divine Will. Then we live as a true sovereign, bowing to the heart as our highest authority instead of external authority figures. This affords us self-respect as we make self-honoring choices, speaking up as an advocate on our own behalf to ensure others treat us honorably. It is self-love that motivates us to set appropriate boundaries with those who demonstrate they lack the awareness to treat us in a loving way.

One who honors the element of water takes time to reflect and become wise, knowing this enhances our capacity for love. To access the wisdom of the heart, a man must learn to revere his sacred tears during his darkest days of Winter, just as a woman dissolves emotionally during the darkest time of her cycle. When we lack wisdom, due to limited self-awareness, we seek others to process our inner landscape for us, as a mother would help a child, rather than doing the work ourselves. That isn't to say, one shouldn't seek a mystic guide to assist them in their process. In fact, those who do are less likely to unconsciously expect their partners and female friends to fulfill this function for them.

The more we reflect on the nature of our wounds, the more we develop compassion for ourselves and those who inflicted our wounds, on the understanding all wounds are inflicted by the wounded. When our heart is full of compassion for the suffering of others, we can forgive those who have trespassed against us and keep our heart open.

When we avoid reflecting on our past hurts, we close the heart to avoid more pain and become miserly towards ourselves and others. When we master the realm of feeling and emotions, we find a balance between giving and receiving love, rather than swinging between over-giving to win love and approval, then retracting into a state of withholding love to punish those who haven't fulfilled our ego's expectations. Someone who awakens the 'cup that runneth over' is free from needing others to fill their cup, so they feel like an empowered adult, not a disempowered child in relationships.

Earth: The Cauldron of Plenty

This is the cornucopia of abundance that symbolizes the limitless potential of the cosmic womb at the Galactic center. We each have equal access to, if we know how to honor the universal laws of creation. Abundance is ensured through understanding and aligning our intentions and actions with the ebb and flow of the natural cycles.

This means understanding and honoring the reason for every season. For men, that means honoring the need to lay fallow in Winter, the season of the Earth element to go deep and still to contemplate one's harvest and future intentions...just as an initiated woman does during her menses. This ensures the time and space needed to be accountable for how our thoughts, words and actions have resulted in our harvest, so we don't seek to blame others and avoid learning necessary lessons.

A man who tends all he seeks to grow with an understanding of the natural cycles will grow his wealth by recognizing the importance of aligning one's actions with divine timing. For instance, *Grail*-initiated women know how to charge intentions during the most fertile lunar phase and release what they no longer need during the moon's waning phase. So too, men initiated into *the Grail* learn how to release what they've outgrown to make the space needed to seed clear intent. Just as a woman's womb releases an egg each month when it isn't fertilized, and her life-giving blood can be given back to the Earth as nourishment for crops, the lesson we must learn to honor the element of Earth is to only take what we need and give away what we don't, as sharing is what promotes the flow of abundance.

When a man learns to release all he doesn't need and only take what he does, he attracts what he needs, when he needs it. If he doesn't learn to release, for fear of not having his needs met, he'll hoard, affirming a lack of trust in divine providence. This keeps him in a mindset of lack, regardless of how much he has. Such a fearful mindset subconsciously drives one to compulsively take more, for fear of not having enough…or make more, for fear of not being enough.

The more we bless what we have, with gratitude, the more we attract all we need with grace and serendipity. It is this trust in the process that manifests as timely miracles. The more we experience such occurrences, the more we trust the process and this lessens a tendency to hoard. Consciously learning how to live in right relationship with the 5 elements of the *Earth Mother* is what grants someone 'common sense' and the ability to meet their material needs.

The concept of the *Cauldron of Plenty* features in the ancient myths of the sacred feminine. The crone

Goddess known as *Ceridwen*, to the Celts and *Hecate*, to the Greeks would place in her cauldron all that was surrendered to her mid-Winter, so it could be returned in the Spring in a

new form...that which was needed to support new growth. Hence, the *Cup of Anwan* (*Avalon*) was considered the 'cup of abundance and fertility'.

The *Cauldron of Plenty* also referred to the cup that *the Grail* bard, *Taliesin* sought. He discovered it contained a herbal remedy with an unforgettable taste, suggesting the blood of the womb, said to be his first taste of knowledge. The *Cauldron* or *Cup of Plenty* also featured in the Irish myth of *Dagda*, who later featured in the *Asterix comics* as the provider of copious amounts of food. The food from her cauldron was said to 'differentiate the brave from the cowards', with magnificent strength granted to the brave. Again, this is a reference to those who felt too 'faint of heart' to ingest the alchemical power of menses. Patriarchy distorted the *Cauldron of Plenty* into a sinister pot where evil sorceresses would brew poisons to exact revenge and assert personal power in unethical ways.

The Ace of Pentacles indicates prosperity comes through mastering one's lessons on the physical plane of existence.

Here we see a pentagram depicted as a gold coin. A pentacle is the 5-pointed star within a circle which distills the power of the 5 elements increasing their value. In divination, this card can portend a financial windfall as an external confirmation of the riches one has found within. Those who have

not taken the journey to discover and appreciate their latent gifts are more prone to overworking and undervaluing their efforts, like a slave working for a master. A pentacle represents the Earthly wisdom of the sacred feminine. Such knowledge ensures justice to oneself and others, hence this symbol was appropriated as a Sheriff's badge to enforce the laws of men. Ironically, when a man observes the laws of nature, he can live as a sovereign without any need for external laws to be imposed or enforced. The lesson of the suit of pentacles is that those who value their time and energy see themselves as a good investment, so they invest time and energy to develop their ideas and passions. Through diligent effort, they can offer their gifts as an exchange to fulfill their material needs. Those who lack self-worth never take the risk on themselves and never fulfill their potential in the world. They are the ones who discourage others from following their dreams, due to their own fears.

Monkey Magic

Mastering the lessons of the 4 elements to transcend the limitations of the 'monkey mind' to become like a God is a theme in Eastern religions. Such as the tale of the Chinese 'Monkey King' who soaked up the power of the *Earth Mother* before being born from a stone egg, whereupon he bowed to the 4 corners of the Earth and set off on an adventure to find immortality to heal his fear of death. This was the inspiration for the 16th-century novel that the hit children's TV show *Monkey*, was based on. Similarly in the Hindu tradition, they have *Hanuman*, the monkey who became a God through an act of complete surrender to Divine Will. This surrendering of the ego, the purpose of *The Holy*

Grail rite, signals one is ready to be trusted with divine power through the activation of their magical gifts and their genius; their soul talents. From this moment of total surrender, one's path becomes clear. This is when we receive a sacred mission to serve the greater good. This realization of our true purpose comes only after we have proven our motives are pure. Without *the Grail* to tame the ego and awaken the gifts of the World Soul, we have been living on *Planet of the Apes.* Our challenge now is to make the shift into the heart so we may collectively fulfill our Divine potential.

CHAPTER 10

The Return:
The Hunt for the Unicorn

Having made the shift from *Muggle* to magical, the hero must now confront his fear of being persecuted for being different. He must face the same prejudice he once held. This is when one is faced with a choice: whether to stay in the 'Special World', where one has received initiation, or start the road back to their place of origin, or a new destination to implement lessons learned. Due to the very real threat of persecution, it's understandable many seekers choose to stay in the 'Special World' rather than make the journey home.

Many avoid the rejection of their clan unconsciously, like Western expats who find life in the East more accepting of feminine traits than in the West. Others do this consciously, renouncing the material world and living in an ashram or monastery, as it's much easier to live an unconventional life when living in an environment that supports it. It is far harder to maintain a commitment to honor one's heart in a metropolis that rewards the ego and punishes the soul. However, if one is to complete the archetypal *Hero's Journey* by returning full circle, they must confront these fears and challenges to humbly serve the greater good, by assisting others to acknowledge and honor the needs of their Soul in an ego-dominant world. In the *12 Labors of Hercules* this is referred to as 'mucking out the group stables'…helping others deal with their shit. By understanding the origin of their fears, one is able to feel compassion, rather than fear them. In this chapter we'll be unpacking the origins of fear that result in prejudice and persecution of those who appear different because they embody the traits of the mystic feminine.

"Quests may not simply be abandoned; prophecies may not be left to rot like unpicked fruit; unicorns may go unrescued for a very long time, but not forever. The happy ending cannot come

in the middle of the story."

Peter S. Beagle

If your soul's calling is to live out your days in an ashram I'm not suggesting there isn't great merit in dedicating one's life to prayer. However it's important to be honest about our motivations; conscious and unconscious. If our choice to not return is underpinned by a fear of 'not fitting in' or being persecuted, that is not reason enough to stay, to avoid facing one's fears. However, such fear is not unfounded, as the road back is not without its dangers.

One who is a carrier of sacred knowledge is in many ways, 'a marked man' someone with a target sign on their back. This is because their insights pose a threat to the status quo. Having undergone a significant personal transformation, they cannot simply blend in with the crowd due to their unconventional outlook and behavior. The challenge is therefore to be proactive and offer ideas as a voice for innovation and leadership or play small to stay safe, and inevitably be scapegoated and persecuted as an outsider. It's interesting to note that the two symbols used to mark a target in our modern culture are sacred symbols signifying allegiance with the *Earth Mother*...

Astrological Glyph for Earth   Pistol Target

The Grail sign of the 'even cross' within a circle is the target symbol one sees when staring down the barrel of a gun. The other symbol is the archery target symbol that consists of three concentric circles. This symbol appears on burial sites throughout the Celtic lands honoring those who served as

Archery Symbol

guardians of the Earth, in life and death. It's also the symbol for the *Earth Mother*, Gaia in the Australian Indigenous culture.

The Persecution of the Sacred

People around the world have long been persecuted for being different by those who fear change. Why? The herd seeks the protection of the group and the group bonds through their common fears so appealing to the lowest common denominator is an easy way to manipulate a mob. The more afraid the group mind is, the more they'll seek a scapegoat to blame and punish, rather than confront their fears. This is why those who seek to oppress the herd lead the vilification of those they deem a threat and feel threatened by people who are soul dominant. Why? Soul-dominant folk only acknowledge the authority of *Infinite Intelligence* and *Universal Laws*, so no amount of ego intimidation or coercion will compromise their allegiance, making them impossible to rule through fear and intimidation. As stated earlier, since our beliefs and values are what motivate our behavior, it is an old tactic of tyrants to incite an angry mob to scapegoat those of a different faith or spiritual outlook. This is why anyone who possessed knowledge of the true *Grail* was persecuted.

The British Coat of Arms

In 2013 when preparing for my first *Grail* speaking tour I noticed the unicorn was portrayed in chains on the *British Coat of Arms* so I 'Googled' why. The answer was, 'According to legend a free unicorn was considered a very dangerous beast; therefore, the heraldic unicorn is chained'[58] There we have it, in plain sight. The empire seeks to enslave the unicorn because they fear the power of the unicorn. In *the Grail* tradition, the unicorn represented the *Sacred King*, one who had been initiated into *the Grail* and sworn his allegiance to serve the Earth and her people…not the empire.

Here we see in the *British Empire's Coat of Arms*, the 'Earthly King of the land' depicted as the lion, who rules the animal kingdom free, while the unicorn, representing the spiritual power of the *Sacred King*, is bound. A unicorn is a mythic beast, one who exists within the inner dimensions, the realm of the

feminine. The unicorn is a white horse, representing purity of intent, like the one shown with *the Grail* knight in the Tarot card, *the Knight of Cups*. Its horn is a symbol of *Cernunnos*, *the Green Man* or 'Lord of the Forest', where *the Grail* rites were performed. The horn protrudes from the third eye, signifying his wisdom is his true power. It's interesting to note that when the pineal gland that governs the third eye is activated it ejaculates, mimicking a male phallus.

Now as the sacred masculine is prophesied to return, we see the motif of the unicorn more popular than ever. The Celts who were conquered by Rome to form

Brittania saw their subjugation continue under the rule of the British Empire. With the gift of hindsight, we can see this was the same enemy, simply operating under a new name.

Today we call it rebranding...hence, we see the same icons on the emblems of those who've sought world dominance during the Piscean Age.

Roman Empire   Nazi Third Reich   United Nations

The empire perceives victory as domination. So those who don't comply pose a threat to their dominion. Like the old saying, 'One bad apple will spoil the bunch' someone who possesses feminine wisdom, symbolized by the apple, is isolated and destroyed for fear of their ideas spreading, like a contagion. A man whose feminine side is enslaved is more easily dominated. Whereas a man empowered with the mystic knowledge of the sacred feminine to liberate himself will inspire others by his example, as *Yeshua* did. This is why it is through liberating the feminine in men that we'll transcend the tyranny of the empire that seeks to dominate and oppress. This is why in heraldry, the unicorn is the symbol of Scotland because this 'proud and haughty beast' would rather die than be captured. Similarly, Scottish soldiers fought fiercely to remain sovereign.[59]

The Hunt for the Unicorn

In both Medieval and Renaissance art, the 'hunt for the unicorn' was a common theme, especially in tapestries.[60] These artworks were a deliberate attempt to preserve *the Grail* tradition by encoding its teachings and its persecution. Creating a tapestry was a true act of service as it cost more to commission than building a castle at the time.

One of the most famous tapestry series that encoded references to *the Grail* was titled, *The Hunt for the Unicorn*. Created in the Netherlands between 1495 -

1505, the series was owned for several centuries by the *La Rochefoucauld* family in France, but fell into a state of disrepair when looted during the French revolution. Eventually they were reclaimed by the original owners and in 1922 *John D. Rockefeller, Jr.* bought them for one million US dollars. Six of the panels hung in his house until 1938 when he donated them to the *Metropolitan Museum of Art*. Like *the Grail*, The *Hunt for the Unicorn* series is surrounded by mystery. While it's not considered a *Grail* tapestry if one views it from the perspective of sacred feminine symbolism, the connection is obvious. *The Grail* awakens the sacred masculine potential within men through initiating them into feminine wisdom, so they become whole, and therefore holy.

Similarly, a unicorn is a magical being with heightened perceptions that has both masculine and feminine qualities. While some art historians acknowledge the unicorn represents *Jesus Christ*, the connection is not made that he is symbolic of the archetypal *Sacred King* who received initiation into *the Grail* and was hunted by Rome for being a direct threat to the power of the empire.

The tapestry series features 7 works, the number that indicates the descent down through the 7 gates to meet one's disowned primal self and nemesis. The first panel, titled *The Hunters at the Start of the Hunt* portrays the gentry class on their horses ready to pursue the unicorn in the forest with their hounds. The catchphrase, 'Release the Hounds' spoken by the tyrannical *Mr Burns* in the TV show, *The Simpsons* now takes on new relevance!

The 7 tapestries in this series are titled:

- The Hunters at the Start of the Hunt
- The Unicorn at the Fountain
- The Unicorn Attacked
- The Unicorn Defending Himself
- The Mystic Capture of the Unicorn by the Virgin
- The Unicorn Killed and Brought to the Castle
- The Unicorn in Captivity

When we first see the unicorn in the second panel he is bearded with cloven hooves, symbolizing the wild man who is one with the forest, wedded to the *Earth*

The Unicorn at the fountain - Artist Unknown

Mother. In this second tapestry, he is found dipping his horn into a stream, detoxifying the water, making it safe to drink. The claim that a unicorn's horn could purify water came from the writings of 5th century Greek physician and historian, *Ctesias,* and later *Aristotle,* who said drinking from a unicorn's horn protected one from disease and poison. In other words, a healthy outlook and disposition created physical health, just as a toxic mindset created physical illness. When a man awakens his inner wisdom he is no longer toxic; a danger to others.

Rather, his emotional intelligence has a healing effect on others.

Another *Grail* motif is the fountain, once synonymous with Goddess worship. The tradition of making offerings in sacred grottos has survived today as the custom of throwing a coin into a *Wishing Well*. Another *Grail* reference is standing next to the unicorn is the stag, indicating he's befriended this aspect. Perhaps the most revealing panel is, *The Mystic Capture of the Unicorn* where he is tamed by a *virgin*; a priestess in a rose garden. Roses are symbolic of Venus and the *Magdalenes* who initiated men and women into the love arts of *the Grail*. Roses were worn as an emblem by those in sworn service to the Goddess of Love. The priestess in this panel is wearing red, the color of the *Magdalene*. The rest of the series details the persecution and incarceration of the sacred masculine.

The Lady and the Unicorn

Another *Grail* tapestry series created around 1500 CE is titled, *The Lady and the Unicorn.* These 6 works of art

The Mystic Capture of the Unicorn
Artist Unknown

were undiscovered until 1844, when they were found by the French dramatist and historian, *Prosper Mérimée* in *Boussac Castle.* It was the unconventional novelist, *Georges Sands* who brought them to public attention in her novels.[61] This series, *The Lady and the Unicorn* portrays a man's initiation by the *Magdalene* through each of the 5 elements via the 5 senses. In this first panel of the series, *Touch,* we see a woman standing between two trees symbolizing the *Tree of Life* and the *Tree of Knowledge* depicted in the Tarot card, *The Lovers*.

The *Magdalene* holds a banner featuring the moon in

The Lady and the Unicorn, Touch compared with the Lovers Tarot card

its waning phase, denoting the mage; a woman who is still fertile but distills the power of wisdom in her *Sangraal*. Bearing shields of the moon in the last quarter phase, are the lion and unicorn that feature in every panel of this series. Again we see the symbolism of both the Earthly 'king of the land' and the *Sacred King*, both of whom are loyal to her. The background is filled with spring blossoms indicating the garden of love that she inhabits - life eternal, an ethos that *the*

Grail preserves. In the second panel of the series, *Taste* we see the same figures of the *Magdalene*, the lion and

The Lady and the Unicorn: Taste

the unicorn on a red background indicating the royal red color of the *Graal*. Both the lion and the unicorn are reared up in anticipation, holding the heraldry of the moon showing their allegiance to the feminine. A new figure, a *Grail* maiden appears holding *the Grail* cup. Forest animals watch on as the rite takes place within a circle.

The Lady and the Unicorn: Smell

In the third panel of the series, *Smell*, we see a *Grail* maiden holding a golden platter. The lion and the unicorn are smiling and kneeling denoting humility.

In the fourth panel of the series, *Hearing*, we see the civilizing art of music employed to connect men with their feeling function, on the understanding a man who is governed by his heart's conscience will make wise choices.

Art is the language of the soul, so it was the responsibility of those who dedicated themselves to

The Lady and the Unicorn: Hearing

serve as sacred vessels to preserve and uphold the status and function of art within a culture. The ancients revered the role of art as a necessary function to reflect the interior of the collective psyche. Art that was an act of devotion moved the soul through inspiration. It was traditionally the role of priests and priestesses to master the arts and employ them to tame the beast (the ego) with love instead of seeking to dominate the ego. Only then would the uncivilized become valuable members of society. This is why art is not valued and patronized as much as competitive sports in a patriarchal culture.

The Lady and the Unicorn: Sight

In the fifth and most well-known panel of the series, *Sight,* the Lady holds up a mirror to the Unicorn while the lion looks away.

This indicates only a *Sacred King* is willing to reflect upon his psyche to become wise. The *Magdalene* illustrates the role of the sacred feminine is to invite a man to see his true self; his soul comprised of all the parts of himself he's unaware of so he may become whole. This panel shows the unicorn has his front legs on the lap of the lady, indicating a personal and intimate connection. This is also reminiscent of the Tarot card, *Strength* showing the Temperance Angel taming the lion, representing the masculine ego, into submission.

Through her loving wisdom he can accept his lower self, seeing himself through the eyes of soul instead of the critical ego. Here we see the hooves of the unicorn are not like a horse but cloven, like a goat. He also has a goatee beard indicating the wild man aspect of Pan, that needs to be integrated as equally divine. The lion, still holding the moon banner may be keeping watch as a protector of their divine union. In this panel we see the tree bearing fruit.

The final panel in the series, *Desire*, shows both the lion and the unicorn holding the fabric of the

The Lady and the Unicorn: Desire

Magdalene's tent open suggesting she has granted them entrance to her private boudoir. The fabric is symbolic of the sacred opening to her body temple. This indicates she is receptive to consummate the act of *Sacred Union*. For only when the masculine has humbled his ego and proven himself a worthy companion is he permitted to indulge his Earthly desire.

A third *Grail* maiden is in attendance holding a chest filled with jewels. This may indicate a dowry of marriage, but it's more likely to symbolize the open lid of *Pandora's Box*. This suggests he's bravely faced his darkest fears and found the inner riches of his soul. The lady also holds in her hands a ribbon, as if to perform a *hand-fasting*, a custom in the ancient Celtic wedding tradition. We now see twice as many trees laden with fruit, including the pomegranate, symbolic of feminine wisdom and regal power. It also signifies the descent to the womb of the Great Mother, to taste of her dark fruit and the bitter seeds that must be eaten to transmute past painful experiences into wisdom.

Mystics: An Enemy of the State

As mentioned previously, patriarchy introduced religious ideology that portrayed the divine as masculine and the feminine as evil, unless subservient to the masculine. The introduction of this misogynistic doctrine instigated persecution of *the Grail* anew, initially by Rome in the 4th century and again from the mid-1400's to mid-1700's. The latter period began with the Roman Catholic church blaming the large loss of life from the Bubonic plague in the mid-1300's on Jews, Moslems and witches, claiming they had used black magic on Christians.[62] Unlike those of the Jewish and Islamic faiths, female mystics lacked the protection of the masculine. This made them the easiest target to scapegoat as a means to bolster the power and influence of the church.

The church seeded superstitions to blame mystic women for natural occurrences such as bad weather that destroyed crops, creating famine and disease. Such claims scared the herd into greater dependency on the church who appointed themselves as their protector. Meanwhile, the medical establishment leveraged the hate campaign against mystic women who possessed a knowledge of herb lore to destroy those they perceived as their direct competitors.

Then came further upheaval when *Martin Luther* created the Protestant church in Germany as an alternative to the church of Rome. When German monarchs converted their faith, the Roman Catholic Church, rather than engage their enemy directly, continued to use female mystics as a convenient scapegoat to unite their flock. They instigated witch trials in Germany and German-speaking countries. These trials targeted single mothers; those widowed by war who offered healing, divination and herbalism to support themselves and their families. Since the patriarchal church taught a women's place was 'in the home' as full-time caregivers, and the only energy healing modality that could be practiced was exorcism by Roman Catholic clergy, countless women were hung, burned, drowned, boiled or stoned to death, often after public torture.

It was during these acts of torture many women confessed to preposterous accusations in a desperate attempt to appease their aggressors. Known as 'The Spanish Inquisition' these trials spread like wildfire with Christian priests using handbooks created by the Roman Catholic church as a guide to 'exterminate witches'.[63] The word, *witch* originally meant 'wise woman' - a woman with her wits about her. The empire benefitted financially from this hate campaign as they seized and claimed ownership of lands and crops of those who were murdered. This persecution continued for four hundred years throughout Europe and formed deep-seated fears and prejudices that continue today.

The roots of this smear campaign date back to the start of Patriarchy, the Greco-Roman era when the mythology of the earlier Paleolithic and Neolithic eras were distorted. This was done to attribute more power to the male Gods while diminishing the role of Goddesses. In the earlier indigenous tradition, the *Earth Mother* was revered as 'Creatress of the material realm' while the *Sky Father* was worshiped as the 'light of Spirit'. Both were revered equally to ensure balance and harmony.

Whereas the era of the Olympiad that emerged until the present day, appointed male demigods as rulers of the three worlds. Rulership was divided amongst *Zeus*; as ruler of the sky, *Poseidon*; as ruler of the sea and *Hades*; as ruler of the *Underworld*. The Olympic Gods were corrupt, unlike the previous stellar race who supported human potential. The Gods of the Olympiad viewed themselves as superior to humans and wanted people to fear them. This is why we see the imposing and intimidating forms of Greco-Roman architecture.

The Olympiads taught man he had dominion over nature; the feminine, so he wouldn't question their assertion that they had dominion over man. They erected statues of themselves to promote a culture where men strived to please them. During this time, the best a human could aspire to was to become entertainment for the elite as an athlete or great artist. This is where our celebrity-worshiping culture has its roots. The message anchored is; aspire to be admired and you'll gain wealth and fame and live a life of privilege, like a God[64] Unlike the earlier *Grail* tradition that taught men to honor and revere the sacred feminine, men were taught to fear women, specifically *Aphrodite*, the Goddess of Love as a force they couldn't control.

The Greeks taught men to value reason; the rational mind, over feeling. Feeling is what creates value. Without feeling one doesn't value life, so they become a dangerous force. The patriarchs warned if a man slept with a woman he would lose his masculine strength. In 700 BC Hesiod told the story of *Prometheus* who sought to steal the 'sacred fire' (*kundalini*) from the Gods, so they punished mankind with women who they referred to as a 'beautiful evil'. A concept reiterated in the patriarchal religions that followed. This thinking engenders a justification to treat women badly on the basis they're the enemy and not to be trusted, just used for sexual gratification. This fuels the hate crime of rape common in times of war that's rampant in today's culture.

The only Goddess the patriarchal Greeks honored was *Athena*, as she devoted her life to the betterment of the city. She was the icon of positive womanhood, a masculine woman with patriarchal values. Today we see women who adopt male values as 'shadow Athenas' being rewarded with a seat at the table in the halls of power, as the immature masculine finds masculine women less threatening. Whatever material gains are made by a 'shadow Athena' will not compensate for the cost to her wellbeing for the compromises made to fit in.

This new pantheon of demigod deities embodied the worst traits of humanity, anchoring a blueprint that lowered the collective consciousness. I speak more about that in my book, *Sacred Union: Awakening the Consciousness of Eden*. Previously, in the earlier polytheistic mystic traditions, the function of demigods was to serve as a template for all the facets of sacred feminine and masculine expression one could embody to create a balanced psyche. In the monotheistic patriarchal religions of Christianity, Judaism and Islam that followed, multi-dimensional spirituality was replaced by a one-dimensional *Father God*.

With the creator re-cast as male, all of his appointed intermediaries were also male. Women were viewed dualistically; as obedient subordinates or evil temptresses. When spirituality became politicized into organized religion, obedience was rewarded and questioning punished. This was justified on the basis that the 'word of God' was only that which had been received by male prophets and was quoted in their official doctrines.

As stated earlier, this split the psyche into fragments so some aspects, like the primal selves, were demonized as evil. Purity was then sought as an attainment of spiritual perfection. While the lower nature - unintegrated, ran amok, resulting in degenerative behavior conducted covertly. This is why those who sought to be most pious; the clergy, became the most dangerous, while yielding power and influence in positions of authority. Priests hoping to feel closer to God through rejecting their physical desires imposed their repressed sexuality on the innocent, while nuns who suppressed feelings of rage exacted psychological and physical violence upon children. Today we see leaders of both church and state who portray themselves as being of high moral standing guilty of the most heinous acts.

This polarization is portrayed in the symbol for *Pisces*, the sign that influenced our collective psyche over  the past two thousand years as we journeyed through the *Piscean* astrological age.

The symbol shows two fish swimming in opposite directions. The fish is the symbol of the mystic, the archetype who unifies light and dark within. Hence, *Pisces* transits evoke the archetypal mystic. This is why the symbol of the mystic fish was appropriated into the symbol for Christianity due to the claim that two of Christ's disciples; Peter and Simon, were fishermen. In the earlier *Grail* tradition, the term *Fisherman*, referred to a disciple of *The Fisher King* and why *Priest Kings*, like *Yeshua* were referred to as *Fisher Kings*.

In this context, a *Fisherman* was one who 'fished for answers' in the subconscious, represented by the depths of water.[65] This is where the origins of the rite of *Baptism* are found as an initiate surrenders themselves completely to the fertile waters of the Great Mother, through dissolving their ego in the salty waters of their sacred tears. By plunging to the depths of their soul, they are reborn. This is why the Polynesian demigod, *Maui* was gifted a fish hook.

The Whole Story

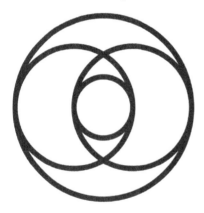

Pisces, is the final sign in the zodiac and represents the end of one cosmic cycle and the beginning of another. *Pisces* offers us an opportunity to enter the

Vesica Pisces; the sacred doorway within the heart of a sacred vessel who embodies the *Mandorla*. Comprised of two intersecting circles, the *Mandorla* signifies the union of opposites within that's needed to open the gate of spiritual ascension. This process awakens the all-seeing eye of inner sight (shown above). This was later distorted by initiates of the dark arts believing they had to ascend a pyramid of power to acquire sacred knowledge. When *the Grail* mysteries were driven underground, due to threat of persecution, initiates would identify each other by drawing a circle on the ground, and if the other responded by drawing

an intersecting circle, to create a mandorla they knew they were amongst sacred kin.

Today, people associate the *Mandorla* with the *Chalice Well* in Glastonbury; a twin spring at the foot of *Chalice Hill* near *Glastonbury Tor*, a man-made mound that was once a sacred site for *Grail* rites. The *Chalice Well* features a red and white spring comprised of water from the Earth, colored by mineral deposits. In *the Grail* tradition these signified the blood of the *Earth Mother* and the semen of the *Sky Father*.

When atop the Glastonbury Tor I had flashbacks to a lifetime consummating the *Beltane* rites of Spring. I also received visions and sounds from the fey nature spirits who live within the Tor showing me Druid initiation rites once held deep within the mound amongst the springs. Today well-meaning guides perpetuate the fiction that the red spring appeared when *Joseph of Arimathea* buried the cup of *Yeshua's* blood. Not surprising in a culture that's blind to the hijacking of *Mandorla by Mastercard, Audi* and the *Olympics*.

The Romans adopted this symbol of 'strength in unity'[66] known also as the *Borromean Rings* which featured in early Buddhist art and Norse art. By multiplying this symbol in repetition they sought to magnify its power on the misunderstanding more is better when in magic, the opposite is true as distilling energy down to a simplified sigil concentrates its power.

The power of the original *Mandorla* is in the fertile interception of polarities, known as the *Vesica Pisces*. The *Vesica Pisces* is the portal that was activated within *Grail* initiates who were 'whole unto themselves', rather than seeking their 'other half' to feel complete. The shape of the *Vesica Pisces* emulates the sacred opening of death and birth within a woman; a *yoni* (vulva) once revered as the 'doorway to the mysteries'. This is why Gothic church doors mimic this shape, and the main body of churches mimic the womb of a woman, with the vestibule being the lozenge-shaped

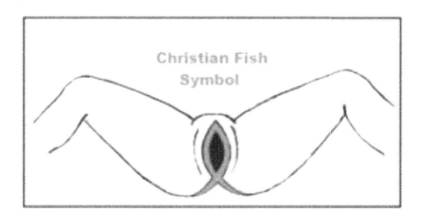

cavity referred to as the *vulva vestibule*. I'm sure most Christians would be shocked to learn this is the true meaning of their fish bumper stickers!

There are also claims made that Michelangelo was reluctant to accept the offer to paint the ceiling of the Sistine Chapel and rebelled against the church by including sacred feminine anatomy and *Sacred Union* iconography to honor the pre-Christian tradition. An attitude that was shared by other Renaissance artists.[67]

 The symbol of the *Vesica Pisces* or 'mystic fish' can also be seen hidden in the glyph for *Virgo*, the zodiac sign of the priestess. *Virgo* is the opposite sign of *Pisces*, the mystic. For Virgoan energy to be expressed positively, as the sacred vessel, it must integrate the lesson of *Pisces*, the opposing sign.

It's through understanding the symbolism of the pre-patriarchal sacred feminine Mystic tradition we can clearly see Christianity was created to cloak and distort *the Grail*, the Mystic tradition that *Yeshua* and *Mari* served.

Diving for Pearls of Wisdom

So yes! Something fishy has been going on for quite some time. In the ancient world, the *Magdalene* or 'Lady of the Waters' was highly regarded as a priestess associated with lakes, wells, fountains and springs. *Mari*, the *Magdalene* was said to spend her final years in France in a grotto renowned for its healing waters. This makes sense as the ancient places of Goddess worship were caves, grottos, groves and mineral springs, both thermal and cool for bathing and drinking. For water and earth are the final two elements in the sacred spiral when we 'cast circle', an act that takes our psyche deep within. This is why the darker seasons of Autumn and Winter are governed by water and earth respectively. Water helps us soften and become receptive so we can transform through surrender and find stillness in the earth.

The element of water was used extensively in sacred feminine ceremonies. A receptive element, it takes on the sacred intention it's imbued with. The work of *Dr Emoto* evidenced this with his experiments that revealed how the crystalline structure of water molecules transform into harmonic mandalas or fractured dissonance according to whether positive or negative intentions are applied. This is why sacred bathing was considered a healing art and is still widely embraced by Eastern cultures like Japan, Bali and Morocco.

The 12th Century *Grail* tale by Chretien de Troyes titled, *Ywain and The Lady of the Fountain*, refers to *la Dompna del Aquae - Mari Magdalene* of the Del Aeqs family. Originally *lac* or *lake* meant a red pigment from the Eastern Dragon Tree.[68] When I traveled to France in 2019 I was called to a crystalline cave at Limousis. It had many 'rooms', some large enough for a circle of thirty people to gather and exquisite springs and grottos. Neither ceremony, nor meditation was possible due to the locked gate erected over the entrance, opened only for geological tourist tours featuring a light show to Pink Floyd! Imagine if mystics dared to desecrate patriarchal churches, synagogues and mosques in such a way.

The Alchemical Colors of the Grail

The springs most synonymous with *the Grail* are the red and white springs in Glastonbury, on account of their colors being red and white. As I mentioned in

Chapter 4, the red downward facing triangle, reminiscent of the vulva, signified the ancient holy trinity of 'maiden, mother, crone' and the gateway to the 'dark womb of rebirth' within the *Great Mother*. To journey this path of initiation was to walk the 'Red Path of the sacred feminine'. The equivalent path was the white path of the sacred masculine. It was symbolized by the upward facing, white *Delta* triangle that signifies one's ascension to experience the consciousness of Spirit, the Heavenly Father.

Together the intersecting triangles of Earth and Sky form another *Sacred Union* symbol; the six-pointed star, symbolizing the union of sacred trinities. An initiate who was a devotee of both the 'Red and White Paths' was considered a *magi*. This is why *Yeshua* was often depicted, wearing the colors, white and red, identical to those in the Tarot card, *The Magician*.

Here we see a figure in the magician's pose illustrating

the idiom, 'As above, So below'. This indicates someone who surrenders their body as a vessel to create 'Heaven on Earth'. Such an initiate strived to awaken the red and white rose within the heart which signifies loving acceptance of both feminine and masculine traits and values. This is the pre-Christian meaning of the rose cross adopted by the esoteric order, the *Rociscrucians* from which magical sects derived, the most famous being the order of the *Golden Dawn*.

In chapter 9, I spoke about *the Grail* colors; red and white featured in the heraldry of the English flag that were originally used by *Grail* knights. The empire appropriated this *Grail* emblem when they declared war on Islam. It was worn by Christian soldiers,

known as *The Knights Templar* who fought in the Crusades.

The crusades were started by the Catholic hierarchy who told all criminals their crimes and debts would be wiped clear if they rode to Jerusalem to fight the Moslems. Given how outnumbered the Christians were by the Moslems, the Crusades were a farce. Those in the middle-East had opulent cities that were far more advanced culturally with populations a hundred-fold greater than their Western counterparts. It was a futile mission to wage war on the basis of a religious claim to sites of cultural significance. Far more credible is the claim the Crusades were a distraction so tunnels could be dug to steal wealth from Solomon's Temple.

The secret order of the *Templars* was said to be founded by nine men from wealthy families in France. It's claimed they dug tunnels for seventy-five years and excavated over two tons of gold and silver. They became the first bankers, holding funds in exchange for bank notes to reduce the chance of theft from those journeying to the Holy Land in exchange for a fee and safe passage. Their motivation was to financially profit from war. Banking was illegal at the time but the church looked the other way, indicating a pact had been struck. Other perks the *Templars* received from the Catholic church included being absolved from all taxes and permission to cross borders freely.

The *Templars* were said to have sworn to serve and protect *the Grail* but instead they were protecting their treasure and newfound power. Some say the *Templars* found the truth; the gospels excluded from the Bible - Solomon's secret texts and the truth about *Yeshua* and *Mari*. I suspect, instead of protecting *the Grail*, the *Templars* betrayed it by giving the information they found to the Catholic church in exchange for financial immunity, making them complicit in suppressing the truth. The *Templars* used their wealth to build churches but also to purchase vast amounts of land to create vineyards, while growing their wealth through manufacturing and trade. They created an elaborate hierarchy in numerous countries with a 'Templar Master' presiding over each order. The overall leader was the *Grand Master* who was elected for life (like the dark lords portrayed as the power hungry *Skepsis* in the film, *The Dark Crystal* or *Darth Moll* in the film, *Star Wars*. My understanding is they practiced an inversion of *the Grail*.

It's interesting to note that July 4, 1097 was the last battle of the *Templars* led by the *Grand Master*, which was the turning point in the crusades. This date is charged each year with nationwide celebrations as the US Day of Independence. After this battle the *Templars* went underground. In 1307 on 'Friday, the 13th' the *Grand Master* tried to start another Holy War in France. Troops arrested the majority of the *Templars* including the *Grand Master* and property was seized. Friday the 13th was originally celebrated as a day sacred to the Goddess since Friday is named after Freya, the Norse name for Venus and 13 is the number of lunar months in a calendar year. Traditionally people celebrated by taking the day off to make love. Selecting this date to start a war was a deliberate attempt to charge the Earth's grid with fear and pain. Hence, we've been conditioned to celebrate the dark on Friday the 13th. Crimes the *Templars* were accused of included spitting and urinating on the cross, denying Christ and 'ritualised homosexuality'. There are claims the Pope is the true *Grand Master*. Today Hollywood portrays the *Templars* as a devout order, despite The 12th-century Muslim view of Crusaders reporting the *Templars* were courageous and skilled warriors, but barbaric in all other aspects.[69] The only representation of the *Templars* I know of where they're portrayed as less than holy is in Ridley Scott's film, *Kingdom of Heaven*.

Here we can see how the double *Mandorla* forms the

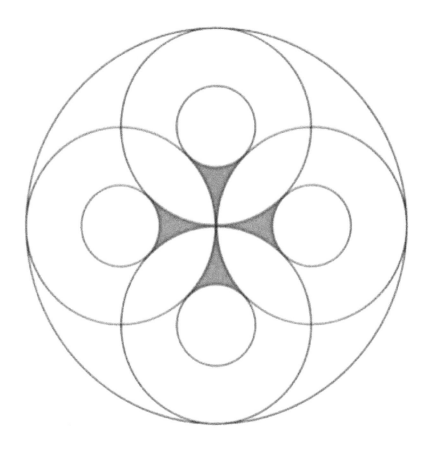

basis of the *Cross Pattie* synonymous with the *Templars* that was later elongated to symbolize the cross of the crucifixion.

It's interesting to note that the *Croix Pattie* was used by the German army in World War Two.

Cross Pattie

Nazi Cross

Empiric Propaganda In Art

Just as *Grail* symbols were appropriated and distorted,

Sir Galahad Wedded to Blanchefleur by
Edwin Austin Abbey

artworks were created that overlaid *the Grail* with Christian themes during the late 1800's and early 1900's. *The Quest and Achievement of the Holy Grail* by Edwin Austin Abbey

The Quest and Achievement of the Holy Grail by Edwin Austin Abbey

is one such series.[70] Here we see priestesses replaced by Christian nuns and monks. Instead of seeking *the Grail* to prepare for Sacred Union, Sir Galahad, considered the most noble knight - a man who honored the feminine, is depicted leaving his new bride, under the false belief only a 'virgin knight' can seek *the Grail*. The misuse of the term, 'virgin' is a flag.

In this context it means 'sexually chaste' whereas in *the Grail* tradition it referred to a woman who dedicated herself to sacred service, regardless of her sexual experience. The Christian obsession with sexual chastity was an attempt to stop men from receiving the initiation of *Shaktipat* to awaken their consciousness. Another example is the series of 6 tapestries created between 1891-1894 by three English men; *William Morris* (heraldry), *Edward Burne-Jones* (figures and overall composition) and *John Henry Dearle* (foreground and background). They were based on a book written in the Middle Ages by *Sir Thomas Mallory* originally titled, *The Whole Story of King Arthur* by Morris, Burnes and Dearle.

The panel titled, *The Knights of the Round Table Summoned to the Quest by the Strange Damsel* depicts a woman in simple clothes, a priestess approaching a dinner table where royals are seated with their closest companions. Her arm is raised as if gesturing to them,

The Knights of the Round Table Summoned to the Quest by the Strange Damsel

'It's time'. It's curious that the flowers in bloom suggest the opposite time of year from when men observed the annual *Holy Grail* rite at Winter Solstice.

The next panel, *The Arming and Departure of the Knights* shows only men, now wearing red tunics and armor and mounted on their horses ready to depart. On one of their shields is the motif of the Roman Empire; *the eagle* and on another, *a turret*. The women who are seeing them off are all young maidens wearing floral

The Arming and Departure of the Knights

garland circlets. Beneath their feet are lilies in bloom.

There are two failures depicted in the series, *The Failure of Sir Gawaine and Sir Uwaine at the Ruined Chapel* and *The Failure of Lancelot*.

The Failure of Lancelot

In the former panel, again we see the Roman eagle depicted on one shield and a lion on the other, signifying Earthly power and an angel wearing the robes of Christian clergy who's not permitting them to enter. In the latter panel, we see a similar angel admonishing *Lancelot*, who is sunken on the ground in a posture signaling despair and shame.

The Vision of the Holy Grail to Sir Galahad, Sir Bors, and Sir Perceval

In the panel, *The Attainment: The Vision of the Holy Grail to Sir Galahad, Sir Bors, and Sir Perceval* we see the successful initiate, *Galahad* wearing red and white robes and kneeling before *the Grail* maidens who sit behind an altar table bearing *the Grail* chalice. *The Grail* maidens have been transformed into angels with wings and three more angels watch over *Galahad*. Here we see again, a Christian overlay. Just as earlier Gods and Goddesses of olde were absorbed into Christendom as canonized saints, *the Grail* has been right under our noses all along, but cloaked in deception.

CHAPTER 11

Resurrection:
The Final Test

Now the hero must apply lessons learned from their quest to transcend their old patterns of self-sabotage to defeat their enemy. After all, knowledge is worth nothing if it isn't applied. This is what reveals how much we've been changed by our ordeal, for the better. So here, at the 11th hour we're tested in a way that takes us to our limits. How we respond reveals our true character. Essentially, that's whether we are still trying to serve our own interests or something greater. Those who are inspired to serve something greater than themselves offer a beacon of hope that inspires others to rise. In tales of injustice, this is the moment when the hero risks all to serve the greater good.

In Hollywood films, this is when we witness the ultimate showdown between the hero and their nemesis in a fight to the death in a 'winner takes all' duel. As the audience, this is when we see how much the protagonist has grown, as they embody living proof of their personal transformation. The stakes are high, because if they don't transcend their former pattern of behavior they will sabotage the fulfillment of their mission; that being, to alleviate the suffering of others.

This is the motivation for the hero now…to do everything in their power to make a difference to the lives of others. Having transcended their personal fears, such as fear of death, they are undeterred in their mission. It is this determination that makes one such a formidable force, as their conviction is unwavering. This usually comes via a revelation so startling it prompts one to take radical action. Ultimately the realization is how much we value someone or an ideal so in the end, love does save the day, as it's what motivates us to take right action and be the hero in our own adventure.

In great romances, this is the moment when the hero risks looking like a fool for love. Such as a demonstration of their heart's courage that enables them to transcend the doubts of their mind. In the quest for *the Grail*, this is when the hero, in search of true love, is reunited with his love interest or a new opportunity for love with someone who reflects their new level of awareness and empowerment. Here the hero is tested to discern whether he has the maturity needed to enter the path of *Sacred Union*. In the case of a reunion this marks the first encounter since the hero has undergone his ego death mid-Winter. The hero's perspective has changed since their last meeting so his challenge is to atone for past transgressions to rebuild trust. In the case of a new opportunity for love, the hero will need to summon their courage to transcend his old fear that he's not enough to win the heart of a Queen/King. Alternatively, it could be risking the fear of being judged by others if he leaves an unfulfilling relationship to follow his heart. Whatever the situation, this stage marks the hero's last chance to pledge his allegiance to the will of his heart. This indicates how much he has come to understand and value the feminine part of himself - his soul, known in myth as *Psyche*, who journeys to the *Underworld* in search of true love. Only with this commitment to himself can he embrace the soul of another wholeheartedly.

This is where the hero revisits the *Supreme Ordeal*. Where previously he confronted his greatest fears to humble his ego in private. Now he must publicly humble his ego, whether that's before someone who's very significant to them, or the wider community. This conveys an ego death has taken place, making true love and justice possible. This is the elixir contained within all great romances and epic sagas. It's the moment we wait for to reassure us that our faithful wait has not been in vain.

Despite the ego being the masculine part of the psyche, it is not always the male ego that needs taming. The film, *Far From the Madding Crowd* based on the novel by Thomas Hardy enacts this reverse scenario beautifully with Bathsheba Everdene, the immature and stubborn female lead (played by Carey Mulligan) called to surrender her ego to embrace the steadfast love offered by Gabriel Oak (played by Matthias Schoenaerts). I can't help but wonder if the name of the male protagonist is an intentional tip of the hat to the *Oak King* of olde; the archetypal *Green Man*. Another very entertaining example of this dynamic is in the film, *The Proposal* starring Sandra Bullock and Ryan Reynolds.

The Christos: The Resurrected Man

In *the Grail* tradition, a man who successfully returned from his descent to 'come full circle' was celebrated as an embodiment of the resurrected Savior God; one who became a vessel for the sacred masculine. This indicated he had embodied *the Grail* teachings to integrate his inner feminine and escape the *Underworld*.

The doctrine of the Roman Empire re-interpreted the 'resurrection' to mean a man who returned to life after a physical death, which is impossible. They set the same impossible standard for women by asserting only a woman who birthed a baby without having sex was a vessel for the sacred feminine.

Happily Ever After

If we consider that the loss of love is usually what catalyzes our descent to the *Underworld*, like *Orpheus*, it is equally the finding of true love that announces our return; our resurrection. In other words, our true Beloved appears when we have done the deep inner work. Like the saying, 'when the student is ready, the teacher appears' our Beloved in our teacher in love who appears when we are ready.

True love with our divine complement is only possible after we have found self-love and fallen in love with life itself, appreciating the divine in all things. If we meet our true Beloved before we're ready, we destroy any chance of love. Self-love and a love of life are the qualities that attract people to us and keep love alive. These essential love affairs; with the soul within and the beauty of life is wonderfully portrayed in the film, *Shirley Valentine* starring Pauline Collins. It features a housewife who embarks on a journey of self-exploration. The book, *Eat, Pray, Love* is a more contemporary version.

Since this is the climactic moment of our adventure, it's worth noting that the Greek word *climax*, means ladder. Everything has been building towards this epic moment. This is the moment that signifies an experience of transcendence; when we overcome all inner and outer obstacles in the *Underworld* and *Everyday World* respectively, to access our own divinity in the *Upper World*. This moment can only occur when we've left behind the safety of all we've known, to enter the mystery of life without hesitation. This is what makes our greatest dreams possible, including true love. To ensure we experience such transcendence, let's unpack what threatens our salvation.

How We Sabotage Love

To experience transcendence we must experience a pivotal moment of self-realization, when we acknowledge our own part in our suffering, instead of blaming others or circumstance for our fate. This may be recognizing we've outgrown a relationship and to stay, merely out of duty, would not be authentic and honoring of our inner truth. Alternatively, we may glean how we've played a part in our own wounding in our previous relationships. This frees us from avoiding intimacy for fear of being hurt by others.

As illustrated in our journey through the *Suit of Cups*, we mature emotionally when we take responsibility for healing our past hurts. This is when we take 'the bull by the horns' by identifying the biggest wounds we enact in our intimate relationships. Wounds that are universal and taboo as they speak to our desperate attempt to win the love of our opposite-gender parent. These are the core wounds responsible for sabotaging love. Yes, the degree to which we felt love denied by our opposite-gender parent determines our success in love, until we heal that wound so buckle up as we're about to navigate the icebergs that lay ahead, unseen in the dark waters of every intimate relationship once the 'honeymoon is over'. To navigate those perilous waters it is essential we acknowledge what's hidden, knowing if we don't, it will shipwreck our hopes and dreams, despite our best intentions. Since I'm a mystic, not a psychologist I'm going to summarize these wounds from both my experiences in intimate relationships and as a guide assisting others.

Men's Core Wound: The Mother Complex

All men, regardless of their gender identity or preference experience this inner mythos to varying degrees. It is therefore essential all men seek to identify this wound to heal it. If this wound is neglected it will fester, resulting in behavior that undermines both personal wellbeing and intimacy. Essentially the Mother Complex refers to how much a man secretly craves his mother's love all for himself. If a man didn't feel his mother's love was abundantly clear while growing up, this wound will rule him in one of two ways. Firstly; his unacknowledged rage at his Mum will manifest as *misogyny*; a fear of the feminine that will poison interactions with the feminine (in men and women). For example, this can manifest as the dualistic nature of the *lover/destroyer* - one who sees themselves as a great lover, but turns like a viper should their love interest remind them of their mother, due to a fear of being hurt. This leads to punishing their love interest emotionally and psychologically by being absent or detached, but should their partner leave, he'll protest how much he loves them.

Secondly, he will constantly strive to earn his mother's love, be it from his own mother, known colloquially as a 'Mummy's Boy' or the mother figure he's projected on to his partner, regardless of their gender. For example, he may strive to play the role of the perfect husband or father as provider/protector, rather than risk being authentic and connected with his own needs. This leads a man to be a people pleaser who over-extends himself, only to later resent the fact his own needs are overlooked. Should his partner leave, frustrated that they always had to lead by making all the decisions due to his tendency to always look to them for direction, he'll feel angry and victimized on the basis his best effort wasn't considered 'good enough'. The majority of men are oblivious to this wound as it's far easier to punish an ex-lover as the cause of one's suffering, than unpack one's neurosis and take responsibility for enacting patterns of self-neglect. Either way, if one is to avoid rejecting the feminine due to their unprocessed fears, they must examine their relationship with their mother or childhood mother-figure to be free. This universal wound is portrayed in the Greek myth, *Oedipus*, so let's explore the story...

The Myth of Oedipus

When *Oedipus* was born, his father, the *King of Thebes* consulted the oracle who told him his son would one day kill his father. Terrified of being usurped by his infant son, he ordered his servant to kill his son. The servant, unable to slay an innocent, placed him in the safekeeping of a shepherd. The shepherd took the baby to Corinth and gifted him to the childless King who raised him as his own.

When *Oedipus* came of age he heard a rumor that he was not the King's son, so he went to the *Oracle at Delphi* who told him he would one day kill his father and mate with his mother. To avoid such a fate, *Oedipus* fled Corinth and traveled to Thebes. On approaching the city, he encountered the man who was his biological father, unbeknownst to him. The two men argued over whose chariot had right of way on the bridge until Oedipus threw the old man from his chariot, killing him. (This is similar to *The Fisher King* who, in his youth, attacks a foreigner he encounters on the path, without stopping to first ask questions.)

Having unwittingly killed his father, *Oedipus* then encounters the guardian of the city. A mythic being, known as the *Sphinx*, who has the head and breast of a woman, the body of a lioness, the wings of an eagle and a serpent's tail. She is multi-faceted; a cryptic riddle to an uninitiated man. Like *Lilith*, the Sumerian 'Goddess of the Underworld', who possessed the head of a woman, the body of a serpent, and the talons and wings of an owl, the *Sphinx* represents the shapeshifting wild feminine who has awakened her *kundalini*; her primal power. As such, she acts as an agent of the *Earth Mother*, serving as a guardian of sacred knowledge and the mantle of earthly power. She was honored in advanced pre-patriarchal civilizations like Egypt where she is still seen today guarding the pyramids of Giza and on the inner planes, esoteric treasures, such as the Emerald tablets of Thoth.

The Greco-Roman patriarchs recast the *Sphinx* as a monster, sent as a punishment by the Gods. It is telling that the word, Sphinx has the same origins as the word, asphyxiate, meaning 'to squeeze one's neck'. This indicates the *Sphinx* is the aspect of a woman who 'goes for the jugular' to elicit truth, on the understanding truth is what sets everyone free. She is another emanation of the dark feminine as the slayer of men's egos. Her role is to test a man to determine if he's ready to access what she protects…whether that's the gate to the inner 'Stairway to Heaven' within her body temple, the mysteries of life or the heart of a city.

In the story of *Oedipus*, the *Sphinx* tests *Oedipus* by posing a cryptic riddle to discern his level of awareness. She does this to determine whether he may pass and enter the city gates - a euphemism for the pearly gates of the feminine. (Yes, long before the term 'pearly gates' was appropriated to a locked gate guarded by male Christian angels, the pearl referred to the clitoris atop the sacred opening of a woman).

Back to the story...so the *Sphinx* asked *Oedipus*, "Which creature has one voice and yet becomes four-footed, two-footed then three-footed?" *Oedipus* contemplates this for a long time, then he responds, "A person: as a crawling baby, then as an adult, then using a stick in old age." Pleased with this answer, the *Sphinx* decides to ask him another riddle." There are two sisters. One gives birth to the other and she, in turn, gives birth to the first. Who are they?" Again, *Oedipus* takes his time to consider her question and then responds with the right answer, "Day and Night."

The patriarchal version of this story claims when *Oedipus* offered the correct answer, the *Sphinx* got so upset she fainted. It also asserts the *King of Thebes* had been so afraid of the *Sphinx* he had offered the crown, his wife and his daughter to any man who could slay the *Sphinx*, making *Oedipus* the new King. This version echoes the betrayal of the feminine by the father in *The Handless Maiden*. In this version, we are told the Thebans were very upset because somebody had killed their king, but happy *Oedipus* had solved the riddle of the *Sphinx*, so they made him king. Whereas from the perspective of the sacred feminine we derive a different meaning. The *Sphinx* is a sacred feminine gatekeeper, both of her riddles test the hero on his cyclic wisdom and how he responds determines if he loses his head or enters her gate to become king. These are *Grail* themes. 1. The hero meets with the dark feminine to be initiated. 2. She has a knowledge of cyclic wisdom. 3. He must demonstrate he possesses the cyclic wisdom of the feminine to gain access to what she guards. His answer will determine is he dies (signifying an ego death) or claims his power as a sovereign. The *Sphinx* would've been glad to award *Oedipus* the mantle of rulership. After all, this was the custom in the ancient world. A man could only rule over the land and her people if the *High Priestess* deemed him mature and wise enough to be responsible with such a mantle of worldly power. A similar testing of wits is shown by the *Queen of Sheba* who refuses to entertain the advances of *King Solomon*, unless he can correctly answer her riddles. I write about that in my book, *Creating Sacred Union in Partnerships* listed in the resource section.

So...*Oedipus* accepted the title and unwittingly married his mother, the widowed queen. They consummated their marriage and bore four children. After many years, a plague struck the city, and the oracle proclaimed it would last until the murderer of the previous king is discovered. *Oedipus* diligently begins the search. When the truth is realized; that *Oedipus* slay his father and copulated with his mother, fathering her children, his mother hangs herself. *Oedipus*, upon finding her body, sticks pins his eyes in an attempt to destroy the image of the pain he has inadvertently caused through his unaware actions.

The Meaning of the Myth

This story shows us how much destruction we can cause when we don't know the truth, as our actions aren't tempered with awareness. It also illustrates the power of fate; the *Universal Law of Cause and Effect*. For we can't avoid making choices that hurt ourselves and others unless we truly know who we are and unpack our story of origin. Put another way, without understanding our past, we will create an unfortunate future, despite our best intentions.

Without truly knowing his father, *Oedipus* unwittingly tries to compete with and usurp his father. This manifests as an unconscious need to assert his dominance to validate his power and identity through compulsive action motivated by a chip on his shoulder so when he encounters his father he 'shoots first and asks questions later'.

This is what destroys many of our relationships. Instead of adopting an attitude of curiosity, enquiring as to the true motivation of the other's actions, we attack based on our projections. Without seeking to truly understand our father by knowing his backstory, we destroy our chance of truly knowing him as a man.

So too, if we persist in viewing our parents through the eyes of the wounded child, we judge them harshly and seek to destroy them as punishment for not being who we needed or wanted them to be. This may surface as an unconscious urge to prove our father (or masculine- dominant mother) wrong or outdo their achievements. This attitude also undermines our happiness and confidence as we fear our best effort is never enough for the critical father we've internalized. If we don't seek to heal this internal dynamic we will remain a defensive child who seeks to destroy perceived competition to impress our love interest; our mother-surrogate.

For modern men who reach maturity, there comes a moment where they realize they have inadvertently 'married their mother', whether that's in a hetero or same sex union. Not literally, but figuratively as their partner reminds them of their mother. This is an opportunity to heal unresolved mother issues. Mature men accept this challenge to explore triggers as an opportunity to heal their core wound, rather than continue to project their unresolved hurt onto their partner.

When an immature man senses that he's 'married his mother' he may feel trapped and powerless, like he did as a boy due to his emotional and psychological dependence on his mother. If not directly confronted, this fear can haunt men and cause destructive patterns of behavior. This stems from ignorance about the cyclic nature of women. For example, when men discover their female partner has the same cyclic nature as their mother, they may feel as if they've been tricked into marrying the *dark feminine*, when they consciously chose someone who seemed like the opposite to their mother's dark side.

Men not initiated into *the Grail* lack understanding of the cyclic nature of women, so they sabotage love due to their fear of the *dark feminine*. This manifests as an unconscious expectation that women must always be happy and fulfill the role of the 'all-giving, caring nurturer' who's kind and supportive. When they inevitably experience their partner as the opposite, the *dark feminine* who sees and identifies the shadow aspects they fear facing in themselves, they may 'run for the hills'. This immature reaction often results in them abandoning their partner when their partner most needs support, when they feel inward, dark and vulnerable.

This usually occurs during the two weeks each month when biological women lose up to 80% of their life force as their bodies prepare to menstruate. This makes them more susceptible to irritability, volatility and illness. Immature men (and masculine-dominant women) find this behavior triggers their mother wound so they withdraw their love and attention to avoid feeling the hurt they did as a child.

Unbeknownst to them it reminds them of the time each month when they felt unloved by their mother, due to a lack of understanding about her cyclic nature.

Women sense when their partners are pulling away. If a woman is immature, she may fight her nature to appear as linear and consistent as her solar-governed counterpart. This may include not taking time to go within to acknowledge and process her feelings. She may self-sacrifice her needs to remain 'ever-available' as a mother-surrogate to her partner, in an attempt to provide constant proof of her love. This dysfunctional dynamic can contribute to breast cancer from 'over-mothering'. Whereas when men and women activate their *inner mother* they no longer struggle to fill the hole left by their mother as an infant, or place that burden of unconscious expectation on to their partners.

The other factor that exacerbates the *Mother Complex* is when a mother leans on her son for emotional support from an inappropriately young age. Essentially this is psycho-emotional incest. This dynamic has been a very common occurrence since the industrial age saw men work long hours away from home, despite it being an unacknowledged taboo.

We hear a lot about pedophilia being perpetrated on daughters by fathers and step-fathers, but psycho-emotional incest is more covert. This shadow feminine behavior is as damaging as sexual molestation and results in misogynistic behavior by boys when they grow to manhood. Why? Boys who perceive their main function in life is to make their mother happy, grow into men who resent women and fear being swallowed emotionally by the feminine...with their needs considered less important than those of their feminine partners. This is one of the main reasons men fear commitment and fantasize about dominating the feminine in pornographic scenarios.

A man who harbors this wound often has unacknowledged rage towards his mother which he projects onto his female (and feminine- dominant male partners). He may even derive a sense of satisfaction or power from punishing them by withholding attention, affection or sex. A woman (or feminine-dominant man) in a relationship with such a man (or masculine-dominant woman) will find their partner will react with cold, cruel and callous behavior when they are upset, instead of offering emotional support. This is because the emotional pain of their partner evokes the overwhelm they felt as a boy, when their mother was unhappy and burdened them with a responsibility beyond their years by confiding in them.

Since they felt unable to effectively counsel and console her, they feel powerless whenever their partner looks unhappy. This is why wounded men (and masculine-dominant women) lash out, traumatizing their partners. The degree to which a man feels rage at his mother will correspond to the degree he felt betrayed by her. Since the role of the mother is to nurture her young, if he felt she was more focused on his achievements, he will feel rage at her for failing to love him for who he is, rather than basing her love on his performance. This rage is accentuated if he felt pressure to compensate for his father's shortcomings by fulfilling his mother's idea of the 'perfect little man'. Men may also harbor rage at their mothers if she was so busy working to provide financially, embodying more of the masculine role of provider/protector that she was unable to adequately nurture his psycho-emotional needs.

Without *the Grail*, husbands and fathers have inevitably struggled to mature, making them ill-equipped to offer the psycho-emotional support needed by their wives. When we add to this picture, how many men returned home to their wives after experiencing the horrors of war, with no trauma-informed therapy, we can start to gain a deeper understanding into why so many husbands were a source of anguish, rather than support, to their wives. Behaviors such as substance abuse, philandering and violence directed towards themselves and their children, along with a cultural expectation to 'keep it in the family' rather than access community support, made for a toxic environment where mothers were dissolving in grief or venting their rage and resentment onto their kids. This has perpetuated the *Mother Complex* as endemic intergenerational trauma.

It's worth noting the incestuous relationship between *Oedipus* and his mother wouldn't have occurred if his father was present in the role of fathering his son. This illustrates the cost of the 'absent father' on a child, psychologically and emotionally, as well as physically. Rather than scapegoat mothers for oversharing information that isn't age-appropriate with their children, we need to provide social structures to adequately support parents, such as the monthly sharing circles that were once part of *the Grail* tradition.

A man (or masculine-dominant woman) with an unresolved mother wound may project their fear of failure into their interactions with the opposite gender polarity. Such a fear undermines their ability to ask potential partners on a date. This is why many uninitiated men avoid rejection by paying for sex or having virtual sex, where there's no chance of rejection. The fantasy of the feminine worshiping the masculine also appeals to the immature masculine who fears he's not enough of a man to fulfill a woman (or feminine-dominant man).

If a man's mother was very dominating, his fear of being dominated may be so acute that he feels repelled by women as potential partners and only safe with the feminine within a male form. That isn't to suggest homosexuality is simply the result of a wound, rather than two souls recognizing one another as kindred spirits, it's simply a key to unlocking the subconscious issues that sabotage love being expressed in a healthy way, regardless of one's gender preference.

The more severe the wound, the more a man (or masculine-dominant woman) will reject or denigrate the feminine in order to feel powerful. This is why porn shows women worshiping men, no matter how badly men treat them. Every act of humiliation a woman endures illustrates her loyalty for an immature man who's seeking unconditional love. Such scenarios fulfill the ultimate fantasy of the immature masculine, which is, that they will never be rejected. Both offer reassurance for the deep-seated fear of rejection, until they unpack their *Mother Complex*. Only then, can they release the sense of burden they feel towards the feminine, on the understanding, their mother's happiness was not their cross to bear. Knowing this, men are less likely to be manipulated by advertising campaigns that show a man making a woman smile by making a large purchase, such as a home.

How the Mother Complex Undermines Relationships

A man (or masculine-dominant woman) with an unhealed *Mother Complex* may sabotage their relationships by subconsciously testing their partner to see if they really love them. They do this by mistreating them to see if they'll stick around, as a demonstration they love them unconditionally, just as a mother would tend to a child, regardless of their infantile behavior. This is the toxic root of abusive relationships. Not just physically abusive relationships, but psycho-emotionally abusive relationships which are far more common and yet not considered, 'domestic violence'. In such a dysfunctional dynamic, a wounded man (or masculine-dominant woman) will constantly reject their partner to prove they don't need their mother. Despite their inability to be loving, they may be shocked when their partner leaves, as they assume because they feel love for them, they should stay. It may not occur to them to reflect on their own behavior and question how loving their words and actions have been towards their partner.

I experienced this dynamic with a partner whose favorite film was, *Leaving Las Vegas* starring Nicholas Cage and Elisabeth Shue. Described as a 'romance drama' it features Cage as a suicidal alcoholic and Shue as a hooker who loves him unconditionally. As the film progresses, the destructive behavior of the male lead impacts more and more negatively on the wellbeing of the female lead. The endgame is the ultimate act of narcissism; after drinking himself to his deathbed, he asks her to grant him sexual favors, after he has repeatedly denied her sex and been unfaithful. This scene illustrates a man who is in the ultimate state of passivity, giving nothing in return and asking a woman to self-sacrifice her needs until the very end. This indicates the fantasy of a man with an unhealed *Mother Complex*. That being, a woman (or feminine-dominant man) will love them completely by remaining loyal, when they offer only pain in return. Portrayed as 'love', this dynamic is a narcissistic projection that a 'good woman' will prove her love by denying herself in every way to prioritize her partner.

Men with this unresolved *Mother Complex* also sabotage their own health and wellbeing by manifesting illness/injury to subconsciously manipulate their partners into mothering them. Some do this when a relationship ends as a last ditch attempt to hook their partner back into a dysfunctional dance, prioritizing their needs over 'her' own. I experienced this dynamic when I ended my marriage. My ex-husband broke his shoulder and asked me to tend to his daily needs. While I initially complied, when he recovered, he returned to say he was homeless and needed to sleep on my couch. Initially I consented, but when I finally put an end to the dysfunctional dance, he quickly found a new mother-surrogate online and moved in with her. Once he had a new mother-surrogate he punished me psychologically and emotionally for years by withholding access to our child at every opportunity. I share this personal account simply to illustrate how devastating this punitive dynamic is on both mother and child.

Acknowledging the Mother/Son Bond

It is perfectly natural for boys when they are young to declare from a place of innocence that they want to marry their mother when they grow up. However as a boy becomes a youth, he may feel increasingly conflicted and guilty if his mother is more emotionally and psychologically bonded to him than to his father. This can be the underlying dynamic that escalates tension between a father and son who has entered puberty, resulting in a showdown where the two men fight to assert dominance like a stag and a young buck. This is why when a boy enters puberty a *Welcome to Manhood* ceremony is so vital to 'cut the apron strings'; the psycho-emotional umbilical cord between mother and son. This sets a boy free so his childhood bond with his mother doesn't become a dysfunctional form of bondage he enacts in his adult relationships.

Women's Core Wound: The Father Complex

All women, regardless of their gender identity or preference experience this inner mythos to varying degrees. It is therefore essential women seek to identify this wound in order to heal it. Like the *Mother Complex* in men, if the *Father Complex* wound is neglected, it will fester and undermine their wellbeing and relationships.

The *Father Complex* refers to the subconscious associations and impulses a woman has with her father that are projected onto men (and masculine-dominant women), such as authority figures. The root of the wound is how much they secretly craved their father's love all for themselves as a young girl. Growing up, if they didn't feel truly valued and protected by their father, this wound will result in dysfunctional interactions with men (and masculine-dominant women). For example, latent rage towards a woman's father may manifest as *misandry*: a fear of the masculine projected towards men or the masculine part of women. This may also manifest as the dualistic lover/destroyer aspect. Such as someone who uses their sexual allure to seduce men (or masculine-dominant women), only to discard or denigrate them once they've validated their ego with their attention. This type of psycho-emotional abuse can also include sarcastic remarks, disapproving looks, the silent treatment or angry outbursts resulting in personal attacks. When a woman (or feminine-dominant man) misplaces rage at their father towards their partner, they may escalate their verbally abusive behavior, using their partner as a whipping dog until their partner leaves or finds the self-esteem to set self-honoring boundaries. To be fair to my ex-husband who I mentioned earlier, I was guilty of the latter due to my unhealed *Father Complex*!

Alternatively, a woman (or feminine-dominant man) with an unresolved *Father Complex* may constantly strive to earn their father's love by playing one of the following roles.

❖   Daddy's Girl.

This describes someone who is trying to fulfill the role of the perfect wife, by embodying the patriarchal ideal of 'homemaker/mother' in an effort to please her man. This subconscious attempt to please her father-surrogate is to validate her identity as a woman. Those in a higher income bracket, where domestic help is employed, may instead strive to fulfill the role of the perfect 'domestic manager/social host' or 'trophy bride'. Such a woman may be so dependent on external validation she overlooks her inner needs and then feels resentment towards her partner. She may complain her partner doesn't truly know and value her. This is a reflection of her underdeveloped relationship with herself. Should her partner reject her, despite her best efforts to fulfill the patriarchal expectation of the 'perfect wife/mother' she may demand financial provision and protection via the courts before seeking another Sugar Daddy to take care of her, rather than unpack her *Father Complex*.

❖   The Good Girl.

This describes a woman who aspires to be 'just like Dad' to earn his approval. She may project 'father-figure' on to her boss or seek recognition from established authorities, such as respected institutions and publications. Due to an obsessive compulsion to gain external validation, she may seek personal achievement, overlooking her personal needs due to her work demands. Impressing Dad is the unconscious motivation for many businesswomen, even those who dare risk their father's disapproval by following their passion. Meanwhile others opt for a conventional career path that Dad would approve of, such as working in the corporate sector or within a male-dominated industry; like law, medicine or engineering...one that affords a woman status within a patriarchal culture. If the *Good Girl* role is really anchored, she may even wait until her father dies before finally pursuing her heart's unconventional calling. I suspect this expression of the *Father Complex*; pursuing recognition outside the home is more likely if she's observed the efforts of her mother within the family home not being respected and valued. Either way, if one is polarizing between rejecting and punishing or seeking approval from the masculine, struggle will inevitably follow until she's explored her unprocessed fears and feelings about men, by examining her relationship with her father or formative father-figure. To assist with that, let's explore the story of *Electra*, the myth that illustrates the universal *Father Complex* in women.

The Myth of Electra

Electra was the daughter of *King Agamemnon* and *Queen Clytemnestra* of Mycenae in Greek mythology. When her uncle, *King Menelaus* discovered his wife had been abducted, her father left abruptly to avenge the abduction of her on the basis she was his brother's property. On his way he kills a stag deer, sacred to the Goddess, *Artemis*. To gain favor with the Goddess, he offers up *Electra's* sister, *Iphigenia*, as a human sacrifice. He then lies to his wife and daughter, saying *Iphigenia* is to be sent away to marry *Achilles*. His lie is discovered when *Electra* and her mother go to the port to see *Iphigenia* off. Fortunately, *Artemis* does not take the life of *Iphigenia*, but instead brings her to Tauris, where she becomes a priestess in service to the Goddess.

The Trojan War that resulted from this retaliation lasted 10 years. When *Electra's* father finally returned home at the end of the war, accompanying him was *Cassandra*, the daughter of *King Priam of Troy*. *Cassandra* was a gift from her father, as a spoil of war. *Cassandra* was a famous prophetess who had foreseen, both the war and the death of *Agamemnon*, so she went willingly, knowing the arrangement would be short-lived.

Electra's mother, *Queen Clytemnestra* was furious at being so publicly betrayed and disrespected. This was compounded by the earlier deceit and treachery of her husband who sacrificed their daughter, *Iphigenia* and murdered her first husband, so he could wed her. Having taken *Agamemnon's* cousin as a lover during the 10 year Trojan War, together they plotted and murdered *Agamemnon*.

When *Electra* learned her Mother was responsible for her father's death, she convinced her brother, *Orestes*, to kill both their mother, and her lover, to avenge their father's death. The Goddess, *Athena* vindicated *Orestes*, on the basis that killing their mother was 'not as serious as the killing of their father'. And we wonder why mothers are devalued in a patriarchal society!

The Meaning of the Myth

In the opening scene of her story, *Electra* witnesses how precarious life is for women in her patriarchal culture. Her aunt is abducted, indicating how essential the protection of a male ally is to one's survival. Such an event would certainly anchor a need to please one's father figure to ensure protection. However, instead of remaining close as *Electra's* protector, her father leaves suddenly and doesn't return for 10 years, leaving his family vulnerable.

Next we witness her father betraying her sister by trading her life for his own gain. This is reminiscent of the wounded feminine theme illustrated in, *The Handless Maiden*. He then betrays *Electra* and her mother by lying to them in an attempt to cover his treachery, thereby breaking trust.

It's then revealed that rather than courting her mother, he took her against her will, by killing her former husband. This indicates a complete lack of morality and disrespect for the sanctity of union. It is now clear *Electra* is a child born of a loveless union. Her mother is viewed as the property of her husband. She is a prisoner who feels no loyalty towards her jailer. *Electra* is raised in a domestic war zone. This is a dynamic that's all too common behind the veneer of civility.

So how is it that, given his psychological profile, *Electra* remains so fiercely loyal to her father? Initially, her loyalty is instinctual to address her survival fears. However, during her father's long absence it seems feasible *Electra* would compensate for the loss of her father by creating a fantasy father figure who can do no wrong. She does this to avoid confronting the pain of his rejection and abandonment.

She places him on a pedestal and redirects her anger at her absent father onto her mother. Why? Her mother is a safe receptacle for her inner torment. Her mother will not reject or abandon her, but will instead hold the space for her daughter's rage. Her mother is also a victim of circumstance. This makes her an easy scapegoat. In addition, *Electra* sees her mother's human flaws on a daily basis, while her father remains perfect in her own mind, fueled by the public accolades he receives as a war hero. This is compounded by the cultural devaluing of women, which is why this dynamic remains common today.

As a youth, *Electra* would've been aware of her mother's indiscretions with her father's cousin. This would further fuel judgment and derision towards her mother. So when *Electra's* father finally returned home, with a younger woman as his new companion, we see the double-standard that is applied to women. Her mother's affair is covert and not accepted, while her father's indiscretion is overt and publicly accepted, indicating a much higher moral code of behavior placed on women, justifying vilification of the feminine.

Electra's pent up misdirected rage at her father is finally unleashed on her mother in a final act of double homicide with *Electra* manipulating her brother into doing her malicious bidding.

Electra is a tragic warning of the fate that befalls a woman who embodies the toxic feminine due to her inability to question her father and the unjust social rules placed on women living within a patriarchy. The origin of her wound is that she feels unseen by her father and society. She internalizes this wound by devaluing the feminine - a product of her cultural conditioning. This is what causes her to betray the feminine, internally and externally. Her distorted relationship with the masculine justifies her destructive behavior towards the feminine.

Her tragic story illustrates how the psyche of a child is damaged when they experience love as betrayal in their family of origin. This anchors a subconscious belief that becomes a self-fulfilling prophecy. This is why the ancients placed such an emphasis on initiations to prepare men and women emotionally and psychologically for partnership.

Just as a mother may impose her emotional needs on her son, creating the *Mother Complex* in boys, here we see the equivalent damage done when a father imposes his psychological needs on his daughter. How? A daughter who is not permitted and supported to form her own ideas and opinions remains stunted, unable to individuate from her father's view of the world by freely expressing her own values and viewpoints. This is psychological incest. It implies the narcissistic belief, "You belong to me and are an extension of me." Rather than perceiving one's progeny as beings in their own right with intrinsic human rights that are worthy of understanding and respect. Such behavior imposes the will of the dominant ego inappropriately on one who is too young to adequately defend and protect themselves.

Electra is a story with a feminist theme, personifying a woman's right to know and express herself intellectually, rather than exist purely for her father's gain. Equally we must honor men's right to know and express themselves emotionally, rather than feel pressured to exist primarily for their mother's happiness. This makes *Oedipus*, a story with a masculinist theme, suggesting perhaps an equivalent social movement be afforded a title to legitimize the need for its existence rather than deny the need for feminism out of resentment.

In a patriarchal culture, where the masculine dominates the feminine, the *Father Wound* is overt so the feminine is sacrificed equally by men and women in big and small ways to afford one greater acceptance in society. Our halls of power, our learning institutions and our information networks all perpetuate the *Father Wound*. Those who regurgitate the conventional viewpoints and behaviors of their forefathers are rewarded with recognition and funding. While those who explore ideas beyond the bounds of patriarchal convention are marginalized and financially disadvantaged. Hence the stereotype of a 'starving artist living in a garret'. It's accepted that if you choose a more feminine profession you will be destined to suffer for your choice.

As I write this, censorship is escalating as the *4th Reich* try to contain the truth to avoid accountability for their actions by punishing those who don't comply with their *Fatherland* propaganda; the name given to Nazi Germany who embodied the *Father Wound* in the extreme. Not that those who opt to live within the society of a *Fatherland* thrive. Those who are enslaved by the *Father Wound* are most at risk of being dominated by the toxic masculine, whether that's an abusive government, work culture, social circle or partnership. This current attempt at totalitarian control is the last gasp of Patriarchy, a paradigm we can each contribute to dismantling by healing our *Father Wound*, so we're not intimidated into submission by the *dark father*.

Why? Children who aren't encouraged to think for themselves and question others, including the status quo, conclude their ideas are of lesser importance or of no value at all. This results in compliance, without question, as they defer to external authority figures. This is how we are groomed to be complicit in our own psychological abuse. As thought leader *Noam Chomsky* observed in the media, consent is manufactured through the repetition of the same idea imposed until it is inevitably accepted. Similarly, to impose our beliefs and allegiances on to a child's developing mind is a form of child abuse. Whether that's done via a religious doctrine, patriotic allegiance to a nation or sports team or the taking on of cultural prejudice…if a child must comply with a parent's perspective or risk exclusion or persecution, that is abuse. Such indoctrination is perpetuated on the misguided premise that children are the property of their family of origin, rather than appreciating them as sacred and sovereign individuals in their own right, with their own minds and inalienable rights.

Such abuse is not deliberate. In fact, quite the opposite. Imposing limiting fear-based ideas as 'truths beyond question' is often a desperate attempt to keep a child safe by imparting all one has learned about life to date. Since the role of the father is to protect his child, if the father has not learned to think for himself, he will instill the prejudices of his own conditioning. For example, if a father's sense of selfhood is underdeveloped, he will fear those from different cultural backgrounds as a direct threat to his own existence. Without exploring his fear, he may feel justified in vilifying those who trigger his fear. This causes xenophobia in the next generation if his children feel unsafe to question his authority. When we consider how prevalent prejudice is in our modern society, it's clear how psychologically immature the group mind has become due to the unhealed *Father Wound*.

A child who fears the unknown and those who are different is rendered powerless to explore the world. In the extreme, these are the children who never leave home. While others may physically leave the nest, they may still defer to their father for advice on big decisions on the belief, 'Father knows best'. Usually as children pass through puberty they question the legitimacy of their father's authority and begin the inevitable process of individuation. However, just as the patriarchal Greek *Sky Father* God, *Zeus* modeled the *Father Wound* by swallowing his daughter, *Athena*, women who are intellectually astute are often the ones who most struggle in a battle of wits and wills with their father. This is because a man who is psychologically immature, will take any form of disagreement as a personal attack and try to take down his perceived opponent due to an inability to separate his identity from his beliefs. In the myth of *Electra* it's telling that the Goddess, *Athena* betrays the feminine by downplaying the gravity of the murder of *Electra's* mother. This illustrates how *Athena* is also a daughter of the patriarchy who perpetuates the devaluing of the feminine. This may seem incongruent when we consider her origin story and her own struggle to exist in her own right. *Athena's* father, *Zeus* feared his daughter would possess an intelligence that would surpass his own, due to her mother being *Metis*, the Goddess of wisdom so he pre-emptively tried to avoid the embarrassment of being usurped by his daughter by swallowing her whole. Similarly, immature fathers may compete with their daughters or shun their efforts for fear of being outdone.

Until daughters dare question the belief that 'Dad's always right', they may struggle to know their own mind, find their purpose and choose partners their Dad may not approve of. Until they question their father's values and the origins of those values, they may struggle to value their time, talents and ideas. The patriarchal custom of the father-of-the-bride 'giving the bride away' at the altar indicates how socially acceptable it is to view daughters as the property of their fathers. This is anchored by giving children the father's name indicating a father's ownership of his family within Patriarchy. When we acknowledge the root of the wounds that undermine our human relating we can create a new interpersonal dynamic via relationships that heal rather than harm. With this knowledge we are ready to enter *Sacred Union*.

In intimate relationships a woman (or feminine-dominant man) with an unhealed *Father Complex* will compete with her partner in a subconscious attempt to prove her worth to her projected father-figure. For info on how to deconstruct that dysfunctional dance, check out my *Conscious Relating* course listed in the resource section.

CHAPTER 12

The Hieros Gamos:
The Alchemy of Love

Having identified the origins of their suffering, the hero is now liberated from the bondage of his saboteur. Without the confusion of distorted beliefs he is clear his purpose is to serve love, on the understanding love conquers all. How? By following his conscience; the wisdom of the heart, that is the voice of Divine Will. By choosing love over fear, he will be a force for healing, wherever there is division.

While *the Grail* quest was always a search for true love, it is only now the hero comprehends the true power of love. Having discovered the gifts of self-love, brotherly / sisterly love, devotional love and romantic love, he is now ready to discover the power of erotic love, as a force for transformation and renewal. For it's through the reclamation of our sacred sexual power we'll experience a true sexual revolution...not a politicized gender war that creates division and trauma.

Dragon Kings and Queens

In the ancient world, those who completed their archetypal *Hero's Journey* were celebrated as *Year Kings and Queens*. Today's appropriation of this custom is the crowning of 'Homecoming Kings and Queens' at high school formals. This patriarchal custom sees teens awarded royal status based on their popularity, rather than their character and effort. The extreme distortion of this ancient custom are beauty pageants, where girls as young as toddlers are awarded symbols of royal power, such as crowns and scepters, based on their appearance and ability to please those in authority.

By way of contrast, in *the Grail* tradition *Year Kings* and *Queens* were those who had 'faced the dragon' and lived to tell the tale by returning to share their gifts.

My understanding is those who successfully completed 7 cycles of *The Hero's Journey* were afforded the title of Dragon *King/Queen*. To mark this achievement they received dragon tattoos or wore serpentine jewelry. In the book, *The Mists of Avalon* by Marion Zimmer Bradley, *King Arthur's* father, *Uther Pendragon*, is portrayed with dragons tattooed on his forearms.

In the ancient world in times of conflict, when the armies of different kingdoms were conjoined, an overall leader was chosen and he was called the *Great Dragon* meaning 'the King-of-kings' or in its old Celtic form, *The Pendragon*.[71] It is by his dragon tattoos Uther was recognized by his future wife, *Igraine*, a noblewoman trained as a priestess at *Avalon*. On sighting the mark of the dragon she acknowledged his level of self-mastery. Today, people get inked without any test of initiation. This lessens the impact of this ancient sacred art and fosters a compulsive desire for more in an unconscious search for initiation.

Previously, those who bore the mark of the serpent/dragon were those whose values and commitment had been thoroughly tested and endured. This meant they could be trusted with worldly power, making them eligible for positions of authority within their community. Known in *Mesopotamia* as *Priest Kings* and *Priestess Queens*, those in positions of rulership were those who had been initiated in the Mystery Schools as a precursor to bearing civic responsibility.

Throughout *Europa* and *Brigit's Isles*, the title of *Dragon King/Queen* granted one the protection of the *Earth Mother's* elemental forces and the ability to summon and direct them at will, as a conduit for healing. Having awakened the ability to traverse the 3 worlds, ancient rulers took vows to serve, not just humans but all the beings who inhabited the realms, which is why the elemental beings were happy to grant their allegiance and assistance. This is also why ancient leaders performed sacred ceremonies on the dragon lines; the major energy meridians within the Earth. By way of contrast, today's world leaders lack the consciousness to perceive the 3 worlds so they unwittingly destroy the habitat of elemental beings, dismissing their existence as mere fantasy.

Prior to the rise of the empires people sought to live in harmony with the elemental forces and beings. The resurgence in popularity of so-called fantasy films, like *Lord of the Rings* and *Harry Potter*, indicates awareness of beings in the other realms is growing as the veils thin between the worlds.

The Return of Magic

The mundane *Muggle* society created by the empires is a form of torture for the multi-dimensional soul, as it denies the truth of who we are and the truth about existence. This is one reason people seek an experience of the other realms through taking mind-altering substances. By way of contrast, our ancestors, instructed by advanced stellar races, considered the power of magic so important, they erected temples where the dragon lines of the Earth intercepted.

They built ceremonial sites in the formation of sacred geometries to conduct the flow of energy upwards. Ceremonies were conducted within stone circles, medicine wheels, barrows (man-made hills) and *pyramids* during the seasonal energy vortices. The intention being to charge the energy grid of the Earth and raise the frequency of the collective consciousness. Ceremonies were held at dawn/dusk when the Earth's magnetic field is strongest on eclipses, solstices, equinoxes and seasonal cross-quarter festivals. This is why the *pyramids* were built with limestone and contained high amounts of magnesium, which conducts *kundalini*; the bio-energy of the Earth. The ancients also built aquifers beneath their temples, such as the *Pyramids of Giza* as water creates a mild electrical charge and acts as a conduit.

The Roman Empire erected patriarchal churches and state buildings on the dragon lines. This caused stagnation within the Earth's energy grid, so the consciousness of the group mind descended, just as illness occurs when the energy meridians within our bodies become blocked.

Covert ceremonies were then conducted in the basements of many churches during the seasonal and lunar power days to raise the power of dark forces to serve the interests of the ruling elite. This was done through committing depraved acts on the innocent. Fortunately, thanks to many brave survivors of ritual abuse, the extent of Satanic cults is now being exposed. This is why we were taught to fear magic - so we wouldn't be aware of how it was being against us and how to use it consciously as a force for good. Every person who meditates and does sacred ceremony to raise the frequency of our *Earth Mother* and all her children during these 'power windows' counteracts these inversions. To recreate *Heaven on Earth* we need to clear the gateways through which the life force flows...that's why so many people have been drawn to visit sacred sites. The more clear vessels who do energy raising practices along the dragon lines help to clear the blocks.

Reclaiming the Power of the Dragon Lines

The Holy Grail was performed on special ceremonial grounds that were created specifically for this rite, such as the *Hill of Tara*. Known as *Temair* in Gaeilge, it was once the ancient seat of power in Ireland where 142 kings were said to have reigned in prehistoric and historic times. Mounds known as *barrows* were also dug to create man-made caves, simulating wombs as incubation chambers, for men to retreat within the Earth for rebirth at Winter Solstice. You can still see many today throughout the south of England.

It's no coincidence they are built along the Earth's dragon lines. These are the same energy meridians where crop circles have been strategically anchored by our stellar neighbors to energize and awaken our collective consciousness, despite media blackouts and claims of hoaxes disseminated by those who own the airwaves. The *Glastonbury Tor* in the south of England is the largest mound I know of built for this purpose. While today, tourists climb it to meditate and contemplate the vista, once it was within this man-made hill that many men undertook their ancient *Grail* rites. *Newgrange* in Ireland is another man-made structure built specifically for this purpose. It's constructed so at the exact time of Winter Solstice the solar light enters the inner chamber for 17 minutes, revealing sacred carvings. The ancient Celts covered the roof in clear quartz crystals so the mound would be charged by solar and lunar light, all year round. This ensured the crystals remained clear and energized to assist *Grail* initiates to change their state of awareness, by piercing the darkness of confusion with the light of insight. Unfortunately renovations to this popular tourist destination have seen the crystals removed from the roof and placed around the sides for 'aesthetic purposes' indicating ignorance or sabotage, or a combination of both! None of the information at the site acknowledges *the Grail* rites. Similarly, *Stonehenge*, a well-known circle of standing stones in England restricts access to those seeking to conduct sacred ceremonies for its original purpose. The only value perceived is that of historic significance, exploited by gift shop souvenirs and walking tours. Having personally persisted to follow guidance to conduct a private ceremony there for a specific astrological event, I can attest as to how frustrating it was paying thousands of dollars for an hour on a date determined by bureaucrats, only to have disrespectful security guards ever present.

Raising the Dragons

Souls who incarnate specifically to raise the power of the dragons within the Earth in service to the *Earth*

Mother first prepare their vessels by activating the twin serpents of sacred masculine and feminine energy within their energy bodies. This practice was taught by the advanced stellar races who lived amongst the *Egyptians* and *Sumerians* and taught them alchemy; the raising of *kundalini* to transform. This is why they chose to settle between the *Tigris* and *Euphrates* rivers, on the understanding this delta was fertile land between the two meridians of energy representing the twin serpents. In these advanced civilizations, *kundalini* was revered as *The Force*; the elixir of life. It was everyone's divine birthright to access this sacred power. This is why the ancient symbol for healing depicted 'the raised serpent on the rod', symbolizing one's spinal cord. If one had not raised their sacred power they lacked moral strength, known as 'backbone'. Whereas those who awakened their 'serpent power', like a cobra, would not cower in the face of an aggressor. This is also why pharaohs and queens in ancient *Egypt* wore cobra insignia on their cobra-shaped headdresses.

The empires appropriated this sacred symbol for their

Rod of Askelpius

Dollar Sign

man-made power; money. Why? The subconscious speaks in symbols, so this switch programmed the group mind to worship money as the ultimate power, sacrificing their life force to the warlords; those who controlled the flow of this measure of energy. This is why it's called currency. That which flows between 'banks', impersonating the current of a river between river banks that provide a natural flow of energy and abundance needed for all life to thrive.

This is why indigenous people fight to protect the free flow of rivers on the understanding that without water, there is no life and those who seek to control the water, by damming and selling it to private interests for their own personal gain, deny our most

Caduceus Symbol of Alchemy   Medical Symbol

basic human right - our right to live freely upon the Earth, our mother. The children's animated film, *Riverdance* speaks to this.

Similarly, the sacred symbol for alchemy, the *caduceus*, was appropriated. It depicts the inner twin serpents known in Sanskrit as *Ida and Pingala*. They are the meridians that lay dormant within our energy field and are awakened through initiation. Since the microcosm reflects the macrocosm, these meridians reflect the energies within the Earth, which we can activate and raise. The serpents are entwined around a central staff, intercepting at each of the 7 energy vortices, known as *chakras* in Sanskrit. When the feminine and masculine archetypal energies that govern these 7 centers are empowered and expressed, the energies of the twin serpents flow unimpeded from the base of the spine to the crown, awakening consciousness, empowerment, wholeness & healing.

The wings atop the staff indicate the transcendence of the ego that grants one a higher perspective. The wings signify the brain's lateral ventricular structures. Between these wings, above the spinal column, is shown an orb, signifying the pineal gland that governs the third eye, considered the 'seat of wisdom'. The combination of the central pineal and its lateral wings has been referred to as the 'Swan'. In *Grail* lore the Swan is emblematic of the fully enlightened being. This is why the *Lady of the Lake*, is often shown in a boat fashioned to look like a swan, in honor of *Caer Ibormeith*, the Celtic Goddess of dreams and prophecy who was accompanied by 150 swans and shape-shifted into a swan at Samhain every alternate year.[72] In the East, the Hindu Goddess *Saraswati* attained inner marriage and was depicted riding a swan.

This is why *Grail* knights, such as *Perceval* and *Lohengrin* were referred to as, *Knights of the Swan*.

The shape-shifting magical or 'winged serpent' is a theme in all indigenous cultures. From the Aztec winged serpent, *Quetzacoatl* who embodies both masculine and feminine energies, to the rainbow serpent of Indigenous Australians and the 'rainbow body' sought by Tibetans to the Islamic, *Melek Ta'us*,

King Arthur asks the Lady of the Lake for the Sword of Excalibur

described as a 'living rainbow'. In the Zuni tradition, the plumed twin serpents/dragons came from the oceans and collected sacred water from springs for ceremonial ritual drinks to assist participants to become like kachinas meaning 'star beings'.

Here we see the archetypal *Holy Hermaphrodite* as the embodiment of a soul who's attained the inner marriage in *The World*, the final card of the Tarot. They're holding the rods

488

of rulership that were once bestowed upon the raising of one's serpents, illustrated by the Minoan 'Snake

Minoan Snake Goddess

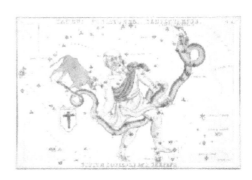

Asklepius as the constellation, Ophiuchus

Goddess' and *Askelpius,* shown as the constellation of *Ophiuchus,* the awakened man.

Just as the power of 'The Force' was later attributed to money, the power of healing was later attributed to pharmaceutical medicine; chemicals. It's a bitter irony that the toxicity of the chemical industry poisons both our bodies and the Earth, destroying fertility, in the name of healing. Whereas, natural medicines and energy-based healing detoxify and promote fertility within us and the land. (More about that later.)

The Alchemy of Erotic Love

Initiates who awakened the twin serpents to create the inner marriage were deemed ready for the *Hieros Gamos*, meaning 'Sacred Union'. This was a practice that was part of the *Wheel of Eight* discussed in chapter 9 as a service to the *Earth Mother* and all her realms.

The sacred art of lovemaking was a key component of this practice, as both parties surrendered themselves as energetic conduits to anchor the union of 'Heaven and Earth'. Prior to lovemaking during specific 'power windows' they would prepare their respective channels by opening the 7 gates, invoking the God and Goddess, by all their names and setting clear intent. That being, to direct the energies raised into the energy grid of the Earth, to anchor the harmonic balance of opposites. They did this on the understanding that everything is interconnected, so the macrocosm of the land and the collective would be renewed with fertility through the harmonious joining of opposites within the microcosm of their energy bodies. These sacred love rites were consummated on energy vortices within the energy grid of the *Earth Mother*. Dedicating oneself to the practice of the *Hieros*

Gamos is what it meant to serve the dragon lines. This is why Dragon Kings/Queens were buried on the dragon lines[73] in honor of their service to the *Earth Mother* and her people. This is why we see the red dragon, symbolizing the life force of the Earth, and the colors of white and green, symbolizing the purity of consciousness and courage of heart, that the sacred masculine embodies, on the Welsh flag that *Uther Pendragon* served.

The origins of the Welsh flag are attributed to an ancient king called, *Vortigern,* who was seeking a suitable site to build his castle and eventually settled on the hill of *Dinas Emrys* that was situated on an

The Welsh Flag

underground lake, where two dragons were said to be sleeping.[74]

The red dragon also symbolized royalty in the ancient Chinese tradition where the energy lines of the Earth are referred to as dragon lines. Hence the celebrations on Lunar New Year with theatrical red dragons and red firecrackers set off to wake them up! So too, in *Mesopotamia*, the entrance to the temple of the *High Priestess*, known as *The Gate of Ishtar* featured dragons, along with *Sphinxes* and bulls. It was here the king of the land would visit on the Spring Equinox to meet with the reigning *High Priestess*. If she deemed him mature, humble and wise, she would consent to participate in the *Hieros Gamos* with him to raise the serpents, blessing the land and her people with fertility, through ensuring the balance of opposites needed to create sustainability.

" In 1408...the Dragon Court was formerly reconstituted as a sovereign body...by Sigismund von Luxembourg, king of Hungary, a descendent of the Lusignan Dragon Kings of Jerusalem. The founding document stated that members might wear the insignia of the dragon incurved in a circle, with a red *cross, the very emblem which had identified the Grail*

succession from before 3000 BC"

Laurence Gardner. Genesis of the Grail Kings

The Beloveds: The Emanation of the Holy Couple

Today there's a lot of talk about *soul mates* and *twin flames*. I speak about the differences in detail in my book, *Sacred Union: Awakening the Consciousness of Eden*. To recap, a *soul mate* is a being we've known in another incarnation so there is a karmic bond that attracts us in order to resolve past lessons. A *twin flame* is a soul who is our extreme polar opposite, so the attraction is magnetic and dynamic but often, dramatic. Why? The role of the *twin flame* is to trigger our unintegrated aspects. This accelerates our self-awareness through a process of inner alchemy. Those who transcend the interplay of intense love and war inherent in these connections do so by committing to self-love and redirecting their focus to create *Sacred Union* within. This is what eventually attracts their *Beloved*; the divine complement who is a reflection of their inner marriage.

My intuitive knowing is that many Beloveds will be united in 2022. Why? In numerology the number, 2 represents the inner balance needed to harmoniously co-operate and co-create. Ever since the start of the millennium in the year 2000 we've been collectively undergoing a 'relationship revolution' examining our patterns of relating to prepare for a new era of 'conscious community'. For those who have been doing the preparatory work; healing and empowering the multifaceted aspects that comprise the soul, this is an exciting time of harvest; being truly met in a way we've not experienced in relationship for many lifetimes. I see this as a time in our evolution when the *Beloveds* shall be reunited and together, co-create *Eden* with like-hearted soul groups known as monads.

When *Beloveds* unite they embody the archetypal *Holy Couple* comprised of two beings who have empowered all 7 feminine and masculine aspects to become balanced and whole. I want to emphasize this doesn't mean one must become perfect to attract their *Beloved*, as our journey to heal and become whole is eternal. En route, our challenge is to accept we all are perfectly imperfect.

Those who master this internal balance to become clear vessels for the sacred feminine and masculine create an energetic template for higher love that is expressed through joint world service. This is what fairy tales portray as the 'happy ending' that ends with 'true love' found and expressed between the royal couple. When we understand this from a mystic perspective, rather than an empiric one, we can appreciate fairytales as wisdom parables rather than dismiss them with cynicism - a mindset which is evident today when we consider the term, *happy ending*, is more commonly associated with a Thai massage that gratifies a primal urge! This is because we've been conditioned to seek quick gratification, so we assume something is wrong if we haven't found 'the one' before each milestone birthday.

Many sabotage their chance at finding 'true love' with their *Beloved* by staying in the familiarity of existing unions that aren't truly uplifting and soul-fulfilling. This is due to a conditioned fear of change and a societal perception that divorce is both a failure and a betrayal. So while patriarchy celebrates long marriages, regardless of their quality of relating, many unconsciously choose to stagnate their personal growth, rather than face their fear of being alone. This amounts to a betrayal of one's soul. That isn't to say, we should strap on our chastity belt until we meet our *Beloved*. Intimacy is a skill we learn through practice.

Beloveds inspire great love, both singularly and together. Like the historic couples; *Yeshua* and *Mari*, *Sheba* and *Solomon*, *Arthur* and *Guinevere*, they are legendary lovers whose embodied union of sacred feminine and masculine energies, individually and together, serve as role models. Hype manufactured by the ruling elite's propaganda has tried to convince us that impersonations of the *Holy Couple*, such as royal and celebrity 'It' couples, are worthy of our constant admiration and attention, simply because they have societal status afforded by wealth, power and fame.

Beloveds experience love at first sight, which is instant recognition of the other. However, such a union is not entered into with haste and seduction. It is understood by both parties that their union serves a higher purpose and its sacred power must be deeply honored and respected so a conscious courtship is entered into. This ensures a meeting of all aspects before physical union takes place. I offer a template for conscious courtship for *Beloveds* in my book, *Creating Sacred Union in Partnerships* listed in the resources section.

It is through the sex act that *Beloveds* initiate each other to higher levels of self-mastery energetically. They also inspire each other to fulfill their divine potential through daily acts of love, beauty and wisdom. Unlike codependent couples where one party is over-responsible and the other irresponsible regarding their psycho-emotional growth, *Beloveds* take equal responsibility for their self-actualization. This is evidenced by their actions prior to meeting.

The closer the time of their meeting, the more they are tested to determine whether they are ready. This involves the burning away of past karma experienced as interactions with past lovers who resurface to determine whether they will be hooked back into old patterns of dysfunction. Potential new suitors will also appear to test their inner resolve to remain chaste until they meet one truly capable of meeting them at the 7 gates. Essentially, both parties have to activate their inner *Tree of Life*, indicating their ability to consciously traverse the 3 worlds and the inner *Tree of Knowledge*, indicating their ability to transcend duality and see the divine working through both polarities. This results in the awakening of plasma energy within their personal energy fields. This occurs through a quickening of their awareness and vibration which intensifies the full spectrum of their inner light.

Union with the *Beloved* amplifies our ability to manifest our intent into form. This is because both have walked the white and red paths of the magi; integrating the lessons of spirit; the sacred masculine and matter; the sacred feminine. This prepares them to create the union of 'Heaven on Earth'. This is why *Beloveds* are such a powerful force for good in the world and threaten the power base of those who seek to rule through imposing fear and separation.

This is why *Yeshua* and *Mari* were persecuted by the Roman Empire and those who assumed power fostered competition, division, shame and confusion about our gender polarities in an attempt to prevent *Beloveds* reuniting. This is also why the cult of Rome replaced the iconography of the *Holy Couple* with the image of a 'mother and son' as the dominant relational image between the sexes. This anchored an immature expectation in the subconscious of the group mind that 'true love' is the feminine mothering the masculine, perpetuating the mother wound that sabotages 'true love'.

When we comprehend the alchemical power contained within our light bodies, and the threat the *Beloveds* pose to the empire, it becomes obvious why the Roman Empire's religious doctrine demonized sex for any purpose, other than increasing the numbers of their flock. With this awareness, we can better understand the programming imposed on the collective masculine to replace *Shakti*-activated women with uninitiated women who act like submissive dolls.

From there it wasn't a big leap to promote the acceptance of sex dolls. This trend began in the early 70's with films like, *The Stepford Wives* that showed men replacing their feminist wives with domestic and compliant sex-slave robots. Since then we've seen films like, *HER* and *Bladerunner* that show men in love with artificial women, rather than just who act with artifice. This is the dystopian trajectory for a society where the majority of men are addicted to virtual sex.

Now we're seeing a growing number of brothels offering silicone robot women in the wake of the 2007 film, *Lars and the Real Girl* that depicts a man whose girlfriend is a sex doll. When we observe the misogynistic trend instigated by the empire to 'dumb down' and demonize women and more recently eradicate biological women with virtual women and AI replacements, it begs questioning whether this plays a part in the fact there are twice as many gay men as there are lesbians and twice as many women transitioning to become male than there are men transitioning to become female.[75] Just as indigenous people have been systematically exterminated because of the threat they posed as mystics and shamans, women who are awakening their *kundalini* and initiating men through an experience of *Shaktipat* threaten to bring down the empire as they disarm the walls around men's hearts.

CHAPTER 13

The Great Rebirth:
Restoring the Sacred Balance

T hanks for coming full circle with me to help reawaken *the Grail* codes within the collective consciousness. In this final chapter I'll share how we can all play our part as heroes creating the 'New Earth' by fulfilling the *Whirling Rainbow Prophecy*. This is a *Hopi* prophecy that foretells a time when all colors and creeds would restore the Earth back to green through reclaiming ancient wisdom teachings and sacred customs.

" They will move over the Earth like a great Whirling

Rainbow, bringing peace, understanding and healing

everywhere they go. Many creatures thought to be extinct or

mythical will resurface at this time; the great trees that

perished will return almost overnight."[76]

This prophecy speaks of the start of the *Aquarian Age,* a 2000 year 'Golden Age' when humanity will experience a quantum shift in consciousness that will transform the world as we know it. This has been anticipated since the 1960's when we witnessed the Aquarian ethos gain momentum as we entered the cusp period between the astrological ages. This is when both genders started questioning the polarized roles assigned to them and a role reversal began in an effort to restore the balance.

It was during the 1960's men started rejecting the expectation they sacrifice themselves as pawns. The catalyst was conscription being imposed on young men to recruit enough 'man power' for the Vietnam War. As a result many men sought more connection with the Earth and strived to embody their feminine traits, rejecting their masculinity along with conventional expectations. Many men adopted a more feminine and earthy appearance by growing their hair. Men were heard singing about their feelings in falsetto voices on the airwaves as the collective masculine set their sights on the moon; the feminine luminary.

Meanwhile, as men descended to reconnect with the Earth, women rose to publicly assert their power, using their voices to demand R-E-S-P-E-C-T with Aretha for themselves and the Earth. They started gathering and organizing themselves strategically to create a better world for their children by instigating rallies for positive social change.

As I write this, 60 years later as the cusp between the ages draws to a close, we are experiencing extreme social unrest as the old guard tries to assert its power over the people in a last gasp for absolute power and dominance. This is serving as a catalyst to awaken the 'power of the people' that has lain dormant along with their 'serpent power'.

Our Personal Metamorphosis

The prophecies written for this time tell us prior to our shift into the 'Golden Age' we will experience *Armageddon*. *Armageddon* means the 'conflict of polar opposites'. Many have feared this would eventuate as *World War 3* and some claim never before has a planet been so polarized and not destroyed itself.

The truth is we are experiencing World War 3, but it's a covert war being enacted by the 1% on the 99% rather than between countries, so many don't recognize it as a war. The start of *Armageddon* began in March 2020. This was a world-wide psychological operation designed to create a 'great divide'. This coincided with the lunar nodal axis moving into Gemini/Sagittarius.

The lunar nodes, known as the head and tail of the Cosmic Dragon indicate our collective karmic lessons. The sign of the south node signals our collective past; the origins of our present day conditions, whereas the north node represents the course of our collective future - like due north on a compass. When the nodes moved into Gemini/Sagittarius May 5, 2020 until Jan

18, 2022 a huge deception was launched through all global information channels; announcing a global pandemic to create hysteria so people would abdicate free will in exchange for safety.

During this nodal transit, our collective lesson was to discern truth from illusion by questioning what we'd been conditioned to trust was true. Depending on where people sourced their information from; the corporate-owned media or independent sources, society divided into those who were questioning everything they were being told and those who believed everything they were being told, without question. This was not a conflict of opposites between cultures or countries, but between families, friends and loved ones. Since wherever there is polarization, conflict follows, this social conditioning enabled 'medical' apartheid policies to be justified and introduced, rewarding compliance and punishing those who refused to waive their human rights.

However, everything that unfolds is always part of the divine plan so when we adopt a higher perspective we can see how these events, while corrupt in origin, have served us, both personally and collectively. For instance, the imposed lockdowns forced people to confront themselves; their choices and the state of their lives, without the usual distractions. This held up a painful mirror, demanding they acknowledge what they'd outgrown, such as relationships and jobs being clung to out of a sense of duty or security.

While many responded by escaping into virtual realities and substances, others embraced the opportunity to adapt and transform, utilizing their imposed isolation as a chrysalis for rebirth. They did this by daring to identify what was toxic and personally unsustainable. This resulted in a purging, just as a pregnant woman detoxes when gestating new life.

This was an intuitive urge to prepare for the 'Great Rebirth' instigated by high frequency solar flares that upgraded our light bodies during this time - a phenomena experienced by the more sensitive as headaches, vertigo and extreme lethargy. Since the light illuminates the dark, these waves of solar light catalyzed revelations about ourselves along with a call to acknowledge and integrate what we'd denied.

As a result, people are now daring to be less conventional and express disowned aspects they had previously been afraid to acknowledge. Society is becoming more accepting of diversity. Hence we're seeing the rainbow flag flown with pride, indicating a collective desire to make the world a safer place for all our colors to be expressed, not limited to gender choices. Just as Dorothy had to cross the rainbow to find her magical self to feel at home in the world, we are each being called to acknowledge our dissatisfaction with the limitations of the ego-based lives we've been leading and take a journey into the unknown. We are being asked to broaden our perspective and become multi-faceted, like the diamond blueprint that is our soul. This process is depicted beautifully in the film, *Pleasantville*, which shows everyday folks awaken to live life in full color, rather than being confined to the limitations of black and white reality instigated by adhering to rigid notions of 'right and wrong'.

Our Epic Call to Adventure: The Apocalypse

In order for an abscess to heal, it must be leeched and the wound cleaned to stop the infection festering. So too, for us to heal ourselves and our soul sick world, we must acknowledge and deal with what lies beneath. So in this final chapter I'm going to acknowledge the toxicity that's festering beneath the surface and what we can each do to heal it.

The word, *Apocalypse* is derived from the Greek word, *Apocalypsis* meaning, 'revelations of truth, disclosure and divine intervention'. This is the exact opposite of what we've been conditioned to expect; end times resulting in a wasteland.

As prophesied, we are now awakening from a sleep state of blind trust in the systems of governance and power structures of banking, education and medicine as a cascade of revelations continue to unveil the depth of deceit and corruption that has lain at the foundation of society as we know it. For many this is too overwhelming to even contemplate, as such a shift in thinking requires a complete psychological death of one's identity and belief systems. It is therefore much easier to remain in a state of cognitive dissonance and dismiss the mounting evidence of the 1% ruling elite's hierarchical agenda. A plan that's been strategically implemented over centuries with a far-reaching architecture that asserts dominance through an interconnected web of agencies increasing the status, wealth and influence of those in power by escalating degrees of enslavement upon an unsuspecting populace.

Like the torture technique, *frog boiling,* they have raised the heat of oppression incrementally to avoid detection, while leaving us clues 'in plain sight' like the *Georgia Guidestones,* like a criminal mastermind who can't resist the urge to boast about their 'great work'. The first two intentions carved into stone on this public monument state:

❖ Maintain humanity under 500,000,000 in perpetual balance with nature.

❖ Guide reproduction wisely – improving fitness and diversity.

The first goal would require the extermination of 9/10th's of the 2020 global population. In a final insult to our intelligence, the narrative being programmed via the ruling elite's propaganda machine; the syndicated global media* infers we, the people are to blame for the state of the world, rather than the 1% who have systematically orchestrated widespread destruction to further their agenda of total world dominance. This rhetoric precedes the final act of their 'Great Reset', an attempt to induce total compliance through Draconian methods that dehumanize the individual through the complete stripping of basic human rights. *It's worth noting that collectively almost all mainstream media worldwide is owned by just 6 companies.[77]

How we respond in these 'transition times' determines our trajectory. If we are impotent to act, passive in the face of increasing top-down control and escalating infringement of our human rights, we allow further implementation of their dystopian New World Order to prevail. The NWO endgame is a technocracy where one is robbed of their own free thought. This began with the introduction of 'politically correct' speech and has escalated with censorship of those who speak the truth in public forums. Methods used to try and limit the sphere of influence of whistleblowers include algorithms that preach to the converted and limit organic reach, access to accounts being temporarily denied, posts, articles and videos being shadow banned (not visible on search engines), labeled false by censorship agents called 'fact checkers' or information deleted without warning and social media accounts being canceled. Meanwhile, 'wearable' data collection devices like *Fitbits and Pokemons* were rolled out to track and collect human movements. The data collected was sold and used to further manipulate human behavior.

Where once mind control was delivered externally via television 'programming' in 2020-21 the ruling elite introduced internal programming via MRNA gene-altering injections that implant nanotechnology into unsuspecting recipients. This is AI that self-replicates within the spinal cord and attaches to the brain stem connecting one's brain function to a centralized 'hive mind'. The result is your health status can be accessed directly and stored in the cloud, and equally, your mind can be programmed directly via the cloud. This is a direct inversion of the awakening of *kundalini* that raises consciousness within the spinal cord, connecting one to the quantum field of infinite intelligence.

Meanwhile, 5G mobile phone towers were installed worldwide during the imposed lockdowns, with many placed next to water reserves, magnifying their radiation and causing flu-like symptoms. 5G is a military grade wifi network that enables targeting of non-compliant individuals with weaponized levels of radiation. All independent scientific studies show it is dangerous to all life forms. The film, *5G Apocalypse* provides more information.

These strategic measures to restructure society into a 'new normal' are part of the global roll-out of *Agenda 21*, an initiative of the *United Nations* funded by globalists, *Bill Gates* and *George Soros*. *Agenda 21* uses the rhetoric of 'sustainability' in an attempt to implement their globalist agenda; to centralize power, strip human rights and depopulate. Implemented in the year 2021 it claims by the year 2030 we will 'own nothing and be happy'. In 2015 it was updated with specific goals and renamed, *Agenda 2030* and later promoted by political parties as, *The New Green Deal*.[78]

It's worth noting that *Bill Gates*, a eugenicist like his father, sought to become a member state of the UN in 2009,[79] to acquire the equivalent power of a 'one-man country'. When he lost the vote he paid the UN $300 million a year to ensure his power of influence[80] while rebranding himself as a philanthropist. This 'charitable good guy' persona was the same strategy previously employed by fellow globalist, *John Rockefeller* to enhance his public image. Upon closer inspection however we discover these so-called 'philanthropists' avoid paying tax by placing their assets in not-for-profit foundations. This enables them to covertly assert their influence through funding political parties, establishing training institutions and influential organizations to ensure they make the rules of the game. For 'he who makes the rules' rules.

This is a conspiracy, but not a theory. The term, *conspiracy theory* was coined by the CIA to deflect questions about the discrepancies surrounding *JF Kennedy's* assassination. It's a term that's been used ever since to discredit those who question the status quo and the tactics employed by global power brokers.

We see the evidence of this global agenda exposed by all countries that co-signed as UN member states, who were legally bound to endorse *Bill Gates* COVID-19 vaccine before it was even available for sale. This included the 193 heads of state who each held a press conference the same week that featured the logo of *Bill Gates* vaccine org, *GAVI.* Each prime minister / president read the same generic script word-for-word like a puppet indicating their true sphere of influence is akin to that of a paid actor. That wasn't all that was scripted. In 2010 the Rockefeller Foundation published a step-by-step playbook detailing the game plan to instill the *New World Order*, via a centralized global government aka, the United Nations. Part one, titled 'Lockstep - Tighter Top Down Government Control and Growing Citizen Pushback' outlined how a global pandemic would kill 8 million people in 7 months and be a catalyst for introducing a new era of tighter civil compliance with mandatory lockdowns, face masks, temperature checks and social distancing as an entrainment tactic for biometric surveillance.

The script read, "Even after the pandemic faded, this more authoritarian control and oversight of citizens and their activities stuck and even intensified." Despite this document being shared on social media before censorship intensified, the majority of people remained oblivious and complied with the spin doctors who implied blind obedience was 'kindness' and those who questioned the false narrative were 'selfish'.

When we understand the *Rockefellers* funded the UN and created the World Health Organization, which is also heavily funded by *Bill Gates*[81] we join the dots to see the big picture. One month before COVID-19 was declared a pandemic in Wuhan, China, a pandemic response simulation exercise event called *Event 201* was staged and attended by globalists including *Bill Gates.*[82]

This doesn't come as a surprise when we understand the origins of Western allopathic medicine and the pharmaceutical industry, both of which are the brainchild of *John Rockefeller*, the US oil tycoon whose motives were profit, not public health. *Rockefeller*, who built his wealth by accruing 90% of the oil industry in the US, capitalized on his existing product by paying German scientists to develop petroleum-based drugs that masked symptoms rather than cured illness.[83] This enabled him to expand his power base to include the domination of both the chemical and medicine industries.[84] His reformation of the health industry began with the *Flexner Report* which he funded in 1910 and catalyzed the closing of natural medicine schools that were replaced by those touting *Rockefeller's* chemical medicines.[85] He then used his financial might to lobby policy makers to remove the threat of competition via legislation, while favoring his own pharmaceutical medicines that have since undermined public health with escalating rates of dependence and harmful side-effects.

It's interesting to note the timing of the release of the *Flexner Report*. 1910 was also the year the *Rockefellers* met with *JP Morgan* and a handful of others including *Paul Warburg*, who represented the *Rothschilds* on Jekyll Island where they created the *Federal Reserve* bank[86] - a privately owned banking system that generated profit for the few, by taxing the many. This came after they sank the Titanic that carried most of their competitors on board, including *Jacob Astor, the 4th*, who was then the richest man alive. *Astor* fiercely and publicly opposed the creation of the *Federal Reserve*.[87] *JP Morgan* built the Titanic and canceled his booking just days before and didn't equip the boat with red rescue flares.

The *Rockefeller's* have also been at the forefront of eugenics, the science of population control since 1902. In 1952 they began developing bio-warfare for this purpose. Prior to that they funded *Adolph Hitler*. So while the *Nazi's* appeared to have lost the second world war, the United Nations was established in 1945 to continue the vision on a global scale as the *4th Reich*. The 'new normal' quoted repeatedly by UN member heads of state, refers to this new system of global governance dictated via a central government; the UN. In this dystopian scenario global citizens would be controlled via a digital currency linked to a social credit system, like the one already in place in communist China that excludes dissidents from participating in the exchange of goods and services. The digital 'vaccine passport' introduced in 2021 is the social credit system.

It's Not All Doom and Gloom

Most people are aware the systems of power and governance are corrupt, they just don't know to what extent, or what to do about it. It's been obvious for a long time from the actions of those in power that they do not represent the people and the Earth. So while we are seeing the plot of the evil masterminds implemented in our waking world, this stage is necessary for the culprits to show their hands completely. The consequences of their ill will is what will eventually serve as a 'wake-up call' for people around the world to take back their free will and assume greater self-responsibility. How?

As I write this the number of deaths and adverse reactions from the engineered bioweapons masquerading as 'vaccines' far outnumber those from COVID. These tragic consequences are explained away in the media as new flu strains, unexplained blood clots and heart attacks despite these being side-effects of the inoculations.[104] The 1% know they have a very limited window before the whole world wakes up, so they have started injecting children as young as

5 and added tromethamine, which increases the chance of Myocarditis and cardiac arrest.[88]

When the critical mass awakens to the deception and genocide that's been executed on a global scale we will see pandemonium erupt in a public outcry of grief and rage. This is when we will experience the full force of the *Apocalypse*; 'divine intervention'.

This is anticipated as a solar flare event that will instantaneously shift the World Soul from the solar plexus to the heart. The solar plexus is the energy center that governs the lower rational mind. When we're solar plexus dominant we perceive reality as dualistic; seeing situations as black and white, right and wrong etc This causes polarization and conflict. When we operate from this energy center we base our identity on our beliefs, so we feel personally threatened by those who have a different outlook. If we are solar plexus dominant we seek approval by doing what the group mind and authority views as the 'right thing'. So long as the group mind is centered in the solar plexus, there will be power struggles, competition, greed and deception.

Prior to this solar event, we will witness the clash between polarities intensify. This has been very evident in Australia, where I am located. Here abuses of power have been overt due to the global solar plexus chakra being situated at the sacred site of *Uluru* (re-named *Ayers Rock*) in central Australia. Like many, I followed a soul call to do ceremony at *Uluru* during the *Great Conjunction* of Saturn and Jupiter on the Solstice, Dec 21, 2020 to serve as a midwife for our impending shift, despite rigorous opposition. Australia is a society founded on abuses of power with indigenous Celts incarcerated and transported so they could be used as a free labor force to establish a new colony for the empire, who assumed ownership by committing a genocide on indigenous Australians.

This time of chaos, directly before the *Apocalypse* is the transition phase of our 'Great Rebirth'. This is the phase in traditional labor when one is stretched beyond their coping abilities and starts bargaining with a higher power in a desperate attempt to end their prolonged state of suffering. This is why so many people are experiencing acute depression and suicidal ideation. It's worth remembering this is the darkest moment before the dawn and while it may seem counter intuitive, the only way out of the darkness is to go through it. The more we try to deny what's really happening, the more the pain and tension will persist. In order to process and resolve the darkness evoked in our psyche in response to the darkness we see in the world, we must go 'down the rabbit hole'. Like *Alice in Wonderland*, to discover for ourselves the illusions that have kept us blind, so we may awaken to our power to create a new future.

Know Thy Enemy

When the masculine isn't balanced by the feminine, internally and externally the expression becomes toxic, in both men and women. For 2000 years, since the dominion of the Roman Empire, the Western world has been living in a war zone, at war with the feminine. This has manifested as a war on nature; all that is alive. The inversion of LIVE, when spelled backwards is EVIL. That which is anti-life, the true 'anti-Christ' has portrayed itself as our savior - the church, the government, banks and medical institutions.

Perhaps the greatest agent of evil is the chemical industry owned by the 1% who are responsible for destroying life on our planet while conditioning us to assume the blame. Their media machine constantly programs us via billboards, television, digital, print and radio to fear nature, so we'll buy their products to combat the programmed shame and phobias created within the group mind. For example, those most disconnected from the *Earth Mother* seek to destroy any sign of dirt for fear of looking 'dirty'. This leads them to judge others who aren't obsessive-compulsive cleaners as 'dirty hippies' to avoid examining their phobia. Ironically, the smell of *mycobacterium vacii*, a microorganism found in soil, lights up neurotransmitters in our brains releasing *serotonin*, the hormone that eases depression and anxiety.[89]

The mass hypnosis that perceives nature as the enemy creates a constant demand for the ruling elite's toxic chemicals that have poisoned our water, food, bodies and habitat, all of which are essential for our survival.

Their corporate propaganda repeatedly instructs us to:

- ❖ Fear and kill germs compulsively by disinfecting our hands repeatedly and using toxic chemicals to clean our homes

- ❖ Take painkillers that contain neurotoxins and petrochemical drugs with dangerous side-effects that undermine natural immunity and bodily functions

- ❖ Fear insects as 'pests' and kill them with poison, rather than seek to understand and support ecosystems that naturally circumvent infestations

- ❖ View menstrual blood as 'dirty' and shameful so we'll buy carcinogenic 'sanitary' products instead of using recycled cloth pads and menstrual cups

- ❖ Use toxic cosmetics, skin care and hair care that clogs our lymphatic system with dangerous carcinogens

- ❖ Freshen' our cars, homes, clothes and bodies with toxic candles, air fragrances, cologne, aftershave, perfume, laundry detergent and fabric softener

❖ Use toxic chemicals to whiten our teeth, tan our skin, plump our lips, apply fake nails and eyelashes, remove body hair, brighten our eyes and hide our naturally aging hair

❖ Drink chlorine, fluoride and drinks colored and flavored with chemicals

❖ Use Mercury in our teeth, inject it into our bodies and inhale it from the vapors of aircraft, car parts and lightbulbs, causing nervous disorders

❖ Eat processed food laden with highly addictive monosodium glutamine, aspartame, herbicides, pesticides, insecticides, chemical fertilizers and wax

❖ Wear clothes and use money laced with fungicides that contain copper that contributes to eczema and psoriasis

❖ Inhale noxious fumes from filling our cars with petroleum/diesel

❖ Expose our bodies and brains to dangerous levels of radiation with mobile phones, digital devices, airport security, X-Rays, CT scans and MRI's

❖ Ingest petrochemical plastics through using plastic wrap, containers, bottles, hair accessories, jewelry, shoes and bags[90]

Put simply, their strategy undermines health while creating a demand for their harmful products and pharmaceutical medicines, while profiting at our expense. This is why educating ourselves on how our psyche, bodies and energy fields function and what we need to thrive is the ultimate form of activism. Instead of blindly 'trusting the science' of so-called 'experts' that tout the corporate narrative. Our survival depends on us becoming well-informed by seeking truth. That is the ethos of the *Grail*; to seek the truth, knowing the truth sets us free. The more ignorant we are, the more we are enslaved we become through highly calculated methods of mind control that are all pervasive.

Just as the physical aspects of the feminine that nourish physical life have been undermined and poisoned, all that supports our psycho-emotional and spiritual growth has been appropriated, distorted and demonized. I am referring to the perceptions, insights, teachings and practices of the sacred feminine embodied in the ancient indigenous paths of *Mysticism*, *Shamanism* and *Tantra*. As discussed previously, in a patriarchal society, the more one aligns with the feminine and the *Earth Mother*, the more one experiences marginalisation, discrimination and persecution. Now is the time to stand with the *Earth Mother*, embodying the strengths of the sacred feminine knowing the stakes have never been higher…as our stand will inspire others.

Bless Thy Enemy: Love Conquers All

Just as it's not time to cower in fear and compliance, it's also not the time to react with hate and condemnation, as plotting revenge towards those who have caused unimaginable harm, only fuels their fire as a force for destruction. It is far more powerful to send perpetrators of pain and trauma loving compassion and healing, as this ends the karmic cycle of 'tit for tat' vigilante justice that escalates conflict. To avoid feeling powerless as victims of circumstance, we need to reside in the power of the heart; the center of true power, embodying 'power from within' rather than seek 'power over' another to avoid feelings of powerlessness.

It is also essential we comprehend this war perpetuated upon the *Earth Mother* and her children was done by those who were most wounded and felt most separate from her. Those whose *Father Wound* was so great, they unconsciously sought to destroy their mother in order to prove their own power to create. I'm not suggesting they not be called to account to atone for their sins; their 'crimes against humanity' but for our own salvation, we need to rise above the old dance of seeking retribution; 'hurting those who hurt us' or the cycle of destruction will never end.

This is our ultimate test to evolve beyond duality and enter a new paradigm. Can we forgive the unforgivable? Only through recognizing the potential for such evil lies in all of us, given the right circumstances. Only someone who is disconnected from the loving wisdom of their own soul can inflict grievous harm onto others. Those who are capable of such deeds have themselves been horrendously abused: psychologically, emotionally, physically and energetically. It is this cycle we must now break, by acknowledging that it exists.

WARNING: this section contains disturbing information.

Power Feeds on the Innocent

As stated earlier, when we don't believe 'true love' exists, we seek power as a substitute, so when the path to 'true love' - *the Grail* was lost, abuses of power followed. This began during the lunar month of Winter Solstice in ancient Rome when courts were closed so the ruling elite could do their private rites during the most potent time to seed intentions to ensure their stronghold of power.

During this time all crimes were allowed and drunken orgies encouraged as this amplified the dark energies invoked by their rites. The *Jubinalia* celebration became *Saturnalia* in honor of the father. *Saturn* is where we find the origin of the word, *Satan* who they worshiped as the 'Father of Darkness' during the darkest time on the seasonal wheel; a direct inversion of *The Holy Grail*. This is where the culture of secret societies or 'dark brotherhoods' began.

Today the ruling elite still meet during the Winter Solstice which, prior to the Roman Empire was reserved for *The Holy Grail*. During the darkest night, the ruling elite perform rites designed to increase their power through acts of domination involving *blood*, *sex* and *death*. These are enacted on the innocent; children who have been abducted, and orphans and children placed in foster care who are seen as expendable. However, the children born into wealthy dynastic families are also at risk of torture, molestation and ritual abuse. Why? This is a torture technique used to break their spirit to ensure compliancy and the ongoing status of their dynasties. This tactic, known as *MK Ultra*, is also used by the CIA. I have personally known 3 women who grew up experiencing this type of ritual abuse. One was terrified for her life, after escaping her town of origin.

Absolute Power Corrupts Absolutely

It stands to reason those in positions of external power are those who most fervently seek power. Such ambition flags an attempt to compensate for a lack of personal power, making them more likely to abuse power through corrupt acts to acquire it. Most people are aware that elected officials are doing the bidding of corrupt corporations to line their own pockets, rather than serve the interests of the people.

What they're not aware of are the depths to which those in power have sunk to attain and maintain their positions of power. I'm referring to the deep shadow acts of those who've climbed to the greatest heights of the pyramid of power, that being the torture and murder of children. Dismissed as 'conspiracy theories' by those keen to deflect suspicion, the mounting evidence is connecting 'the pieces of the puzzle' incriminating the ruling elite, including politicians, CEO's, Hollywood execs, celebrities and royalty.

The ruling elite maintain their stronghold through well-established covert means and traditions. Such as *Ivy League* fraternities that require ritual initiations to gain entry to their secret societies that form the membership of organizations whose alumni are a 'who's who' of power brokers. Their rituals mimic *the Grail* rites, but are vampiric in nature, using the energetic force of *blood*, *sex* and *death* in unethical ways to enhance their insatiable lust for power.

Claims of Satanic rituals involving child sacrifices have been made by independent journalist *Alex Jones* about the gatherings of *Republicans* at *Bohemian Grove* for their annual 'Cremation of Care' ritual. This rite features a small coffin that would fit a child marked, 'Care' which is burned on a forest altar amid much pomp and pageantry in a male-only rite that proclaims, 'weaving spiders not welcome here'. Spiders are a symbol of feminine power; the Creatress who 'weaves the web of life'. They claim these are 'Druidic rituals'. However, these are men who portray themselves as righteous Christians. Publicly they judge other faiths, none more so than Earth-worshiping pagans, so it's completely incongruent they would be practicing 'Druidic rituals'.

Most who participate are groomed from birth, as their rites of passage involve subsequent acts of disempowerment to break their spirit through domination to ensure submission and allegiance to the alpha males. Only by lifting the veil and bringing these dark acts into the light of understanding will they stop. Check out *Fiona Barnett's* book, *Eyes Wide Open*, or *Nick Bryant's* book, *The Franklin Scandal* that detail these dark fraternities and incriminate many influential members of society.

Here in Australia, unbeknownst to many, former prime minister, *John Howard* enacted a 90 year suppression order to prevent the names of 28 high-ranking Australians, including judges and a prime minister being exposed as pedophiles, despite evidence by the federal police revealed at a Royal Commission in 2017.[91] There are growing calls to release the names so justice may be served to protect the innocent and to stop the culture where such secrets are used to blackmail people of influence to do the bidding of the ruling elite.

The Ultimate Devil's Bargain

When I was 10 I saw a film called, *The Devil and Max Devlin* starring *Elliot Gould* and *Bill Cosby,* as the Devil. An ironic case of art imitating life, given the later sentencing of Bill Cosby for sexual assault of women and minors. In the film, the lead character must recruit 3 people who'll sell their soul to the Devil to gain his freedom. The double bind is, one who has betrayed their own conscience is never free. Similarly, the way secret societies function is one is rewarded for each subsequent Devil's bargain they make. Such personal compromises are seen as demonstrations of loyalty to the organization over one's own conscience, like the protocol of the well-known crime syndicate, the *Mafia.* The degree to which one sells one's soul assures greater levels of power within the covert organizations and the external halls of power. Those in the lower levels are unaware of the activities of those in the higher levels, until they gain admission through their own dark acts. Most men who join brotherhood organizations do so to feel a part of something greater and serve the community through good deeds, so they would be horrified to learn their participation in simple ceremonies adds to the power base of those in the top tiers who are committing heinous acts.

As members ascend through the hierarchical ranks, the secrets they harbor become darker and this lowers their personal frequency. This may involve betraying the confidence and trust of loved ones, torture of other members and illegal/immoral acts that are recorded as an 'insurance policy'. If members don't comply with the demands of the organizations that grant their ambitions, they have material to blackmail them, ensuring their silence. Films such as *The Firm* and *Eyes Wide Shut* are an attempt to raise public awareness. *Director Stanley Kubrick* was found dead from a heart attack directly after showing the final cut of *Eyes Wide Shut* to *Warner Brothers* executives. Kubrick was quoted as often stating a very revealing credo of his: "Be suspicious of people who have, or crave, power." He added, "Never, ever go near power. Don't become friends with anyone who has real power. It's dangerous".[92] Turns out it's relatively simple to induce a heart attack in a targeted person. There are a number of chemicals, some of them classified, which can be used to perform the deadly task of producing premature heart failure.

Hollywood's Darkest Secret

It's not just 'old money' families who are involved in these dark rituals. Anyone pursuing fame is a prime candidate to be approached and offered a Devil's bargain. Hence, the entertainment industry is a hotbed of dark rites and abuse. While it used to be common knowledge young women were exploited by Hollywood's 'casting couch', as our collective consciousness descended, the abuses extended to children. In 1977 the first case was made public with director, *Roman Polanski* charged with drugging and raping a 13 year old girl. Since then numerous child actors have come forward speaking about their abuse. The most shocking testimony came from *Macauley Culkin*, child star of the *Home Alone* franchise who was shown 'skin trophies' worn by a movie executive boasting of children he'd sacrificed and turned into shoes and belts. The more innocent and pure the victims, the greater the hit of power received by the perpetrators.

Another abhorrent practice indulged in by the ruling elite is *'Spirit Cooking'*- cannibalistic feasts where they ingest the blood and endocrine secretions of specific glands of minors. This is a debauched attempt to gain spiritual power and eternal youth. The disturbing 'art' of *Marina Abramovic*, clearly glorifies this practice 'in plain sight', although she denies any connection. It is only in the past few hundred years that the practice of cannibalism among royals has not been publicized. In Europe, around the time of the American Revolution 'corpse medicine' was very popular among the ruling class, Charles II even brewed his own.[93]

" Jesus! What kind of monster client have you picked up this time? There's only one source for this stuff..." He nodded. " The adrenaline glands from a living human body," I said. " It's no good if you get it out of a corpse." "I know," he replied. " But the guy didn't have any cash. He's one of these Satanism freaks. He offered me human blood – said it would

make me higher than I'd ever been in my life," he laughed." [94]

Hunter S. Thompson, Fear and Loathing in Las Vegas

Adrenochrome is a secretion from the adrenal glands that's produced when one is terrified. The claim is when it's ingested it gives one a hit of life force. The 1982 film, *Death Becomes Her* depicts women who drink a magical brew to prevent aging but the brew has dreadful side-effects. So too, *Adrenochrome* is said to be highly addictive and if supply is interrupted causes instant ageing. The film, *Mirror Mirror* also speaks to this practice indulged in by Hollywood's leading ladies who fear the physical signs of aging ending their careers. Hollywood has also sought to glamorize vampirism and normalize serial killing over the past two decades, descending the group mind into accepting depravity.

Another gland the elite are said to ingest is the pineal gland, known as the 'Eye of Horus' or the 'All-Seeing Eye' that features atop the pyramid of power on *US dollar bills*. This is the gland that governs the third eye energy center that serves as a doorway to clairvoyance. The pineal gland is about the size of a pea and the shape of a pinecone, an icon that features in *Freemason* architecture. The book, *Fear and Loathing in Las Vegas* refers to smoking a pineal gland to get high. Some claim this is an attempt to accelerate their illumination, hence the name of the secret order known as *The Illuminati*.

Anyone who has any understanding of metaphysics knows such depraved behavior could never advance one's consciousness, although one might experience visions while under the influence. The ancient *Egyptians* honored the power of the glands of the body on the understanding they were suppositories for the energy vortices within the body. Today modern medicine harvests *melatonin* and *serotonin* from the pineal glands of dead animals, but these aren't considered as potent as those which exist in the live human glandular system.

The heinous practice of harvesting live human glandular secretions makes more sense when we comprehend the 'metals' of the early alchemists referred not to 'common metals' but living essences prized for their metaphysical nature. The word, *secret* has its origin in the hidden knowledge of glandular 'secretions'. Truth was the *ritu*; the 'redness' or 'blackness' and from the word *ritu* stems the words: *ritual, rite, root* and *red*. The *ritu*, it was said, reveals itself as physical matter in the form of the purest and most noble of all metals: gold. Gold in metaphysics refers to consciousness. Hence, gold was deemed an 'ultimate truth'[95] Those eclipsed by dark forces are so deceived they actually believe their depravity is a way of experiencing the truth of divine union like the *Aghori monks*, a sect of *Hindu Shaivites* in India who also indulge in cannibalism[96] and perform distortions of the original sacred rites involving the holy blood of the womb.

When we understand the power contained within our glands, it makes sense the *Epstein Barr* virus was engineered as a bioweapon specifically to undermine our glandular system to prevent our ascension process. Like the engineered viruses, *Ebola* and *HIV*, which I speak about in my book, *Sacred Union*, EBV was first discovered in Africa; a testing ground for bioweapons. In 1965 scientists started investigating after children began presenting with swollen glands and tumors. They discovered it infected white blood cells, 'B cells' and could transmit to uninfected 'B cells' causing them to become cancerous.[97] This is a category of biowarfare known as a 'stealth virus'. *EBV* is a stealth virus that hides by cloaking itself in the 'B cells'. It remains dormant and undetected in blood tests, while it continues to feed off the life force of its host, causing a range of symptoms including brain fog, chronic fatigue, chronic sinusitis, recurrent strep throat, fungal infections like candida, swollen glands and lymph nodes, food intolerances, chemical and light sensitivity, insomnia, anemia, tingling in extremities, migraines, mouth/genital ulcers and weakened immunity.[98] The longer one has *EBV* in their system, the more symptoms they will experience until they undertake a protocol to starve its source of nourishment.

EBV feeds on adrenaline (stress), heavy metals like iron and mercury and eggs, on account of the live culture having been grown in a petri dish with egg. *EBV* targets the immune system and is the most common virus on the planet. Known as 'the kissing disease', *glandular fever* or *mono*, it enters the body easily; via expressions of love.

I contracted a second strain of *EBV* in 2019 after experiencing chronic symptoms ever since I was very young, causing me to conclude I contracted it in the birth canal of my mother who has it, along with my siblings. So while the world searched for a novel Coronavirus (still yet to be isolated, despite a worldwide effort indicating there never was a novel Coronavirus) I focused on healing myself of stage 4 chronic *EBV*. I found the protocol of the book, *Medical Medium* by Anthony William helpful along with personalized tinctures and remedies prescribed by my naturopath as well as liver cleanses, an Ayurvedic diet, removing amalgam dental fillings and bio-resonance sessions.

It was author, *Anthony William*, a medical intuitive who pointed out 80% of the body's reserves go into menstruation and that those with an underlying viral load crash energetically during their pre-menstrual/menstrual phase, resulting in extreme mood swings, severe depression, rage and suicidal ideation. The medical system labels this condition, PMDD: premenstrual dysphoric disorder and removes women's uteruses as a 'cure'. I have experienced this condition for most of my fertile years and witnessed my mother and trans son, who also have *EBV* experience PMDD. In light of all the evidence, it seems a deliberate ploy to undermine the emotional balance and wellbeing of women when their psychic abilities are most pronounced.

It's not just glandular secretions the ruling elite have been targeting and harvesting. The *Olympics* were originally created as a ritualistic event.[99] Women were not allowed to attend as either athletes or spectators. The young male athletes performed nude in what was essentially a homoerotic spectacle. In ancient Greece is was socially acceptable for older men to take on underage boys as students and initiate them into pedophilic sex acts in return for mentoring and lodging. The purpose of the *Olympics* was to worship 'an expenditure of ritual energy for the God's' and young men's sweat was collected as a sacrifice for this purpose.[100]

Similarly, the patriarchal religions introduced the blood rite of circumcision for newborns; those too young to give informed consent, making this an act of ritual abuse that is still socially accepted. Done without anesthesia, this invasive and violent act, results in trauma and severs the bond of trust with the mother, possibly anchoring a mistrust of women and rage at women for the betrayal. It's not surprising to learn that statistics of sudden infant deaths are higher in circumcised babies.

The documentary film, *American Circumcision* presents compelling evidence that the tradition of male circumcision was originally introduced as a ritual act to harvest the foreskin of young men to offer it to the Gods. Originally male circumcision removed only a small piece of skin from the top of the foreskin but over time the practice changed, so a much larger piece was removed, with the incision made along the frenulum, where the most nerve endings are, impacting a man's ability to become fully orgasmic.[101]

This widespread genital mutilation limited men's ability to directly experience ecstatic oneness with the divine through sacred sexuality, a practice that was once revered in the earlier Mystic traditions and if experienced, would challenge the monotheistic idea that sex is lowly and profane and celibacy is pure and divine. This intervention also undermined the sacred sexual energy that could be raised in the mystic practice of the *Hieros Gamos*.

Recently Hollywood celebrities, *Sandra Bullock* and *Cate Blanchett* openly stated on the *Ellen Degeneres* talk show that they use skin products that contain stem cells from the foreskin of Korean newborns on their faces to enhance their youthful appearance.[102]

Bringing Down the Vibe

Another way the elite have tried to lower the frequency on planet Earth to enhance their power and dominion is through music. In 1885, the Italian Government declared that all instruments and orchestras should use a tuning fork that vibrates at 440 Hz, which was different from the original standard of 435 Hz and the competing 432 Hz used in France. In 1917, the American Federation of Musicians followed suit with a further push for 440 Hz in the 1940s. In 1953, a worldwide agreement was signed.

432 Hz has 'a pure tone of math fundamental to nature' and is consistent with the divine design pattern of the

universe, the 'Golden Ratio'. 432 Hz resonates with the *Schumann Resonance*, the documented fundamental electromagnetic 'heartbeat' of the *Earth Mother*. Its resonance feels soothing to the nervous system and stimulates the heart. *Nazi* propaganda minister, *Joseph Goebbels* insisted on 440 Hz tuning in Germany because he believed, it made people think and feel in specific ways, making them "a prisoner of a certain consciousness."

Today we are saturated with noise pollution that undermines the health of our subtle energy bodies. Every time we hear a digital notification we experience a hit of *cortisol*, the stress hormone, which undermines our immune system. Those who live in the inner city and lower socio-economic areas hear constant sirens from police whose charge is ironically to, 'keep the peace'…and today most cars and appliances such as kettles, dishwashers, ovens, washing machines and dryers come with built-in ear-piercing alarms that demand our instant attention. Add to that the noise pollution of power tools invented to 'tame nature into submission' such as leaf blowers, brush cutters, lawn mowers and chainsaws and you can see it isn't just daily caffeine addiction putting everyone's nerves on edge! Meanwhile, practitioners who use powerful frequency healing devices such as bio resonance machines are legally forbidden to make any public claims that they assist healing.

This war on our 'collective frequency' is a deliberate tactic to destabilize our health and wellbeing. Many recording artists have come forward to expose the music industry that pressures them to include Satanic ritual iconography and chants in their video clips, in conjunction with low frequency music. This is an entrainment technique to manipulate the group mind of our youth. When we understand what young celebrities are exposed to, it's easy to see why they use drugs to cope and have very public breakdowns that undermine their credibility, should they start exposing the truth. It's also why we see many celebrities try to redeem their sworn allegiance to the dark; by dedicating themselves to charitable causes or rebelling publicly against the ruling elite in an effort to counteract the compromises made in their youth.

Monkey See Monkey Do

Many years ago I saw an episode of *Oprah* where she showed undercover footage of a dark initiation rite that was a pre-requisite to join a senior girl's cheer squad. The rite involved the degradation and humiliation of new members who had to eat human excrement in order to be accepted into the squad, an acceptance that would ensure their social status. This is a clear case of youths mimicking rites they have been exposed to as victims, by re-enacting them as perpetrators in an unconscious way to process the trauma of what they experienced.

This also highlights how important it is that we, as adults, provide rites of passage for teens that heal and empower their psyche, since it is human behavior to create rituals in order to process change, and without guidance, the rituals uninitiated teens create are harmful. Such as gang initiations that require one to execute dares to do reckless, demeaning or illegal acts or girls who are expected to humiliate themselves sexually. A number of years ago a friend confided in me that a daughter of a friend who attended a private girl's college in Melbourne, Australia had complained to her about 'sex games' being played at weekend parties. These involved girls lining up to give oral sex to boys in a race to see who could bring a boy to climax first and a competition where boys compared how many different shades of lipstick they could boast on their penis by the night's end.

Addressing the Cause

While there are many non-profit organizations and *pro bono* legal counsel working tirelessly to rescue women and children from the daily torture of human trafficking and abuse, like those working with the *Humanitad Foundation* and Pulitzer prize winning authors, *Nicholas Kristof* and *Sheryl WuDunn*, we need to address the underlying cause, or the problem will persist. We do that by seeking to understand the psyche and the reasons people act out in these ways.

Examining Our Own Relationship with Power

Just as porn is addictive for those lusting for greater power, the ultimate high for those governed by their lower self is to dominate a submissive to the point of death. That may start by experimenting on oneself with asphyxiation or choking others in the sex act. This is why pornography is so potentially dangerous. It is designed to excite one energetically using fantasies of domination. This is how pornography is different from *eroticism*. Porn features degradation, humiliation and violence whereas *eroticism* uses pleasure, portrayed in artful ways to excite. Someone who is emotionally and psychologically immature is susceptible to porn addiction. Why? Consider how small boys torture bugs to see how they respond. They inflict harm on a defenseless creature to see how much it will take. This is like a child testing the boundaries of a parent…'Will you still love me if I behave badly?' This is the dynamic portrayed in the popular series, *Fifty Shades of Grey* which highlights the societal fascination with power as a pathway for sexual gratification.

Many assume they're not hurting anyone if they indulge in dark fantasies in the privacy of their own home. This attitude doesn't take into account the energetic repercussions of their acts. This is perfectly understandable given the lack of awareness we have culturally about the conscious and unconscious use of energy; magic. We're fascinated by magic because it's hidden and misunderstood, hence the success of *Harry Potter* and *Lord of the Rings*. Porn is a form of black magic. To charge one's energy, while focusing on domination, charges a paradigm of 'power over' within our collective consciousness. Men have been targeted and unwittingly used as human batteries to 'power up the grid' with domination fantasies. Just as *Shakti* is siphoned by dark magicians who claim to initiate women sexually, the sexual energy of men predominantly is being siphoned via porn to charge up the entity that is the, Military Industrial Complex that enslaves humanity. I highlight this, not to judge men or those who use porn by inferring they should feel guilty about being complicit in the violence being perpetuated on the innocent, but rather to raise awareness to inspire them to unplug from porn. For in doing so, they will regain their life force and contribute to a world free from violence and inequality.

Another incentive to unplug from porn is that it evokes an urge in many to act out their virtual sadomasochistic fantasies. Sadomasochism is sexual expression at the level of the solar plexus, the lower mental body. It uses power in the form of mind games as an aphrodisiac, instead of love. This is what lays at the core of pornography, pedophilia and Satanic rituals. Just as the blood sacrifice of soldiers, orchestrated on set dates with occult significance, charges the power and dominion of the Military Industrial Complex, human sex trafficking, demonic rituals and sadomasochistic sex acts performed during the *Wheel of Eight* all keep the sacred feminine, in both men and women enslaved. Only by accessing authentic 'inner power' can we raise our energy and be centered in the heart. When we are heart-centered, we are available to experience love. This frees us up from the pursuit of external power. So how do we shift from being solar-plexus dominant to heart centered? Through reclaiming *the Grail* rites that initiate us into the archetypal energies of the inner mother and father who reside in the heart. If these aspects are disempowered, we continue to enact power struggles and perpetuate endemic trauma. This is the key to breaking the cycle of psycho-emotional pedophilia that perpetuates our pedophilic culture; a society that preys on the innocent to accrue personal power. Only when we learn how to return to a state of innocence, through integrating our shadow, will the innocent be safe from our shadow being projected on them. Here is a diagram showing the cycle of unconscious manhood followed by the cycle of conscious manhood. This is how men can access their inner power to transcend compulsive behaviors that are an attempt to feel powerful.

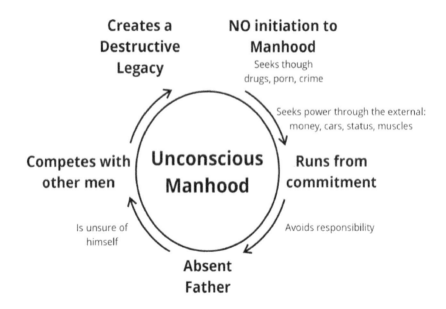

The first diagram shows a sequence of events where the wounded masculine is embodied as the 'distant/absent father' who disempowers the next generation of men. This is followed by a regenerative cycle via initiation into *The Holy Grail* which awakens the power of the heart.

Those who are not centered in the heart lack a strong center, so they are easily influenced by those who don't have their best interests at heart. Without *the Grail,* the majority of people remain centered in the lower energy centers. This low level of awareness is what creates an experience of' Hell on Earth'.

The Energetics of Human Evolution

When we operate within the first dimension we perceive reality primarily through our *base/root* energy

center, located between our genitals and rectum. At this level of awareness we have the maturity of a 0-7 year old and we're primarily concerned with meeting our physical survival needs. We're motivated by the fear we'll never have enough materially to feel safe and secure from external threats, so our primary focus is on creating physical security. We do this by generating money and accumulating possessions. This creates debt and a fear of losing what one has. Simply put, we want more toys and don't want to share the ones we have!

When we operate within the second dimension we perceive reality through our second energy center; the *sacral*. At this level of awareness we have the maturity of a 7-14 year old and we're primarily concerned with meeting our emotional survival needs. Driven by a fear we're unlovable, we seek emotional security by trying to gain acceptance to social groups. We may compulsively seek a partner who won't leave us, so we can avoid our fear of being alone. We create mutual dependence as an emotional bond. The search for the 'love object' and the fear of losing them, provides a source of endless emotional drama.

When we operate in the third dimension we perceive reality through our third energy center; the *solar plexus*. At this level of awareness we have the maturity of a 14-21 year old so we're primarily concerned with meeting our psychological survival needs. This plays out as a need to express our opinions and find those who validate our viewpoint. At this level of awareness we identify with our beliefs, to the point where we feel threatened by those with a different perspective. When the rational mind feels threatened, it reacts by trying to assume greater power and control. This mindset creates polarization and conflict.

Our current world events are an external initiation calling for us to mature and respond as adults from the heart, acting on behalf of future generations, rather than reacting in fear to serve our own interests, like a child or teenager. This is how we transcend the perpetual stress and struggle of 3D 'Hell on Earth'.

Love transcends power. Just as the heart center is located above the seat of will; the *solar plexus*, love will always triumph in the end over power. Why? Power offers only short-term gratification, while love endures by offering long-term solutions. We are now awakening from an obsession with power, to pursue an ideal that's higher; love. Not dependency on a surrogate parent to appease the fears of our wounded inner child, but love for ourselves and humanity as a whole that extends to all living beings, including our *Earth Mother*.

The Shift into the Heart

If you're feeling overwhelmed by the darkness now coming to light, take heart as all that has been covert must be brought into the light of awareness in order to make the quantum shift into the light of love. Now is not the time for 'spiritual by-passing' affirming everything is love and light to avoid acknowledging the dark that coexists in our realm. In the not too distant future, just when we thought things couldn't get any stranger, we will find ourselves entering a 'whole new world' as our solar system enters a new part of the galaxy; *the Photon Belt*. Comprised of light particles that have zero mass, no electrical charge and an indefinite long life, this is 'The Force' - the light of the divine that emanates around the *Alcyon*; 'the Great Central Sun' that is the brightest star in the *Pleiades* star system. Every 12,000 years, during the astrological ages of *Leo* and *Aquarius*, we transit through this forcefield of quantum light particles.

Our entry into the *Photon Belt* will be heralded by us moving through, *The Twilight* Zone (yes, turns out the 60's TV show was predictive programming). This is the null zone comprised of the outer edges of the main band, that is expected to create an experience of 'twilight' followed by 3 days of darkness, when neither the sun or stars will be visible, creating a potential for extremely cold temperatures. We will then awaken to a new dawn of a light-filled world where we will rediscover latent abilities, such as telepathy, bi-location, levitation, precognition and instantaneous manifestation. There are claims our bodies will be less dense and we'll be able to see colors and other dimensional beings previously not perceived. Within this forcefield anything that is not of natural origin will cease to exist, including man made electricity, putting an end to the total surveillance technocracy plans of the ruling elite.

Prior to our shift into The *Twilight Zone* we will experience a solar flare so intense it will shift the group mind from the *solar plexus* into the *heart* in an instant. This is because one can only withstand the high frequencies of the *Photon Belt* if they are centered in the heart. This is why the ruling elite have tried so hard to anchor fear within the group mind, fearing we will leave them behind and no longer serve as their free energy source. I feel intuitively this preparatory event will happen in 2022, which adds up to 6, the number of harmony symbolized by the union of the trinities of sacred feminine and masculine that meet in the heart as the marriage of 'Heaven and Earth'.

While it is likely we will also experience a 'pole shift' in the not too distant future that sees some lands return to the sea to replenish and others rise, creating the physical 'New Earth'…this catastrophic event will be preceded by an unprecedented amount of divine intervention and benevolent assistance from our galactic neighbors, so there is no need to panic and hoard supplies in a bunker with an arsenal of weapons!

We are on the threshold of the era John Lennon envisioned where a true 'brotherhood of man' prevails, beyond the 3D constructs of borders and religion. If you'd like to know more about the Photon Belt and the 'pole shift' watch my presentation, *Shift into the Light*. Details in the resource section.

Love shall overcome…and 'thy will be done on Earth, as it is in Heaven'. In the meantime we are being impulsed to be a conduit for anchoring 'Heaven on

Earth' by following our heart's calling, even if it makes no sense to our rational mind! Then together we will create a world inspired by love. My heart's calling is to create a temple of love that heals the World Soul from the paradigm of war through providing an experience for people to live in alignment with the natural cycles and initiate men and women into *the Grail* and *Sacred Union* practices and train facilitators to create socially sustainable communities. To find out more, visit my website listed in the *About the Author* page.

Thanks so much for taking the time to read everything I've shared from my journey decoding *the Grail*. Please do a shout out about this book on social media if you think it has something valuable to say to your tribe. It would be my absolute pleasure to meet you in person at one of my events at the temple of love I see in my heart named, Rainbow Haven Retreat!

Blessings in Sisterhood,

Tanishka

P.S. I had to share this beautiful artwork gifted to me by a dear brother, Venn, the morning I finished the final draft of this book. After a conversation about the ceremony I'd led at Stonehenge he told me he had a Stonehenge related gift for me...unbeknownst to him, it featured *the Grail* and its power to awaken the caduceus, the symbol of healing through the harmony of opposites.

Pistis Sophia by Amoraea Dreamseed

ABOUT THE AUTHOR

Loved as Facebook's 'Moon Woman' with half a million followers of her daily lunar guidance, Tanishka is a former stand-up comic who's passionate about creating positive social change through the power of authentic soul-centered connection. She loves empowering individuals to understand and embrace all facets of the soul within safe spaces that foster liberated self-expression, essential for healing patterns of dysfunction that otherwise result in relationship breakdown and intergenerational trauma. For the past 25 years, since her kundalini awakening at age 26 she has followed her inner guidance to create a range of initiations and practices she came to realize were once part of *the Grail* tradition. Via her mystery school she offers a range of *Grail* practices for men and women to promote social sustainability through living in alignment with the natural cycles.

A leader in the global *Red Tent* movement, she has trained women in 44 countries to facilitate *Red Tent* women's circles as a community building initiative to support women during their most challenging time of the month. In 2008 she received guidance to 'awaken *the Grail* codes'. This was followed by wisdom teachings and practices detailed in her *Sacred Union* books. In 2013 she began captivating audiences around the world by decoding the greatest mystery of all time, *The Holy Grail* from the perspective of the sacred feminine.

A popular keynote speaker at conferences, summits and festivals online and worldwide, her articles and interviews have been featured in leading women's magazines and consciousness raising publications both in print and online. In addition to online seminars and courses she has conducted speaking tours and retreat intensives for men and women around the world. Her book, *Goddess Wisdom Made Easy* published by Hay House in conjunction with an online course has now been translated into French, Turkish, Slovenian and Chinese.

The Grail is her 6th book. To find out more about her work or submit a request for an interview, go to: https://themoonwoman.com/

RESOURCES BY TANISHKA

Other Books by Tanishka

The Inner Goddess Makeover
https://themoonwoman.com/the-inner-goddess-makeover/
Goddess Wisdom Made Easy
https://themoonwoman.com/goddess-wisdom/
Sacred Union Vol 1: Awakening to the Consciousness of Eden
https://themoonwoman.com/creating-sacred-union-within/
Sacred Union Vol 2: Creating Sacred Union in Partnerships
https://themoonwoman.com/creating-sacred-union-in-partnerships/
The 28 Day Happy Challenge
https://themoonwoman.com/the-28-day-happy-challenge/

Video Masterclasses for Men and Women by Tanishka

Sacred Union and the Holy Grail
https://themoonwoman.com/sacred-union-the-holy-grail/

Ancient Wisdom Series
https://themoonwoman.com/online-masterclasses/#sacredunion
Initiation: The Sacred Power of Blood, Sex and Death

https://themoonwoman.com/online-masterclasses/#initiation
Shift into the Light
https://rumble.com/vp1yea-shift-into-the-light-photon-belt-update.html

Short Courses for Men and Women by Tanishka

Conscious Relating
https://themoonwoman.com/conscious-relating/

Initiation Journeys for Women with Tanishka

The Descent of Ishtar
https://themoonwoman.com/inner-goddess-course/
13 Moons
https://themoonwoman.com/13-moons/

Initiation Journeys for Men with Tanishka

The Descent of Orpheus
https://themoonwoman.com/rainbow-warrior-multidimensional-masculinity/
The Hero's Journey
https://themoonwoman.com/make-it-happen/

Grail Facilitator Training for Women with Tanishka

Magdalene Training Level 1 - Red Tent Facilitator:
https://themoonwoman.com/red-tent-online-course/
Magdalene Training Level 2 - Feminine Rites of Passage:
https://themoonwoman.com/rites-of-passage/

Grail Facilitator Training for Men with Tanishka

Merlin Training
https://themoonwoman.com/12-suns-mens-facilitator-training/

Podcasts with Tanishka and Kiki Maree (formerly Kristin Murray Alexi)

Love, Blood, Sex, Death podcast
https://themoonwoman.com/love-blood-sex-death-podcast/

LINKS & FOOTNOTES

Acknowledgements / Links

Military Industrial Complex Money Trail

https://https://www.lewrockwell.com/2021/04/bill-sardi/who-runs-the-world-blackrock-and-vanguard/the-world-blackrock-and-vanguard/

http://themillenniumreport.com/2016/03/who-owns-and-controls-the-military-industrial-complex/

Crop Circle June 5, 2016 photographed by Lucy Pringle

https://cropcircles.lucypringle.co.uk/crop-circles-2016-june/#jp-carousel-6992

Pistis Sophia artwork by Amoraea Dreamseed

https://divine-blueprint.com/

Footnotes

1. https://anxietyhub.org/anxiety-disorder-statistics/

2. https://www.ancient-origins.net/myths-legends/warriors-rainbow-prophecy-001577

3. https://en.wikipedia.org/wiki/Holy_Grail

4. https://en.wikipedia.org/wiki/Peredur_son_of_Efrawg

5. https://en.wikipedia.org/wiki/Parzival

6. https://www.bibliotecapleyades.net/sociopolitica/sociopol_brotherhoodsnake06.htm

7. https://www.gotquestions.org/sacred-stone.html

8. https://en.wikipedia.org/wiki/Robert_de_Boron

9. https://www.atlasobscura.com/places/holy-chalice-of-valencia

10. http://time.com/5210705/mary-magdalene-controversial/

11. https://prophecyinthenews.com/articles/legend-of-the-holy-grail/

12. https://genesis6conspiracy.com/chapter-61-legends-of-the-holy-grail/

13. https://watson.brown.edu/costsofwar/costs/economic.

14. Blood, Bread and Roses by Judy Grahn.

15. The Hero Has a Thousand Faces. Joseph Campbell

16. The Magdalene Legacy by Laurence Gardner

17. The Genesis 6 Conspiracy by Gary Wayne.

18. https://awomensthing.org/blog/artemisia-gentileschi/

19. https://www.youtube.com/watch?v=09maaUaRT4M

20. https://www.economist.com/international/2020/05/10/pornography-is-booming-during-the-covid-19-lockdowns

21. https://www.stopthetraffik.org/about-human-trafficking/the-scale-of-human-trafficking/

22. http://genesis6conspiracy.com/chapter-15-isis-ishtar-gaea-and-ninkhursag/

23. https://nwhn.org/hysterectomy/

24. https://rense.com/health3/hyster.htm
25. http://nuff.org/health_statistics.htm
26. https://www.betteraging.com/aging-science/does-a-hysterectomy-or-oophorectomy-increase-the-likelihood-of-dementia/
27. https://www.webmd.com/women/features/health-risks-after-hysterectomies
28. https://www.hormonesmatter.com/hysterectomy-experiences-organ-dysfunction/
29. https://www.bibliotecapleyades.net/biblianazar/esp_biblianazar_13a.htm
30. https://www.alcohol.org/guides/alcohol-fueled-emotions/
31. https://greatergood.berkeley.edu/article/item/can_connection_cure_addiction
32. https://www.slideshare.net/ConnectionCulture/physiological-effects-of-positive-human-connection
33. https://www.academia.edu/RegisterToDownload#RelatedPaper
34. https://www.britannica.com/art/courtly-love
35. https://tarotinstitute.com/tarot-cards-origins/
36. One of Us. Release Date: October 20, 2017 (USA) Loki Films
37. https://www.primaveradreams.com/post/2017/04/21/the-origins-of-the-words-bride-and-groom
38. https://www.worldhistory.org/Labyrinth/
39. https://www.monroecc.edu/ArchAnnou.nsf/Attachments/17EB75C995AC01BF05257B0100696A15/$FILE/A%2520Brief%2520History%2520of%2520Labyrinths.pdf
40. https://www.who.int/news/item/17-06-2021-one-in-100-deaths-is-by-suicide

41. https://www.worldometers.info/demographics/life-expectancy/

42. https://www.medievalchronicles.com/medieval-knights/famous-medieval-knights/the-knights-of-the-round-table/gawain/

43. https://jocelynmercado.com/blog/deer-mother-winter-solstice

44. https://fantasticfungi.com/the-mush-room/connection-between-christmas-and-mushrooms/

45. https://en.wikipedia.org/wiki/A_Visit_from_St._Nicholas

46. https://en.wikipedia.org/wiki/Jack_in_the_Green

47. https://en.wikipedia.org/wiki/Green_Knight

48. https://en.wikipedia.org/wiki/Sir_Gawain_and_the_Green_Knight

49. The Women s Encyclopedia of Myths and Secrets by Barbara Walker

50. https://genesis6conspiracy.com/chapter-15-isis-ishtar-gaea-and-ninkhursag/

51. https://www.learnreligions.com/the-origins-of-santa-claus-2562993

52. https://religion.fandom.com/wiki/Kykeon

53. https://genesis6conspiracy.com/chapter-15-isis-ishtar-gaea-and-ninkhursag/

54. Genesis of the Grail Kings by Laurence Gardner.

55. https://lostsymboltweets.blogspot.com/2009/09/do-you-masons-really-drink-from-skulls.html

56. https://www.historyextra.com/period/medieval/king-arthur-facts-real-round-table-holy-grail-death-buried-lancelot-guinevere/

57. https://www.psychologytoday.com/us/articles/201912/8-truths-about-intuition

58. https://en.wikipedia.org/wiki/Royal_coat_of_arms_of_the_United_Kingdom

59. https://www.ancient-origins.net/myths-legends/magic-unicorn-horn-0010750

60. https://www.orencooriginals.net/blogs/news/the-hunt-for-the-unicorn-tapestries

61. https://www.streetdirectory.com/travel_guide/14566/education/the_lady_and_the_unicorn_tapestries.html

62. https://www.streetdirectory.com/travel_guide/14566/education/the_lady_and_the_unicorn_tapestries.html

63. https://teaandrosemary.com/european-witch-trials-hunts/

64. Gods & Goddess History channel

65. The Magdalene Legacy by Laurence Gardner

66. https://www.ancient-symbols.com/symbols-directory/borromean-rings.html

67. https://www.dailymail.co.uk/sciencetech/article-3768950/Does-Sistine-Chapel-hide-secret-feminist-code-Michelangelo-concealed-symbols-female-anatomy-great-ceiling-fresco.html

68. Gods & Goddess History channel

69. https://3brothersfilm.com/blog/2012/02/medieval-as-modern-the-historical-accuracy-of-kingdom-of-heaven

70. http://quetedugraal.over-blog.com/the-quest-and-achievement-of-the_holy-grail-by-edwin-austin-abbey/

71. https://www.bibliotecapleyades.net/biblianazar/esp_biblianazar_21.htm

72. https://feminismandreligion.com/2017/05/21/shapeshifting-goddesses-by-judith-shaw/

73. Pyramid Code documentary

74. https://www.visitwales.com/en-us/info/history-heritage-and-traditions/dragon-spirit-legend-welsh-dragon

75. https://psychology.stackexchange.com/questions/23841/why-are-trans-women-more-common-than-trans-men

76. https://rainbowmessenger.blog/2016/02/08/the-whirling-rainbow-prophecy/

77. https://www.webfx.com/blog/internet/the-6-companies-that-own-almost-all-media-infographic/

78. https://www.gracevanberkum.com/post/we-are-being-played-please-read

79. https://www.facebook.com/100004006819810/videos/2314851648658373

80. https://qz.com/1396994/where-does-the-un-get-its-money-a-simple-explanation-of-a-complex-system/

81. https://www.gracevanberkum.com/post/2010-rockefeller-lock-step-document-coming-to-life-right-now-time-to-wake-up?fbclid=IwAR0Uw_hW2c3we6OcVjBtozZShvyTbrxSLFFfxkbMmvOE7tlKYAiTJPkEoM

82. https://www.corbettreport.com/gates/

83. https://thefreedomarticles.com/western-medicine-rockefeller-medicine/

84. https://meridianhealthclinic.com/how-rockefeller-created-the-business-of-western-medicine/

85. https://pubmed.ncbi.nlm.nih.gov/21966046/

86. https://www.amazon.com/Creature-Jekyll-Island-Federal-Reserve-ebook/dp/B00ARFNQ54

87. https://anonews.co/did-j-p-morgan-titanic-conspiracy/

88. https://apdillon.substack.com/p/what-is-tromethamine-and-why-is-it?s=r

89. https://www.facebook.com/100004087092380/posts/2758448890967987

90. Cleanse to Heal by Anthony William.

91. https://awakeaustralia.org/pedophiles-in-government/

92. https://suspiciousdeaths.blogspot.com/2010/09/stanley-kubrick.html

93. https://thefreethoughtproject.com/elite-ingesting-blood-conspiracy/

94. https://www.reddit.com/r/conspiracy/comments/5igy00/a_possible_reason_for_the_elites_obsession_with/

95. https://genesis6conspiracy.com/chapter-15-isis-ishtar-gaea-and-ninkhursag/

96. http://www.cultofweird.com/culture/aghori-cannibal-hindu-monks/

97. https://news.cancerresearchuk.org/2014/03/26/50-years-of-epstein-barr-virus/

98. http://www.ebva.co.uk

99. http://www.tonyperrottet.com/nakedolympics/

100. Gods & Goddess History channel

101. American Circumcision documentary.

102. http://www.huffpost.com/entry/penis-facial_n_5b02df5be4b0463cdba4a6fa

103. https://www.facebook.com/watch/?v=780752749944113

104. https://thehighwire.com/videos/episode-276-turning-the-tide/